Taboo and Transgression in British Literature from the Renaissance to the Present

Taboo and Transgression in British Literature from the Renaissance to the Present

Edited by

Stefan Horlacher, Stefan Glomb, and Lars Heiler

TABOO AND TRANSGRESSION IN BRITISH LITERATURE FROM THE RENAISSANCE TO THE PRESENT
Copyright © Stefan Horlacher, Stefan Glomb, and Lars Heiler, 2010.

All rights reserved.

First published in 2010 by
PALGRAVE MACMILLAN®
in the United States—a division of St. Martin's Press LLC,
175 Fifth Avenue, New York, NY 10010.

Where this book is distributed in the UK, Europe and the rest of the world, this is by Palgrave Macmillan, a division of Macmillan Publishers Limited, registered in England, company number 785998, of Houndmills, Basingstoke, Hampshire RG21 6XS.

Palgrave Macmillan is the global academic imprint of the above companies and has companies and representatives throughout the world.

Palgrave® and Macmillan® are registered trademarks in the United States, the United Kingdom, Europe and other countries.

ISBN: 978–0–230–61990–6

Library of Congress Cataloging-in-Publication Data

    Taboo and transgression in British literature from the Renaissance to the present / edited by Stefan Horlacher, Stefan Glomb, and Lars Heiler.
      p. cm.
    ISBN 978–0–230–61990–6 (alk. paper)
     1. English literature—History and criticism. 2. Taboo in literature. 3. Social norms in literature. 4. Social control in literature. 5. Deviant behavior in literature. I. Horlacher, Stefan. II. Glomb, Stefan. III. Heiler, Lars.

PR149.T33T33 2010
820.9'3552—dc22   2009031634

A catalogue record of the book is available from the British Library.

Design by Newgen Imaging Systems (P) Ltd., Chennai, India.

First edition: March 2010

10 9 8 7 6 5 4 3 2 1

Printed in the United States of America.

Contents

Part I   Theoretical and Historical Perspectives

I   Taboo, Transgression, and Literature: An Introduction   3
Stefan Horlacher

II   Taboo and Transgression: A Socio-Historical and
Socio-Cultural Perspective   23
Uwe Böker

III   Against Censorship: Literature, Transgression, and
Taboo from a Diachronic Perspective   49
Lars Heiler

Part II   Literary Analyses

IV   *Hamlet, Macbeth*, and 'Sovereign Process'   75
John Drakakis

V   The Taboo of Revolutionary Thought after 1660 and
Strategies of Subversion in Milton's *Paradise Lost* and
Bunyan's *The Holy War*   99
Jens Martin Gurr

VI   Worshipping Cloacina in the Eighteenth Century:
Functions of Scatology in Swift, Pope, Gay, and Sterne   117
Jens Martin Gurr

VII   The Organic Uncanny: Taboo, Sexuality, and
Death in British Gothic Novels   135
Stella Butter and Matthias Eitelmann

VIII   The Age of Transition as an Age of
Transgression? Victorian Poetry and the Taboo of
Sexuality, Love, and the Body   159
Sarah Heinz

vi   Contents

IX   Metrical Taboos, Rhythmic Transgressions:
Historico-Cultural Manipulations of the Voice in
Nineteenth- and Twentieth-Century Poetry   177
Clive Scott

X   'Logicized' Taboo: Abjection in George Eliot's
Daniel Deronda   193
Anna-Margaretha Horatschek

XI   Revaluating Transgression in *Ulysses*   211
Stefan Glomb

XII   Taboo, Transgression, and (Self-)Censorship in
Twentieth-Century British Theater   227
Folkert Degenring

XIII   The Holocaust and Aesthetic Transgression in
Contemporary British Fiction   243
Lars Heiler

Editors and Contributors   259

Index   263

PART I

THEORETICAL AND HISTORICAL PERSPECTIVES

CHAPTER 1

TABOO, TRANSGRESSION, AND LITERATURE: AN INTRODUCTION

Stefan Horlacher

Absolute freedom from taboos is a taboo as well, and not even a humane one

—*Kaltenbrunner*

[T]aboo, by carving out a part of the world, carves out a self

—*Gell*

Both temporally and geographically, the phenomena of taboo and transgression can be considered omnipresent, that is existent in all societies or cultures and at all times. If the ubiquity of taboos and their influence on social structures is generally accepted with regard to the past, which a narcissistic and supposedly enlightened present all too often views with condescension if not outright derision, what is remarkable is the fact that taboos not only continue to exist but that they can actually be said to be flourishing. A brief reference to the recent debates on political correctness, to shibboleths in relation to the terrorist attacks of 9/11, or to the ongoing question of how to deal with topics such as the Holocaust,[1] should suffice to make this point clear. Specifically with reference to the British literary scene, one could, of course, also mention the more than thirty years of censorship imposed on D.H. Lawrence's novel *Lady Chatterley's Lover*, the uproar surrounding the staging of Howard Brenton's *The Romans in Britain* and Edward Bond's *Saved*, or the outburst of violence following the publication of Salman Rushdie's *Satanic Verses*, so brilliantly portrayed in Hanif Kureishi's novel *The Black Album*. Thus, even in modern or postmodern and

4   •••   *Stefan Horlacher*

supposedly enlightened Western societies, taboos are still pervasive, the controversies just mentioned being only the tip of the iceberg of an ongoing cultural struggle with, against and in favor of taboos; a struggle which, as the above examples demonstrate, is especially well reflected, documented and hard fought in literature and the arts, and which ultimately can be traced back to the very origins of human-kind. Wilhelm Wundt has called taboos "the oldest unwritten code of humanity" (Thody 312),[2] Sigmund Freud takes parricide and the ensuing incest taboo as constitutive of society,[3] and Philip Thody correctly concludes that "the impression given by most anthropologists is that the incest taboo is an even more important sign of our humanity than the development of language, the use of tools, or the obligation we feel to care for the old and the infirm" (37).[4]

Considering that taboos are remarkably ambiguous and multi-faceted phenomena, differing from period to period and from culture to culture, it is surprising that there has been no detailed, histori-cally oriented and theoretically up-to-date study that analyses how British culture and literature in particular have dealt with this topic. It is for these reasons that *Taboo and Transgression in British Literature* undertakes to offer exemplary model analyses of representative pri-mary texts. The approach adopted here traces the complex dynamic and ongoing negotiation of notions of taboo and transgression as an essential though often neglected facet to understanding the develop-ment, production and conception of literature and literariness from the early modern Elizabethan period through to recent postmodern debates, covering almost fifty representative authors and œuvres. It is, of course, true that the concepts of taboo and transgression have for quite some time been the focus of a whole array of differ-ent perspectives ranging from children's and youth literature or fairy tales via sociology to cultural anthropology, philosophy, media stud-ies, aesthetics, psychoanalysis and psycho-linguistics. Moreover, many popular science books as well as dictionaries on the subject[5] bear witness to the still unbroken interest of a broad public in this interdisciplinary, not to say in several senses paradoxical topic of taboo; paradoxical because the concept of taboo has become a taboo in itself (cf. Thody 4), because taboo is generally accepted as draw-ing the fundamental borders between the sacred and the profane, whereas a critical glance shows that these borders can scarcely be drawn unproblematically, since not only the concept of taboo as such, but also the concept of the sacred turns out to be polysemic, if not aporetic.[6] While in most civilized societies the use of violence is strongly tabooed, it nevertheless remains inherently if not inextricably bound up with the notion of taboo. This does not only hold true for the cultivating potential inherent to relinquishing drives, but, as Christoph Türcke argues, "above all for the fatuousness of a specific ban on thinking that individuals *en masse* subject themselves to in order to be able to endure a society they did not choose themselves and yet allow to remain as it is" (9).

Most commentators argue that there is no consensus any longer on what constitutes taboos today. As it came into common usage in Europe, taboo—already in its original meaning not exactly a precise term—has increased its semantic scope, while diminishing its terminological precision.[7] However, given that seemingly unambiguous definitions of taboo mostly hinder rather than foster the production of knowledge (cf. Eggert 19), an interdisciplinary approach encompassing cultural and literary studies, ethnology, anthropology, sociology, religious studies, and psychoanalysis does create a broad space for reflection necessary for the localization and analysis of phenomena and manifestations of taboo. The broad scope of disciplines involved in theorizing taboo arises from the fact that this concept has proved central to understanding the formation of culture(s). Located at the culture / nature divide, taboos are on the level of the surface structure manifested differently depending on the society, cultural region, and time period, while on the deep structure they appear at least to a certain degree characterized by anthropological and psychoanalytical constants.

Let us, however, begin with some historical definitions and common usages of the term, before moving on to the theorization of taboo within and across a range of disciplines. The term *taboo* is of Polynesian origin and was first noted by Captain James Cook during his exploration of Tonga in the late eighteenth century. "Not one of them would sit down, or eat a bit of any thing...," he notes in his *Voyages to the Pacific*, and continues: "On expressing my surprize [*sic*] at this, they were all taboo, as they said; which word has a very comprehensive meaning; but, in general, signifies that a thing is forbidden. Why they were laid under such restraints, at present, was not explained" (qtd. in "Taboo" 2009, [n. pag.]). In a further entry, he writes: "As every thing would, very soon, be *taboo*, if any of our people, or of their own, should be found walking about, they would be knocked down with clubs" (ibid.). These two quotes from Cook's journals already identify some of the problematic elements associated with modern definitions of the term, including

6 ❧ *Stefan Horlacher*

a comprehensiveness of meaning as "part of a community's social codex" that extends beyond a mere prohibition on certain foods and the fact that over and beyond—indeed in contrast to—prohibitions or laws "[t]aboos are, per definition, non-existing topics" that "cannot be questioned as to their rational background" (Heinschink and Teichmann [n. pag.]; see also Thody 9).

Though there are a few examples of the term used in a transferred or figurative sense already in the first half of the nineteenth century, the notion of taboo was generally restricted to religion, and the study of 'primitive' religions in particular. As Willard Gurdon Oxtoby notes, "two terms in particular came into wide use in the description of primitive religion: mana and tabu ('taboo')," with taboo, denoting, "like 'sacred', that which is set apart from common use or contact" (513). The emergent late-Victorian discipline of anthropology, which in its early manifestations specialized in the study of foreign or alien, non-European, non-Christian cultures or religious traditions, brought the term taboo 'within the pale': "The anthropological reflection on taboo starts with the constatation...as postulated by philosophical Christianity" of the radical dualism of body and soul, the physical and the metaphysical, which "can rarely be found beyond it or similarly minded thought systems" (Valeri 43). Thus, the two leading British theorists of taboo in the late nineteenth century, Sir James Frazer and William Robertson Smith, argue that in contra-distinction to European, Christian 'advanced nations' primitive societies do

> not distinguish between what pertains to the gods and what pertains to the world, between spiritual and physical evil, between the holy and the unclean or polluted: he [the savage] confuses them all under a single notion of 'danger', which corresponds to a single amoral sentiment—fear. (ibid.)

Even if these definitions and distinctions belonging to the Age of Empire have subsequently been superseded, Frazer and Robertson Smith can nevertheless be seen as founding an "anthropological tradition" that firmly connects taboo and the danger of contagion / pollution, the latter being "considered as an automatic reaction from the tabooed object or person" (ibid. 44).

Also writing at the turn of the last century, but from a sociological perspective that focuses on symbolic forms, Emile Durkheim states that "a taboo is a prohibition justified by the sacredness of what is prohibited, and this sacredness, in turn, is embodied by 'puissances redoutables'" (ibid.). For Durkheim rules such as the prohibition of incest "are too fundamental to be enforced by human agency or by human agency alone." Moreover, he also argues that "the sacred is the social in symbolic (i.e. reified) form" (ibid. 52). From this it follows that if the rules mentioned above "must be associated with forces that are as infallible and as unchallengeable as physical forces," these forces in fact derive from society itself and symbolize it. Durkheim's and Alfred Radcliffe-Brown's view that taboo is essentially proscription, "the expression of a renunciatory or repressive form of morality" (ibid. 58), is then taken up by Sigmund Freud, the issues of classification and renunciation / repression being closely intertwined, so that for the latter, in his "attempts to use his theory of the unconscious to account for the two aspects of taboo to which his predecessors attracted attention: ambivalence and contagion" (ibid.), taboo is defined as:

> prohibitions of primaeval [*sic*] antiquity which were at some time externally imposed upon a generation of primitive men; they must, that is to say, no doubt have been impressed on them violently by the previous generation. These prohibitions must have concerned activities towards which there was a strong inclination. They must then have persisted from generation to generation, perhaps merely as a result of tradition transmitted through parental and social authority. (Freud 31)[8]

There are clear parallels between Freud's and Durkheim's theory: They both "identify taboo with renunciation; . . . view contagiousness as symbolic displacement" and "the ambivalence of what is tabooed as the reification of an ambivalent attitude toward it" (Valeri 59). But no matter whether taboo is linked to magic or morality, whether the psychoanalytical, sociological or anthropological dimension is more important, any comprehensive explanation must also take into account the classification of objects and the cosmological ideas that exist in particular societies. This insight prompted several 'classificatory' or 'taxonomic' theories of taboo, amongst them the work of Edmund Leach and Mary Douglas. With Leach, the notion of taboo is considerably widened, so as "to include any kind of 'prohibition, explicit and implicit, conscious and unconscious'" (ibid. 61). This allows him "to treat in the same analytic framework phenomena like aversion, disgust, judgements of inedibility or unmarriageability

8 ❧ *Stefan Horlacher*

(due to danger or a sense of propriety), and formal prohibitions—in sum, the whole spectrum of socially shared avoidances" (ibid.). At the basis of Leach's classificatory theory is a claim about cognition, which views taboo as the manifestation of a "kind of discriminatory repression...necessary to the functioning of conceptual thought." Thus, taboo "serves to discriminate categories in men's social universe," and in so doing "reduces the ambiguities of reality to clear-cut ideal types" (ibid. 63). As such, the function of taboo would be to repress "interstitial states produced by the application of discrete conceptual classes on the continuum of experience." For Leach, the fact that these interstitial states "undermine the work of classification by confusing adjacent categories" explains "their association with 'sacredness,' that is, with powers that are both contaminating and ambiguous." If taboos are considered as rules for the avoidance of such powers, and if they induce mankind to avoid the sacred, they also "keep the destructive powers of confusion at bay and help maintain the unambiguous categorization that is a prerequisite of successful communication" (ibid.).

A second classificatory approach was advanced by Mary Douglas. As the title of her analysis of taboo already suggests, for her the notion of pollution takes precedence over taboo. She combines structural-functionalist elements—"follow[ing] Radcliffe-Brown in considering pollution as a sanction, and thus as presupposing the taboo it sanctions" (ibid. 70)—with a more cognitive approach that "makes pollution primary but only by giving it some of the properties that taboo has in Leach." Drawing on Lord Chesterfield's definition of dirt as "matter out of place," Douglas argues that objects are not considered dirty in and of themselves, but because of their status or classification in a system of categories. If in the most general formulation her theory "states that pollution arises from what is residual in terms of *any* type of classification," Valeri argues that "in practice her most novel and stimulating contribution lies in associating pollution with what is out of place in terms of *one* particular kind of classification—namely taxonomy" (73). The basic issue on which the whole theory of pollution as taxonomic anomaly rests is whether it is "possible to show that everything polluting is taxonomically anomalous and everything taxonomically anomalous is polluting" (ibid. 74). The problem here is that it has been shown that taboo is produced by a "normative classification by means of prototypes, rather than by a taxonomic impulse proper" (ibid. 78), and that the "exclusive linkage of taboo with categorical intermediacy or anomaly leaves

Taboo, Transgression, and Literature ❧ 9

out precisely what epitomizes taboo in both popular and anthropological discourse: the taboos on incest and cannibalism" (ibid. 83).[9] This deficit in taxonomic theories of taboo gave rise to Françoise Héritier's hypothesis that the "avoidance of the identical" is of prime importance, that is "the proscription of associating—at least with regard to eating, reproducing, and having sex—two terms that are in some crucial respect considered the same" (ibid.).[10] If with Héritier "the principle of avoided identity" is still "the counterpart of a principle of balance of contraries and thus of difference," the avoidance of identity becomes even more primary in the work of Alain Testard, for whom "taboo is concerned solely with disjoining a substance from itself, and thus with creating difference where lack of difference is implied" (ibid. 86; cf. Testard 1985 and 1991):

> Testard's theory of taboo, and more generally of symbolic efficacy, seems completely at odds with the usual structuralist and functionalist theories, particularly those of Leach and Douglas. While they stress the preservation of difference, he stresses its creation from the negation of identity. Their presuppositions are dualistic, his are monistic. Identity is for them secondary, for it presupposes a system of differences, but for him the opposite is true: identity is primary and difference is derivative. (ibid. 91)

More subject- and body-oriented theories on taboo have been formulated by Alfred Gell, Anne Meigs, Julia Kristeva and Valerio Valeri himself. Gell, for whom "taboo does not signal a self that preexists it" but is "a form of existence of the self" (ibid. 97), develops a theory that takes "taboo's role in creating a sense of personal identity and agency" into account. Arguing that taboo not only expresses but constitutes the self and that "personal identity consists in a difference from other humans which coincides with a difference in their relationship with the world" (ibid. 98), he maintains that "taboo, by carving out a part of the world, carves out a self." Such a self—and this is where Gell's theory has its shortcomings—must also, however, be located in a body, given that the relations between object and subject regulated by taboo are principally "eating, touching, and penetrating, as in killing and having sex" (ibid. 101). "All these," Valeri points out, "involve the body as desiring, that is as feeding on its objects, consuming them," so that it seems necessary to stress the "crucial element of corporeality inherent in taboo" (ibid.). Both Anna Meigs and Julia Kristeva have subsequently re-emphasized the body-centeredness

10 ❧ *Stefan Horlacher*

of the notion of pollution, and it is the latter in particular who has not only injected "a subjective and developmental dimension into the exclusively classificatory perspective of structuralism," but also shown how a

> subject symbolically constituted, but necessarily located in the body, must be haunted by the fear of its disintegration through the body, since it constantly experiences the body's resistance to the subject's symbolic ordering of itself. The embodied subject's fear of disintegration through the body and by the body is the ultimate basis for the notion of pollution. (ibid. 111)

From this perspective, pollution and abjection coincide as "the cultural form taken by what threatens the subject because it has to do with its precultural stage—that it is the presymbolic making itself felt in the symbolic" (ibid. 110).[11] Working within this framework, and developing upon as well as combining both Freud's critique of religion and Douglas's taxonomy of the biblical system of food taboos, Kristeva postulates a three-stage trajectory of pollution that is premised on increasing levels of abstraction moving from the primitive, via Mosaic and Levitican laws, to Christianity, where "the Christian notion of sin substitutes the Levitican notion of pollution" (ibid. 107): Whereas "Judaism externalises abjection, Christianity internalizes it" (ibid.). Kristeva thus reads the history of morality as "that of a progressive reinforcement of the 'male' principle of symbolic differentiation and order as against the 'female' principle of indifferentiation" (ibid. 106). More specifically, what has taken place in the shift from the Old Testament to the New with regard to pollution is a "reversal of the source of danger, from outside to inside, [which] correlates with a transformation of orality" (ibid.).[12]

Valeri, whose interdisciplinary approach eschews the usual distinction between anthropological and psychoanalytical approaches to the topic, argues "that the phenomenon of taboo and the various dangers that motivate it must be apprehended at the points of articulation and confrontation of the subject and the conditions—symbolic and presymbolic—of its existence" (111). For him, the "greater the embodiment of the subject,…the greater its potential permeability to external bodies," and the greater, also, "the potential that any material undermining of the body (diseases, etc.) be interpreted as the undermining of the subject." From this it follows that potentially

Taboo, Transgression, and Literature ✸✸✸ 11

"any disease can be read as a pollution, and any pollution can turn into a disease" (ibid. 111f.). Thus,

> [t]he focus of the language of taboo and 'pollution' on the body as carrier of a subject that is constituted by symbolic classifications should be made evident by the concern of the symbolic classification with food, excretions, and the processes of transformation and decay of the body that are principally associated with taboo and pollution. A taboo usually marks some event or situation that is likely to threaten the integrity of the body as the seat of the integrity of the subject. But...this integrity of the subject may in turn depend on the integrity of a certain external object, as determined by the classificatory system at large. If the focus of interest of taboo, then, is ultimately the subject, it does not exclude—indeed, it must include—all classifications of objects that have any bearing on the subject....Thus pollution, although focussed on the subject, modelled on the body's permeability to external objects, and principally concerned with the substances and processes where this permeability is located, may stray very far from them. It may...become entangled with all kinds of medical and magical theories and practices where they exist. Furthermore, it may be used to enforce rules, to shore up or even express hierarchical relations, and so on. (ibid. 112)

If this survey has at least given a glimpse of the different approaches to taboo ranging from traditional British cultural or social anthropology, via continental European sociology, structuralism and psychoanalysis, to post-structuralism, and if it has become apparent that these approaches are often hardly compatible in that they emphasize entirely different aspects, it seems—even at the risk of an oversimplification—necessary to offer at least something like a generally accepted working definition of taboo which the following literary analyses can take as a starting point and from which they can diverge into more specialized Durkheimian, Freudian, Kristevan, or Valerian directions and approaches. To produce this kind of general guideline or smallest common denominator of taboo and to propose a non-specialized definition, a combination of the respective entries of the *Encyclopædia Britannica* and the *Oxford English Dictionary Online* proved helpful. In both cases, a shift in the meaning and use of the term can be viewed as a productive instance of the 'margins rewriting the center' and as a measure of the impact that post-colonial discourses have had after Edward Said's seminal *Orientalism* in redefining the field of anthropology.

12 &&& *Stefan Horlacher*

Thus, whereas the original 1888 articles on taboo and totemism by Sir James Frazer for the *Encyclopædia Britannica* "laid the foundation for his work on *primitive* religion" (Cannon [n. pag.], emphasis added), the recent entry defines taboo more universally as "the prohibition of an action or the use of an object based on ritualistic distinctions of them either as being sacred and consecrated or as being dangerous, unclean, and accursed" ("Taboo" 2006, [n. pag.]). While this entry still stresses that taboos "were most highly developed in the Polynesian societies of the South Pacific" (ibid.), it also makes clear that "they have been present in virtually all cultures" (ibid.) and that there is an

> inconsistency between the taboos in which notions of sacredness or holiness are apparent...and taboos in which notions of uncleanliness were the motivating factor.... Generally, the prohibition that is inherent in a taboo includes the idea that a breach or defiance of the taboo will automatically be followed by some kind of trouble to the offender.... These misfortunes would ordinarily be regarded as accidents or bad luck, but to believers in taboos they are regarded as punishments for breaking some taboo. A person meets with an accident or has no success in a given pursuit, and, in seeking for its cause, he or others infer that he has in some manner committed a breach of taboo.... There is no generally accepted explanation of taboos, but there is broad agreement that the taboos current in any society tend to relate to objects and actions that are significant for the social order and that belong to the general system of social control. (ibid.)[13]

Slightly different aspects are emphasized in the entry in the *Oxford English Dictionary Online*, where the meaning of taboo is defined as

> [t]he putting of a person or thing under prohibition or interdict, perpetual or temporary; the fact or condition of being so placed; the prohibition or interdict itself. Also, the institution or practice by which such prohibitions are recognized and enforced.... The institution is generally supposed to have had a religious or superstitious origin (certain things being considered the property of the gods or superhuman powers, and therefore forbidden to men), and to have been extended to political and social affairs, being usually controlled by the king or great chiefs in conjunction with the priests. Some things, acts, and words were permanently taboo or interdicted to the mass of the people, and others specially to women, while a temporary taboo was frequently imposed, often apparently quite arbitrarily.

Taking the survey of theoretical approaches to taboo as well as the definitions offered above as their background, the task of the articles collected in this book is to analyze the complex dynamic of intrinsic (textual) and extrinsic (contextual) transformations inherent to notions of taboo and transgression as these have developed and are represented in British literature from the Elizabethan period through to the present. As noted above, the concept—or even "idiom" (Valeri 113)—of taboo is here not understood in a narrow sense but rather viewed as comprising persons as well as locations, nutrition, the pronouncing of names (e.g., relatives) and certain actions, cultural practices and conditions (such as those regarding the dead). Moreover, the analyses will consider what functions taboos fulfill in British society at different points in time, bearing in mind that, on the one hand, taboos can be functionalized by a society to strengthen its identity (cf. the scapegoat), that they can create security since they exclude objects, actions and persons viewed as threatening and thus produce, albeit *ex negativo*, a legal sphere in which certain topics are precluded from being openly discussed, but that, on the other hand, this function can also be interpreted as a highly effective means of social control, that is as a collective system of repression and negative conventions that draw borders and help secure authority along the temporally and culturally specific axes of the sacred and the profane, the pure and the impure. Since the inherent transgressive potential and the sanctions applied for trespassing taboos provide an insight into the socio-psychological condition of a society and culture, the interdependent, overlapping discourses surrounding the concept of taboo—such as transgression and repression, innovation and conservatism, punishment and pleasure, or sadism and masochism, to name but a few—can be understood as an arena of contestation in which a society negotiates not only its values and beliefs (from the Inquisition via post-Enlightenment secularization to sexual liberation) but also its borders and power structures.

Especially as far as Western or so-called permissive, 'enlightened' or taboo-free societies are concerned, one has to ask whether this supposed liberation from taboos is not also a disguised, deferred and disavowed discursive structure of repression which excludes the abject in the form of impotency, incontinence, incest, cannibalism, insanity, implicit racism, old age and death. If as some critics argue we live in an age that prides itself "in its aversion towards taboos and in which ever more taboos are losing their erstwhile power" precisely because they are regarded as "inhuman, repressive, irrational and archaic" (Kaltenbrunner 7), there is also "much to indicate that under the guise of an emancipatory and critically enlightened rational thinking new taboos have been created that are no less repressive than their predecessors" (ibid. 9). In this sense, maybe "the censor of old" has merely been "replaced by an authority that operates by methods that are more diffuse and subtle, in part because we have ourselves internalized them" (ibid.), and thus behind our total aversion to taboos there continue to operate coercive mechanisms that have yet to be revealed. In any event, the exploration of the paradoxical and polysemic potential of taboos does give rise to the following issues: whether taboos will remain a necessary constituent of human society in the future, in how far their transgression automatically generates new taboos, and whether or not they can be viewed as producing knowledge and furthering progress. As a matter of fact, taboos need not always "be characterized by irrational or repressive qualities; they can equally well have a 'nurturing function'…, that is to say have a life conserving or enhancing role, which is also therefore rational if we accept Alfred North Whitehead's definition that the inherent function of reason is 'to promote the art of life'" (ibid. 14f.). Moreover, as Kaltenbrunner contends: "[the] complete removal of taboos would destroy the fabric of human society. One taboo can be replaced by another, even the conversion of taboos from negative into positive ones (or vice versa) is possible, but taboos cannot be eliminated from people's lives." (16) This is, of course, reminiscent of Alexander Mitscherlich's line of reasoning when he calls those who would merely negate taboos fools who have not yet learned what fear means and understand nothing of the world. Especially from the perspective of psychoanalysis, "the utopia of a taboo-free society" is often considered as compromised by the fact that it was conceived by people with drives for which there are no predetermined limits regarding their satisfaction (cf. ibid. 15). It is in this sense that Thody argues that taboos "embody something of the principle of deferred gratification which Freud sees as the first step towards the process of civilization. They thus represent a practice which any culture rejects completely only at its peril" (307). From this it follows that taboos can be understood "as a means whereby society tries to hold itself together against internal decay as well as external threats" (ibid. 304), and that, although taboos are irrational "in so far as they never allow themselves to be reduced to mere means for determinate ends, it is hard to deny them 'a deeper rationality'" (Kaltenbrunner 12).

Taboo, Transgression, and Literature &&& 15

Since taboos are normally perceived of as having an emotive component, their transgression not only creates tensions and triggers mechanisms of exclusion or punishment, they can also be a catalyst for a controlled release of pent-up aggressions and libidinal energies as is the case with jokes (cf. Horlacher 2009, 17–47) or swear words (cf. Eggert and Golec 9). From this perspective, it is evident that the pleasure-inducing dimension involved in transgressing taboos has to be taken into consideration too—as does the problematic and ambivalent 'nature' of transgression itself. As Chris Jenks has emphasized, to "transgress is to go beyond the bounds or limits set by a commandment or law or convention, it is to violate or infringe. But to transgress is also more than this, it is to announce and even laudate [*sic*] the commandment, the law or the convention." Thus, transgression becomes "a deeply reflexive act of denial and affirmation" (2). But if it is defined as "that conduct which breaks rules or exceeds boundaries," what then "is the character of the cultures that provide for the appreciation or receptability of such behaviour?" (Ibid. 3) Is transgression, as some theorists would have it, central to postmodernity, is it the hallmark of an aesthetic of the modern, or is it an integral part of our history of laws, the symbolic order and taboos? Does transgressive behavior deny limits and boundaries or does it exceed and thus complete them? And doesn't every rule, limit, boundary or edge carry with it its own fracture, penetration or impulse to disobey? If transgression and excess thus become an important component of the rule, they would neither be "an abhorration nor a luxury" but rather "dynamic forces in cultural reproduction preventing stagnation by breaking the rule while simultaneously ensuring stability by reaffirming the rule" (ibid. 7). As John Jervis succinctly argues:

> The transgressive is reflexive, questioning both its own role and that of the culture that has defined it in its otherness. It is not simply a reversal, a mechanical inversion of an existing order it opposes. Transgression, unlike opposition or reversal, involves hybridization, the mixing of categories and the questioning of the boundaries that separate categories. It is not, in itself, subversion; it is not an overt and deliberate challenge to the status quo. What it does do, though, is implicitly interrogate the law, pointing not just to the specific, and frequently arbitrary, mechanisms of power on which it rests—despite its universalizing pretensions—but also to its complicity, its involvement in what it prohibits. (4)

Literature, of course, can also be understood as a phenomenon of transgression which is characterized by the fact that while literary texts bear a clear historical imprint, they nevertheless transcend any narrow notion of mimesis which would reduce them to a mirror or straightforward representation of their 'given' reality. Since taboos are normally not the topic of open discussions but largely internalized, any form of critical questioning is realized, if at all, only through massive outside influence. Given literature's ability to constitute a discursive field in which even marginalized, aberrant voices can articulate themselves, to give voice to something which could be called 'the collective unconscious' and to transcend its time of origin (cf. Horlacher 2004, 291–329), literature becomes an extraordinarily privileged medium for the depiction and analysis of phenomena such as taboo and transgression.[14] And the more so if one considers literature with Kristeva as "the ultimate coding of our crises, of our most intimate and most serious apocalypses" (208) and as "an elaboration, a discharge, and a hollowing out of abjection through the Crisis of the Word" (ibid.). However, if the transgressing of prohibitions—a transgressing of which literature is also part—is not the exception but a constitutive element of the taboo or prohibition, this means that transgression is always already codified (cf. Bataille 63ff.). Very often there exist exact definitions of when and by whom transgressive acts are allowed, one example being killing during a war.[15] Since taboos have to be communicated publicly in order to function— "The taboo is always linked to a collective public. There are no taboos that are not public." (Eggert 21)—the ambivalence between inclusion, exclusion and transgression engenders an ambivalence concerning the representation of taboos. These phenomena of prohibitions (such as aniconism) and precepts regarding representation (e.g., of the naked human body) have the effect that across the arts as well as throughout history "ritualized representations and symbolizations have been constitutive for taboos," that is to say, that "taboos reveal a genuinely aesthetic component which extends from non-linguistic symbolizations through to the standardization of aesthetics" (ibid. 22). From this in turn it follows that an approach that conceives of taboos only as social phenomena misses the point, that textual analyses need to pay attention to the strategies and the contents of symbolizations, and that aesthetic traditions need to be taken into consideration, such as, to give but one example, the modernist aesthetic of innovation which often depends on rupture and on violating taboos. Moreover, inherent to the topic of taboo and transgression is that it raises fundamental questions regarding the limits of art, its self-conception and its aesthetics based on power: "What is art allowed to do?—Is art allowed to do anything?" (Ibid.)

Given the specific qualities of literary texts as discussed above and their careful selection in this volume, the plays, novels and poems analyzed should make it possible to provide a comprehensive survey of some of the most important developments in Britain's aesthetic, religious, economic and political systems of values as these are represented in and negotiated through literature. The literary texts selected are characterized by their contemporary as well as by their historic relevance and cultural influence, so that changes and alterations in the epistemological, ideological, and discursive systems as well as in the literary techniques and aesthetics applied can be shown on a larger diachronic scale. Although aspects from Cultural Studies, New Historicism as well as functional approaches are taken into consideration, the focus is primarily within literary, not cultural studies. This manner of proceeding makes it possible to undertake close readings of major texts—ranging from the works of Shakespeare via Milton and Bunyan to Joyce and McEwan—with a view to the larger synchronic as well as diachronic patterns of thought they are part of and helped to shape, and—in a second step—to link these to the extra-literary world. For this reason, the ten literary analyses are introduced and contextualized with the help of two diachronic survey articles. The first examines the changing legal framework as well as the concomitant transformation of social norms and explores their interaction with the collective imaginary as exemplified by literature. Given the longevity of censorship in the United Kingdom, that is, the tabooing of certain literary texts, the second survey article concentrates on literary strategies for subverting or transgressing taboos, considering as well the fact that the institution or field of literature has in the past operated, and continues to, with its own specific taboo structures.[16]

Notes

I would like to thank Claudia Lainka, M.A., for her precious help in formatting and proofing of the manuscript, and Peter Stear, M.A., for preliminary research and help with translations and stylistic issues.

1. Cf. the debate around Dani Levy's Hitler comedy *Mein Führer—Die wirklich wahrste Wahrheit über Adolf Hitler*, which was released in German cinemas in early 2007.
2. Cf. also: "In so far as they predate the invention not only of religion but also of laws and philosophical speculation, they are indeed a relict of a pre-ethical stage in the evolution of human thought" (Thody 312).

18   *Stefan Horlacher*

3. Cf. Freud 156: "[T]he beginnings of religion, ethics, society, and art meet in the Oedipus complex."
4. Cf. also Edmund Leach, who has called the incest taboo "the great event with which culture began," and Claude Lévi-Strauss, who sees it as "the corner stone of human society" (Thody 37).
5. Cf., for example, Thody; Hoffmann; Graupmann; Holden; McDonald.
6. "Though the fundamental borderline between the sacred and the profane in defining taboo varies across cultures and epochs, even apparent borders have proved themselves paradoxical, or rather ambiguous. The word sacred derives from the Latin *sacer*, which denotes both what is holy and heinous, whereas profane denotes that which lies outside the *fanum* or sanctuary, has not been consecrated, and hence can also mean the everyday or quotidian. *Sacer* means both consecrated *and* execrated, what is both revered and repellent, and has therefore the same inherent numinous ambiguity as the originally Polynesian word *tabu*" (Kaltenbrunner 8). All translations from German texts are by Peter Stear, M.A.
7. "The uncertain etymology and origin, as well as the even more indeterminate meaning brought about through translations and circulation—ranging from 'consecrated' to 'sacrosanct', from 'inviolable' to 'forbidden'—have helped rather than hindered the dissemination of the word in Europe. Besides this, and the attraction of the exotic, one also however needs to consider the productive vacuum of an actual lexical gap. For the anti-norm or prohibition, determined by religious veneration as well as fear, by experiences undergone as well as political intentions, by the replacement of instincts lost by new bonds, for all of these there was no single word in the language, no 'obvious marker'. Taboo filled that gap, has been further 'secularized' in its meaning, reduced down to what is embarrassing and objectionable, with the latter also eventually becoming taboo" (Betz 141).
8. Cf. also Freud 34f.: "I will now sum up the respects in which light has been thrown on the nature of taboo by comparing it with the obsessional prohibitions of neurotics. Taboo is a primaeval prohibition forcibly imposed (by some authority) from outside, and directed against the most powerful longings to which human beings are subject. The desire to violate it persists in their unconscious; those who obey the taboo have an ambivalent attitude to what the taboo prohibits. The magical power that is attributed to taboo is based on the capacity for arousing temptation; and it acts like a contagion because examples are contagious and because the prohibited desire in the unconscious shifts from one thing to another. The fact that the violation of a taboo can be atoned for by a renunciation shows that renunciation lies at the basis of obedience to taboo."

9. For reasons of space, Claude Lévi-Strauss's important work on totemism and his basic thesis that "taboo creates a 'signification' which is reduced to the creation of a social difference, or rather a difference of social units" (Valeri 95) can only be mentioned in passing.

10. Françoise Héritier argues "that taboos maintain the balance of the world by proscribing the reinforcement of either of two contraries which is brought about by the summation of two or more identical (or equivalent) terms.... The taboo on incest belongs to the same logic: in order to reproduce certain relationships of contrariety in the social world, it proscribes the marital and even sexual association of people who are categorically identical" (Valeri 84).

11. Cf. ibid. 105: Ritual pollution "happens when the 'paternal' symbolic order does not sufficiently repress the 'maternal' semiotic order, when a subject that is the function of language does not completely displace a presubject that exists in the instability of the semiotic differentiation of the body." In Kristeva's interpretation, the phenomenon amounts to "a transposition into the realm of the symbolic of the borderline separating 'the territory of the body from the signifying chain'" (ibid.), which she terms "abjection: a loss of the symbolically, linguistically founded subject, a fall into its presymbolic stage, where the subject becomes lost in the object instead of constituting itself by standing against the object" (ibid. 106).

12. Cf. also: "Levitican orality is linked with eating; Christian orality is linked with speaking" (ibid. 106).

13. What we should add to these definitions is that typically, and cross-culturally, taboo appears to be primarily concerned with "the body in its exchanges with other bodies," such as decomposing, excreting, bleeding, reproducing, eating, and to define "basic social rules involved in those bodily exchanges or symbolized by them (for instance, the taboos on murder and incest, both of which are usually symbolized by a polluting flow of blood). Taboo also seems to be involved in the avoidance of sacrilege, that is, of improper relations with divinities and their appurtenances" (ibid. 48).

14. Literary texts are understood as being a central part of that "larger symbolic order by which a culture imagines its relation to the conditions of its existence" (Matus 5) and as a space "in which shared anxieties and tensions are articulated and symbolically addressed" (ibid. 7). Moreover, through active reader participation, literature renders imagination 'livable'—the fictional world can actually be experienced and can therefore be 'tested' and criticized—so that the literary text becomes a privileged space of simulation where the work on a cultural imaginary can take place (cf. Fluck).

15. Hence the 'heinous' act ascribed to the events of 9/11 as referenced above, the concomitant echoes of Pearl Harbor, the subsequent

20 ⁂ *Stefan Horlacher*

       need to invoke a 'war on terror', and the categorical indistinctness in international law when dealing with asymmetrical warfare and failed states.

16. This is exemplified by the act of canonizing certain texts or genres, which may then invite acts of transgression, thereby allowing literature to retain its critical edge and to renew itself continually.

Works Cited

Bataille, Georges. *Die Erotik*. Munich: Matthes & Seitz, 1994.

Betz, Werner. "Tabu—Wörter und Wandel." *Meyers Enzyklopädisches Lexikon*. Vol. 23. 9th ed. Mannheim: Bibliographisches Institut, 1978. 141–44.

Cannon, John. "Frazer, Sir James." *The Oxford Companion to British History*. Oxford: Oxford UP, 2002. July 12, 2009 <http://www.encyclopedia.com>.

Douglas, Mary. *Purity and Danger: An Analysis of Pollution and Taboo*. London: Routledge and Kegan Paul, 1966.

Eggert, Hartmut. "Säkulare Tabus und die Probleme ihrer Darstellung. Thesen zur Eröffnung der Diskussion." *Tabu und Tabubruch. Literarische und sprachliche Strategien im 20. Jahrhundert*. Ed. Hartmut Eggert and Janusz Golec. Stuttgart: Metzler, 2002. 15–24.

Eggert, Hartmut, and Janusz Golec. "Vorwort." *Tabu und Tabubruch. Literarische und sprachliche Strategien im 20. Jahrhundert*. Eds. Hartmut Eggert and Janusz Golec. Stuttgart: Metzler, 2002. 7–14.

Fluck, Winfried. *Das kulturelle Imaginäre. Eine Funktionsgeschichte des amerikanischen Romans 1790–1900*. Frankfurt am Main: Suhrkamp, 1997.

Freud, Sigmund. *Totem and Taboo and Other Works*. The Standard Edition of the Complete Psychological Works of Sigmund Freud. Vol. XIII. London: Hogarth Press, 1975.

Gell, Alfred. "Reflections on a Cut Finger: Taboo in the Umeda Conception of the Self." *Fantasy and Symbol: Studies in Anthropological Interpretation*. Ed. R.H. Hook. New York: Academic Press, 1979. 133–48.

Graupmann, Jürgen. *Das Lexikon der Tabus*. Bergisch-Gladbach: Bastei Lübbe, 1998.

Heinschink, Mozes F., and Michael Teichmann. "Taboo and Shame (Ladž) in Traditional Roma Communities." *Rombase*. July 14, 2009 <http://romani.uni-graz.at/rombase>, orig. publ. October 2003.

Héritier, Françoise. "Symbolique de l'inceste et de sa prohibition." *La Fonction symbolique: Essais d'anthropologie*. Eds. Michel Izard and Pierre Smith. Paris: Gallimard, 1979. 209–43.

Hoffmann, Arne. *Das Lexikon der Tabubrüche*. Berlin: Schwarzkopf und Schwarzkopf, 2003.

Holden, Lynn. *Encyclopedia of Taboos*. Oxford: ABC-CLIO, 2000.

Horlacher, Stefan. "*Daniel Martin, America, Faith in Fakes/Travels in Hyperreality* und das Verschwinden der Realität—Überlegungen zum antizipatorischen Potential von Literatur." *Beyond Extremes. Reflexion und Repräsentation von Modernisierungsprozessen im zeitgenössischen britischen Roman*. Eds. Stefan Glomb and Stefan Horlacher. Tübingen: Narr, 2004. 291–329.

———. "A Short Introduction to Theories of Humour, the Comic and Laughter." *Gender and Laughter: Comic Affirmation and Subversion in Traditional and Modern Media*. Eds. Gaby Pailer, Andreas Böhn, Stefan Horlacher, and Uli Scheck. Amsterdam: Rodopi, 2009. 17–47.

Jenks, Chris. *Transgression*. London: Routledge, 2003.

Jervis, John. *Transgressing the Modern*. Oxford: Blackwell, 1999.

Kaltenbrunner, Gerd-Klaus. "Vorwort des Herausgebers." *Der Innere Zensor. Neue und Alte Tabus in unserer Gesellschaft*. Ed. Gerd-Klaus Kaltenbrunner. Munich: Herder, 1987. 7–18.

Kristeva, Julia. *Powers of Horror: An Essay on Abjection*. New York: Columbia UP, 1982.

Matus, Jill. *Unstable Bodies. Victorian Representations of Sexuality and Maternity*. Manchester: Manchester UP, 1995.

McDonald, James. *A Dictionary of Obscenity, Taboo & Euphemism*. London: Sphere Books, 1988.

Mitscherlich, Alexander. *Auf dem Weg zur vaterlosen Gesellschaft*. Munich: Piper, 1963.

Oxtoby, Willard Gurdon. "Holy (The Sacred)." *Dictionary of the History of Ideas. Studies of Selected Pivotal Ideas*. Vol. 2. Ed. Philip P. Wiener. New York: Charles Scribner's Sons, 1973. 513–14.

"Taboo." *The Oxford English Dictionary Online* (OED). 1989. 2nd ed. Oxford: Oxford UP. July 14, 2009 <http://www.oed.com/>.

"Taboo." *Encyclopædia Britannica 2007 Ultimate Reference Suite*. DVD. Chicago: Encyclopædia Britannica, 2006.

Testard, Alain. *Le communisme primitif*. Paris: Eds. de la Maison des sciences de l'homme, 1985.

———. *Des mythes et des croyances: Esquisse d'une théorie générale*. Paris: Eds. de la Maison des sciences de l'homme, 1991.

Thody, Philip. *Don't Do It! A Dictionary of the Forbidden*. London: St. Martin's Press, 1997.

Türcke, Christoph. *Gewalt und Tabu. Philosophische Grenzgänge*. 2nd ed. Lüneburg: zu Klampen, 1992.

Valeri, Valerio. *The Forest of Taboos: Morality, Hunting, and Identity among the Huaulu of the Moluccas*. Madison: Wisconsin UP, 2000.

CHAPTER II

TABOO AND TRANSGRESSION: A SOCIO-HISTORICAL AND SOCIO-CULTURAL PERSPECTIVE

Uwe Böker

The Taboo: General Remarks

Especially with a view to the two fundamental aspects of human existence, sexuality and death, the following socio-historical introduction will focus on the main religious, political, moral, and social discourses that have regulated the silencing or breaking of taboos since the sixteenth century, that is, since the invention of printing and Henry VIII's institutionalization of an independent Church of England.

Even after the first civil injunction against sodomy in 1533 "as a symbolic token of the supremacy of the secular courts over the ecclesiastical courts" (Norton 1992, 16), it is still possible to distinguish between a variety of transgressions. Ultimately, however, all transgressions—including the breaking of a taboo—fell under the jurisdiction of the state or civil society. Nevertheless, and at least until relatively recently, the Church of England has been a powerful institution that continues to exert its influence on the religious and moral attitudes of the population. One can thus distinguish between a variety of transgressions: the religious and / or legal concepts of sin, offence and crime on the one hand, and the taboo on the other hand, with, as already noted, sexuality and death as fundamental to human existence being the two main areas of tabooing, whereas the state, civil society and the church are the main institutions regulating acts of tabooing.

The concept of taboo may be variously applied to persons, locations, nutrition, the pronouncing of names, certain actions, cultural

24 &&& *Uwe Böker*

practices and conditions, as well as to literary texts. But as prohibitions and transgressions are logical concomitants of the concept, a taboo cannot, from an epistemological point of view, be identified unless it is the subject of a narrative in the broadest sense, that is, a story either told in the act of face-to-face verbal communication, for example in a confession, in a trial account, in journalistic, documentary or literary texts. Taboos are thus always related to social activities that are prohibited in a general way—either by a religious institution or, more usually in England, by common and / or statutory law as well as civil society and are identified through verbalization. Such taboos and prohibitions have a stabilizing function in that they exclude objects, actions and persons viewed as threatening, but also in the sense that they create routines in order to cope with situations such as sexuality and procreation, death and dying. Although taboos and their transgression are embedded in social practices, analysis would not be possible without some form of textual artifact in the broadest sense. Thus P.B. Shelley's *Queen Mab* was considered by a court ruling as blasphemous and seditious, since the writing and publishing of the poem, including the notes directed against the church, religion, monarchy and marriage, were seen as violations of a taboo, as was Lord Byron's incestuous relationship with his half-sister (incest is a capital crime since 1650, cf. Blackstone iv, 64).

According to the logocentric Judeo-Christian tradition, the prohibition of uttering God's name resulted in one of the most powerful taboos in history, that of blasphemy (cf. Marsh). Hence, the act of silencing can be considered as one of the basic features of a taboo. It is therefore necessary to analyze the various forms of religious, political or social censorship by the three primary agents of institutionalized social control and / or moral reform in England / Britain, that is, church, state and civil society. Social control, supervising all kinds of religious, legal, moral or social transgressions, includes (a) censorship of the theater, (b) censorship of the printing press as well as private reading and (c) moral supervision by the ecclesiastical courts and, later on, mostly by voluntary and participatory reform associations, as well as the state. The existence of taboos in contemporary, multicultural British society will be dealt with separately at the end of this chapter.

Silencing can, however, never be absolute, otherwise prohibition, censorship, acts of shaming, humiliation or victimization of the transgressor and transgressions would be impossible. Considering the taboo of sodomy and the standard form of indictment—"a crime

A Socio-Historical Perspective 25

not fit to be named; *peccatum illud horribile, inter christianos non nominandum*" (Blackstone iv, 216)—the injunction to silence would be futile without some euphemistic and metaphoric circumscription, such as "the infamous crime against nature" or "the unnatural offence" (Offence Against the Person Act of 1861), or the association of "buggery" with "bulgarus" (the members of an Orthodox heretical church).

As to blasphemy, during the nineteenth century, "the imperative to silence the blasphemer progressively inflected and obsessively etched itself into legal procedure and reportage" (Marsh 233). It should be noted that in 1883 Judge North abstained from uttering the "blasphemous" words or sentences in the *Freethinker* trial, remarking: "The prisoner Foote...said, among other things, a certain thing which seemed to me to be——. Well, I would rather not touch upon it" (237). The 1888 Law of Libel Amendment Act even declared that forbidden (blasphemous) words ought neither to be spoken nor even silently recorded:

> It is no longer necessary to set out in the indictment the...passages in full. It is sufficient to deposit the book, newspaper, or other documents containing the alleged libel with the indictment, or other judicial proceeding, together with particulars showing precisely, by reference to pages, columns, and lines, in what part of the book, newspaper, or other document, the alleged libel is to be found. (237f.)

In the case of the Oscar Wilde trials, the shorthand writers of the Court "declined to print the proceedings of any of the trials on the ground that the details disclosed by them were 'unfit' for publication" (Foldy xii). The newspapers decided to fulfill their task of 'social control' and to cover whatever was said in the court-room, although dialogue considered improper was left out. Silencing as well as circumlocution are both indications of the "awareness of what not to do or say or think or feel" (Meier 164), and the Victorians seem to have been masters of such circumlocution (cf. Thomas 1959 on the double standard).

Discourses are, however, instruments of power and hegemony, and the principles and legitimacy of a given order are made manifest by means of institutionalized social rules and regulations that serve to shape the basic orientations of actors and to make available relatively permanent and binding norms and values (cf. Böker 2002, 35ff.). This is, for example, the case with blasphemy. Although originally conceived

26   Uwe Böker

as an offence against the Christian religion, with the aim "to pervert, insult, and mislead others by means of licentious and contumelious abuse applied to sacred subjects" (Blackstone iv, 59; Stephen 125 n.2), the 1650 *Blasphemy Act* was meant to suppress the religious and political opposition of the Ranters and other Antinomians and to punish crimes against the state. In the 1676 case of *Rex v Taylor*, the Lord Chief Justice Sir Matthew Hale stated that: "blasphemous words were not only an offence to God and religion, but a crime against the laws, State and Government.... Christianity is parcel of the laws of England and therefore to reproach the Christian religion is to speak in subversion of the law" (*WrigleyClaymon.com*). The court was of the opinion that an attack on Christian beliefs would undermine and endanger society as a whole. As the late eighteenth-century political trial of John Wilkes, M.P., or the nineteenth-century blasphemy trials mentioned below demonstrate, sedition and blasphemy are usually mentioned together. Blasphemy thus came to be "the chameleon phrase which meant the criticism of whatever the ruling authority of the moment established as orthodox religious doctrine" (*Caslon Analytics*).

As some topics are in every society precluded from public or even private discussion, taboos are an important element of the collective system of repression. The social function of taboos has therefore to be considered as the stabilizing factor in social and cultural systems. Taboos related to religion, politics, sexuality and death—such as for instance blasphemy, sodomy, incest, cannibalism, child abuse, infanticide, adultery, bigamy, masturbation etc.—have over the centuries been controlled by prohibitions against verbalizing tabooed acts, except by circumlocution. Taboos indicate or represent social control, especially with regard to class, gender, and race, cultural hegemony, the norms and values of legal cultures, or they can express the attitudes and mentalities of subcultures and countercultures.

Basic conflicts over social norms and values that are taken for granted may then also be subverted or deconstructed by political groups. Thus, Quakers and other religious groups were confronted with "a ban on thought, a form of suppressing a set of political ideas and their utterance by means of censorship and other forms of political and legal repression" (Gurr, this volume), and this despite Milton or Bunyan daring to transgress censorship. Especially during the nineteenth century, 'coarse,' 'shocking,' or 'blasphemous' language was considered as lower-class, linguistic subversion of the existing political system; members of the elite, however, were not prosecuted for the same offence (cf. Marsh 55). When Richard Carlile was tried for publishing Tom Paine in 1820, he was still allowed to read the entire 'blasphemous' *The Age of Reason* aloud to the jury; others were given leave to quote from the texts of canonized (although evidently blasphemous) upper- and middle-class authors (cf. 69); but some years later it was ruled illegal to publish "even a correct account of proceedings in a Court of Justice, if such an account contain[ed] matter of a seditious, blasphemous or indecent nature" (235). Although the control of anti-establishment, reformist and political groupings was intensified, complete censorship could never be realized.

Thus, there are "discursive fields in which even marginalized, aberrant voices can articulate themselves" (Horlacher, this volume). But this requires readers who have learned the norms and values of their culture so that they are, as members of an elite, able to appreciate the qualities of literary texts that are, as a rule, "a major contested category in the production of culture" (Sinfield 2). "Stories of how the world goes" (or should go) in the medium of print do form a special kind of knowledge, although this is then itself defined by the agents of cultural hegemony in contrast to other kinds of every-day, social, theoretical or literary forms of knowledge, especially when these are voiced by competing social groups that tell different stories of their private lives, their concepts of society, or their interpretations of the world.

Taboo and the Agents of Social Control and Censorship

The three primary agents of institutionalized social control in Britain, charged with supervising all kinds of religious, legal, moral or social actions (cf. Cohen 1985; Lowman; Böker 1994), have been the church, state and civil society. One has, however, to distinguish between censorship of the theater, censorship of printing, and religious or moral supervision by the church, which was carried out by voluntary and participatory reform associations, or, later on, by institutions of the state.

Theatrical censorship, in contrast to censorship of the press (cf. Connolly; Johnston; Stephens) had been since the sixteenth century regulated by state intervention (cf. Barroll 3: 41ff.). Since 1589, the Master of the Revels had been authorized to look through "comedies and tragedies, and...strike out such parts and matters as they shall find unfit and undecent to be handled in such plays, both for divinity and state." Thus, the authors of *Sir Thomas More* were told

28 ⚬⚬⚬ *Uwe Böker*

to leave "out the insurrection wholly and the cause ther off and begin with Sir Thomas More att the mayors sessions with a report afterwards off his good service don being Shrieve off London upon a mutiny against the Lumbards only by A short reportt and not otherwise att your own perills" (Clare 171).

Representations of popular protest or references to popular unrest were considered to be taboo. Hence, the deposition in Shakespeare's *Richard II* failed to appear in the first printing, and Jack Cade in his *Henry VI* (2nd part, III, 1, 362–63) was depicted as "a wild Morisco," that is, a demagogue, and his act of rebellion "a sort of saturnalia" (Barber 29), a reversal of the social structure, a topsy-turvydom of egalitarian non-hierarchical order: "the...play contains an unambiguously inscribed political ideology which enables the audience member or reader to understand Jack Cade as pathetic, ludicrous and potentially vicious aberration.... Cade's folly is identified with rebellious intentions, with the consequence that he is exposed to ridicule, expelled and executed." Although Cade's speeches are a political and discursive "indiscretion"; the feelings of the characters represent a "trangressive and illogical discourse," and the "expression of popular resentment...escapes being totally repressed" (Bristol 89) by the hegemonial powers.

In 1605, as Robinson notes: "An Act to restrain the Abuses of Players" made it an offence "[that] any person or persons do or shall, in any stage-play, interlude, show, May-game, or pageant, jestingly or profanely speak or use the holy name of God, or of Christ Jesus, or of the Holy Ghost, or of the Trinity (which are not to be spoken but with fear and reverence)" (397). Both dramatists and theaters had to be careful not to mention politically contentious topics and had to abstain from presenting religious characters on stage. Any discussion of such matters was forbidden,

> wherein either matters of religion or of the governance of the estate of the common weall shalbe handled or treated: being no meete matters to be written or treated upon, but by menn of auctoritie, learning, and wisdome, nor to be handled before any audience, but of graue and discreet persons. (Albright 95)

When in 1642 the Puritans banned public performances for religious reasons, they recommended "to the people of this land the profitable and seasonable considerations of repentance, reconciliation and peace with God, which probably will produce outward peace and prosperity, and bring again times of joy and gladness to these nations" (Montague 172).

At the beginning of the Restoration, the Stuarts allowed new plays to be performed, although expressly forbidding any "profanity" and "immorality": censors / publishers had "to be very Carefull in Correcting all Obscenityes & other Scandallous Matters & such as any ways Offend against ye laws of God Good manners or the knowne Statutes of the this Kingdom" (Pankratz 1998, 52ff., 57). The revival of *The Maid's Tragedy* was prevented due to political reasons, and Nathaniel Lee's *Lucius Junius Brutus* was silenced in 1680 because of some "Scandalous Expressions & Reflections vpon ye Government" (Loftis 27). Censorship was rather permissive on sexual subjects, but severe on political or religious topics. Yet, by the end of the century, censorship was directed at morals and good manners in order to expunge from plays "all Prophanenesse and Scurrility" (29).

In the eighteenth century, in line with the 1737 (pre-performance) Theatre Licensing Act, non-conformist dramatists were effectively silenced, thus preventing them from devoting their attention to certain political, social or otherwise forbidden topics and taboo words or expressions. Subsequently, on the basis of the 1737 law, the performance of P.B. Shelley's *The Cenci* was forbidden (except as a club production in 1886), as were G.B. Shaw's *Plays Unpleasant* about prostitution and capitalism, his *The Shewing-Up of Blanco Posnet* (blasphemy), Granville-Barker's *Waste* (abortion: 1907, first public performance 1936). A license was refused for Edward Garnett's *The Breaking Point* (subsequently published with the subtitle "a Censured Play. With Preface and a Letter to the Censor" (1907), A.E. Housman's *Bethlehem* (1902) and *Victoria Regina* (1935), as well as E. Bond's *Early Morning* (1968), Osborne's *A Patriot for Me* (homosexuality), Bond's *Saved* (baby battering). Theatrical censorship was only abolished after the legal proceedings in connection with Bond's *Saved* in 1968. There were also conflicts between the English Stage Company and the Lord Chamberlain over John Osborne's *A Patriot for Me* (1965), Joan Littlewood's Theatre Workshop-production of Chapman's *You Won't Always be on Top* (1958); in the case of Osborne's *The Entertainer* the censor demanded for example that "ass-upwards" be changed into "cockeyed," "balls" into "whistle" (Liebenstein-Kurtz 92). But there have also been other ways of intervention, amounting to a post-production censorship by taking recourse to the law of libel or the Obscene Publication Act of 1959 (cf. Innes 1992, 152).

30　❧　*Uwe Böker*

During the sixteenth century, censorship of the printing presses was controlled by the state and, in addition, by the Stationers' Company in order to hinder the printing of "scandalous, malicious and heretical books" (Feather 32). The production, distribution and, in some cases, the burning of seditious or blasphemous texts, was supervised by the state (book-burning began in England under Henry VIII) (cf. Perrin; Thomas 1969; Rafetseder).

This situation changed during the Commonwealth, if one considers the flood of the so-called Thomason Tracts or John Milton's *Areopagitica* advocating the abolition of censorship. The backlash came with the beginning of the Restoration period when severe measures of censorship were implemented, as the execution for merely being in possession of a manuscript of the politician Algernon Sidney indicates. These renewed acts of censorship were directed at offensive political and religious writings (cf. Feather 50ff.).

The lapse of the Licensing Act in 1695 proved to be the basis for the proliferation of both publishing and bookselling, and hence the emergence of the 'bourgeois' public sphere (Böker 2002, 35–66), although even here the state used various bureaucratic means of intervention (stamp and newspaper taxes, the law of libel) to silence oppositional voices. After the early nineteenth-century "war of the unstamped," these forms of economic pressure and censorship were abolished (cf. Altick), although other forms of legal restrictions, including indictments in cases of blasphemy, immorality, or pornography, were used as a means of social control. This situation only changed following the Obscene Publications Act of 1959, when the High Court ruled in favor of Penguin, allowing an unexpurgated version of *Lady Chatterley's Lover* to be published (cf. Rolph). Nevertheless, even at the end of the twentieth century, confronted with increasing pressures from the IRA and the threat of international terrorism, Tony Geraghty chose to remark in *Index on Censorship*, a journal founded by Stephen Spender and published by Writers & Scholars International: "The surveillance apparatus of the state marks home and hearth with an odour of fascism that no amount of liberal discussion can deodorise or exorcise" (15).

In order to understand the social functions of taboos in England, it is above all necessary to reconsider the relationship between the church, state, and civil society, which has considerably changed from late medieval times to the present day. The power relationship between the Pope in Rome as God's vicar in matters spiritual and the Emperor as vicar in matters temporal had already been altered

A Socio-Historical Perspective 31

fundamentally by Henry VIII. The Canon Law of the Western church had given way to the "King's Ecclesiastical Law of the Church of England"; and these Courts were the instruments through which the state acted. For example, in 1533, "the detestable and abominable vice of buggery committed with mankind or beast" was made a felony and the so-called Buggery Act (25 Henry 8, c.6) decreed that sodomites be hanged; this first civil injunction against sodomy was aimed at reducing the jurisdiction of the former ecclesiastical courts (cf. Norton 1992, 16), thus institutionalizing secular claims of authority.

However, one has to keep in mind that the old ecclesiastical courts (cf. Outhwaite) had always exercised a wide control over the religious beliefs and the morals of clergy and laity alike (cf. the criminal precedents published by Archdeacon Hale in 1847). The offences dealt with in the *Act Books of six Ecclesiastical Courts* between 1475 and 1640 were adultery, procuration, incontinency, incest, defamation, sorcery, witchcraft, failure to attend church, behavior in church, swearing, profaning the Sabbath, blasphemy, drunkenness, haunting taverns, heretical opinions, profaning the church and usury, that is, including matters of taboo (cf. Outhwaite).

Having been abolished in 1640 but re-established during the Restoration, the jurisdiction of the ecclesiastical courts was finally curtailed at the end of the seventeenth century. Churchmen tried to revive their disciplinary authority over the laity, but the so-called Societies for the Reformation of Manners filled the void (cf. Isaacs). As their members believed that God judged nations by the populace's conduct, they decided to enforce a religious and moral code that would, they hoped, produce governmental and social stability, and thus prosperity (cf. Roberts).

Since associations such as the Societies for the Reformation of Manners acted on a voluntary basis, which denoted the "primacy of the private sphere in the shaping of civil society" (Price 195), it was the task of the Parliament to establish the legal basis for action in society, "but the institutions of civil society derived their legitimacy from the voluntarism of private individuals acting as public citizens" (193). Voluntarist associations, as Price maintains, became "collective expressions of individual interests"; they achieved "purposes that in other countries were the responsibility of the state or of established corporate bodies" (195). Whereas the family remained the quintessential unit of the private sphere and its boundaries could only be violated by official bodies in very special cases, public sites of

32 &&& *Uwe Böker*

discourse became the domains of "policing" by the Societies for the Reformation of Manners, which were broadly middle-class voluntary associations trying to promote civilized refinement, to change collective identities and to purge the public space of transgressive behavior. As the "old" seventeenth and eighteenth-century society was still "an open aristocracy based on property and patronage" (Perkin 38ff.), law and law enforcement remained, although the English lacked the coercive capacities and institutions of a fully developed and centralized police force, in the hands of the political elite (cf. Emsley 8ff.). But the emerging public sphere, which was a concomitant of economic developments, became the culturally-mediating and legitimizing institutional field in which the role of state power and the rights and obligations of the private individual were discussed. The aforementioned societies influenced public debates from 1690 to 1740, during the 1790s and the 1800s, and they shaped Evangelical reform movements during the 1860s and 1870s. They have to be considered as private institutions that sought to exert pressure both on the state (by demanding state legislation) and on certain groups within society by criticizing their way of life (especially the aristocracy, for example, after the Glorious Revolution, the French Revolution or during the Regency period) and institutionalizing taboo-silencing. These societies developed because of the absence of a police force and the emergence of the political and social norms and values of participation and voluntarism.

Types of Taboo: Discursive Changes and Historical Developments

a) The Taboo of Sexuality

As has been said before, sexuality and death are the two main taboos in early (primitive) as well as in modern societies and cultures. Although Michel Foucault maintained that it was only during the nineteenth century that the need to talk about sexuality developed into a discourse of knowledge and power (cf. Adams), this discourse emerged in an earlier period, and prohibitions on speaking about certain aspects of sexuality are clear indications of silencing and taboo. Thus, theologians of the sixteenth and seventeenth centuries had "pass'd over this abominable Sort of Impurity in Silence" and hardly made any mention of for example masturbation. It was only with the pamphlet *Onania; or the Heinous Sin of Self-Pollution, and all its Frightful Consequences* (first edition in 1710), a book that clearly transformed sexuality into an object of knowledge, that readers were made aware of the necessity of expressing themselves "with the utmost Circumspection and Caution, for fear of intrenching upon Modesty" (Kirchhofer 122).

Another phenomenon already mentioned was the taboo on sodomy. Although the term sodomy continued to evoke religious associations, it was clearly considered to be a transgression foregrounding social and political attitudes, and, in post-revolutionary England, linked with pride, idleness, debauchery, extravagance, irresponsibility and often with the behavior of dissidents of all sorts (cf. Cohen 1989). Since the beginning of the eighteenth century, the Societies for the Reformation of Manners had sought to eradicate the meeting houses (molly houses), and they were responsible for the undercover entrapment of suspected sodomites, for bringing sodomites to court, for closing down homosexual clubs; furthermore, Society informers and constables were instrumental in gathering evidence (cf. Bristow; Goldsmith). During the second half of the eighteenth century, the readiness to sentence sodomites rose considerably, and by the 1830s the number of men executed was ten times the average figure in the eighteenth century, sixty men being hanged for sodomy between 1805 and the eighteen-thirties (cf. Gatrell 618). The 1828 "Offences against the Person" bill no longer defined sodomy as a capital offence with the help of arguments culled from the Bible and theological commentaries, but it was now considered to be a normative civil transgression. In 1861, sodomy was removed from the list of capital crimes; the legal injunction under section eleven of the Criminal Law Amendment Act (1885) shifted "the locus of culpability from a particular kind of act to a particular type of actor" (Cohen 1989, 203). The full meaning of the section on "gross indecency" as applied to literary texts in the trial of Oscar Wilde (cf. Hyde) has to be seen in the context of a renewed agitation for social reform since the 1860s and the institutionalization of middle-class voluntarist norms and values as well as in the institutionalization of scientific discourse, especially the "medicalization of homosexuality." In the case of the Wilde trials we have to take into account "the drive to control suspicious inner life" by means of the "medical and judicial monitoring of morality" (Farrell 28). The emergence of a professional medical-scientific discourse resulted in a "controlling" definition of "same-sex passion" as mental illness and psychological disturbance that gave rise to public fears of the potentially dangerous "other"

34   Uwe Böker

(Foldy 69). The fear of the dangerous "other" was the fear of losing the battle in a period when decadence and racial degeneration
were linked together. On the one hand, the ideas of degeneration
and of retrogression (H.G. Wells' *Time Machine*, 1895) had a powerful appeal to the British; on the other hand, the underlying rationale
of scientific reasoning had developed a means to come to grips with
the "other," by institutionalizing a discourse that seemed to be able
to map and thus to colonize unknown territories of degeneration; as
Foldy argues, "the medico-psychiatric model of degeneration should
be understood as an ideological production that was embraced by the
various European states for purposes of social control" (74). Thus,
the institutionalization of definitions of deviant behavior such as
sodomy that had been in the hands of the church, the state and the
public sphere (defined as sin, moral transgression etc.) was, at the end
of the nineteenth century, a by-product of the prevalent scientific
discourse, and the "medicalization of homosexuality."

As Rictor Norton (2005) has maintained, not only gay history but also lesbianism has frequently been silenced. Texts that
depict lesbian love, despite being devoid of explicit sexual details
or even innuendos, have been subject to suppression. Women were
brought up to value discretion, modesty and propriety, and families
took care to protect their reputation so that relationships between
women were presented in letters and memoirs as harmless. Thus,
Christina Rossetti's brother apparently destroyed some poems
because they were love poems addressed to women. Passages were
omitted from the letters quoted by George Eliot's husband when
he wrote her biography in 1885. Sixteen lines of a letter by Mary
Wollstonecraft describing her passion for Fanny Blood were deleted
by some "well-meaning scholar." The dearth of material on British
lesbian life in the 1930s (and the stigmatization of spinsters as lesbians) may be owing to the prosecution of Radclyffe Hall's *The Well
of Loneliness* for obscenity in 1928. In the 1930s, well-known lesbians
wrote autobiographies, and one of Constance Maynard's executri-
ces apparently deleted parts of her intimate diaries. Ann Bannon,
"Queen of Lesbian Pulp Fiction" and author of the *Beebo Brinker*
series of lesbian novels in the 1950s, destroyed all the correspondence she received from women in response to her novels for fear
that it would be discovered by her children (cf. Foote). On the other
hand, a recent article in an *Observer* review declared that "tales of
incestuous abuse have lost their power to shock thanks to fashionable feminist fiction" (Roiphe 9).

A Socio-Historical Perspective 35

Ever since the Jeremy Collier's Stage-"immorality" campaign around 1700, the ostracizing of the immoral and pornographic novel of the early eighteenth century (cf. Behn, Manley) in favor of the type of novels by Richardson and Fielding (cf. Warner), the censorship of the literacy and literature of the lower orders and of reading after 1790, the literary world has been controlled by a kind of "literary police" (Böker 1990; 1994). Other examples of this kind of censorship were the criticism of the "immoral" reading matter during the 1830s and the 1840s (cf. Böker 1992), the criticism of eighteenth-century novelists such as Fielding or Smollett as "immoral," and, on a lower level, the literature for the masses, as well as the new genre of the sensation novel that during the 1860s reflected the female interest in contemporary trials of women accused of "unspeakable crimes," focussing on detection, adultery, and bigamy, and exploiting repressed sexual fantasies (cf. Showalter). One major institution responsible for silencing certain varieties of literature and the moral supervision of writers and readers are the lending libraries, above all influential being Mudie's (cf. Griest). Magazines for Sunday reading and family magazines such as the *Cornhill* were eager to protect their readers, especially "the young lady," from moral shock, while the editor W.M. Thackeray told Mrs. Browning that "there are things my squeamish public will not hear on Mondays," turning down Trollope's "Mrs. General Tolboys" because of the allusion to a man with an illegitimate child (cf. Maurer). Publishing houses advocated bowdlerization (cf. Perrin); voluntary organizations like the National Vigilance Association were responsible for the trial of Henry Viztelly, publisher of French naturalist novelists ("Zolaism" being branded as "a disease"; Thomas 167); and even Hardy—"Jude the Obscene" and "Hardy the Degenerate"— came under attack: "Humanity, as envisaged by Mr. Hardy, is largely compounded of hoggishness and hysteria" (Millgate 369).

Other taboos are at various periods related to incest, infanticide, rape, polygamy, and the genre of immoral, obscene, and pornographic literature, that flourished from the 1680s onward, was driven underground by legislation and eventually silenced in the course of the institutionalization of English Studies. By the time of the *fin de siècle* and the early years of modernism, deep-seated Victorian taboos had obviously been eroded. Nevertheless, Lytton Strachey's question in 1908 as to whether there was semen on his sister's dress was certainly only possible amongst the coterie of the intellectual middle and upper classes. According to Virginia Woolf: "[w]ith that word all barriers of reticence and reserve went down....Sex permeated our conversation.

36　✺　*Uwe Böker*

The word bugger was never far from our lips. We discussed copulation with the same excitement and openness that we had discussed
the nature of good.... It was, I think, a great advance in civilisation"
(qtd. in Adams 125). When H.G. Wells, however, submitted his novel
Ann Veronica (1909) to his publisher, Macmillan objected because it
was not considered as likely to contribute to an uplifting of the morals of the majority; and the *Spectator* condemned it for "undermining
[of] that sense of continence and self-control in the individual which
is essential in a sound and healthy State" (Dickson 206).

Immediately after the First World War, *The Quarterly Review*
described "Mr. Joyce's work as literary Bolshevism. It is experimental, anti-conventional, anti-Christian, chaotic, totally unmoral"
(Egloff 82). A closer look at the 1920s and their discovery of the
Freudian Unconscious, the disrespectful 'red' decade of the 1930s
or the decades following the Second World War will show in how
far taboos have been de-emphasized but still shape cultural life
today. The *Lady Chatterley* trial is usually thought to have promoted
a degree of frankness that was at that moment still strictly forbidden on the stage. Twenty years later the 'voice' in the last chapter of
David Lodge's *How Far Can You Go?* (1981) remarks:

> Many things have changed—attitudes to authority, sex, worship,
> other Christians, other religions....the most fundamental change
> is...the fading away of the traditional Catholic metaphysic—that
> marvellous complex and ingenious synthesis of theology and cosmol-
> ogy and casuistry, which situated the individual souls on a kind of
> spiritual Snakes and Ladders board, motivated them with equal doses
> of hope and fear, and promised them, if they persevered in the game,
> an eternal reward. (qtd. in Kühn 55f.)

There have been, however, during the last few decades, individuals
who have fought for the old Victorian moral values and taboos: Mary
Whitehouse, for example, who maintained a watchful eye on broad-
cast media but also initiated private prosecutions for blasphemous
libel against *Gay News* (1977) and against Michael Bogdanov, the
director of a National Theatre production of Howard Brenton's *The
Romans in Britain* (1980) under the Sexual Offences Act of 1956.

b) The Death Taboo

As stated before, sexuality and death are the two main taboos in
early as well as in modern societies and cultures (cf. Meier 160ff. and

A Socio-Historical Perspective 37

167ff.). According to Clive Seale, social and cultural life involves a continual turning away from death, as the awareness that our bodies eventually die threatens to make life meaningless. There are certain defenses against this awareness which include routine and everyday activities as well as the reliance on "imagined communities," the hope of revivalism and resurrective practices (cf. Seale 3), as well as, since the nineteenth century, the use of closed coffins (the term "casket" is a North American euphemism). According to Geoffrey Gorer's thesis of 1955, there has been a shift from an emphasis on the taboo of sexuality to that of death during the last two hundred years, with the latter "becoming more and more 'unmentionable' as a natural process." But this "denial of death" thesis has recently been questioned by Seale (50) and others.

It is certainly true that during the Medieval and the Renaissance pandemics death became a familiar part of life. The "Black Death" of 1348 killed nearly 40 percent of London's population. When the so-called sweating sickness was visited upon the capital, thousands died within the space of a few hours. Between 1563 and 1603 there were several plague attacks, and for Londoners "Feare and Trembling (the two Catch-polles of Death) arrest every one...no voice heard but *Tue Tue*, Kill, Kill" (Ackroyd 203). Defoe's account of the plague of 1664–65 gives a vivid picture of the ubiquity of death. In addition, there was a religious sense of existing at the end of time. Even during the sixteenth and seventeenth centuries, death was a common phenomenon of life.

In connection with this, one special aspect has to be mentioned, namely the changing attitudes toward the death penalty in England, in particular as represented by the public spectacle of the gallows as a symbol of political hegemony and social control. Henry Fielding, asking his readers "what is the principal End of all Punishment," refers them to the Lord Chief Justice Sir Matthew Hale: "Is it not as Lord *Hale* expresses it, 'to deter Men from the Breach of Laws, so that they may not offend, and so not suffer at all? And is not the inflicting of Punishment more for Example, and to prevent Evil, than to punish?'" (Fielding 166)

Capital punishments have existed for all sorts of crimes in nearly all societies, ranging from stoning, strangling, burning, poisoning to beheading for crimes like murder or high treason. In England, however, a dramatic increase in the number of felonies punishable by death was noticed between 1688 and 1815, although the potential "overkill" of the Bloody Code, which marked a return to Tudor policy, did not actually lead to higher levels of executions (cf. McLynn 257). According to Radzinowicz, out of 389 capital convictions in London and Middlesex between 1749 and 1754, 285 offenders were executed, accounting for an average of five to six every six weeks as reported in newspapers or recorded in trial reports (cf. 1: *passim*).

These draconian measures were in part a reaction to the increase in crimes of property, resulting from an increase in wealth after 1688 and the advent of the consumer society; they were, due to the discretionary powers of the judge and other institutions, primarily a means to ensure social stability and to ensure the deference of the lower orders. The concepts of the "rule of law" and of "equality before the law" were invoked in order to maintain the cultural hegemony of the ruling class, meting out "exemplary rather than certain punishments" (McLynn xviii) under the cover of mercy and pardon.

The public spectacle of the road to Tyburn and the hangings are discussed in Bernard Mandeville's *Enquiry into the Causes of the Frequent Executions at Tyburn* (1725). Mandeville paints a picture of the "Execution Day and the Journey to Tyburn": the "undisciplined Armies" of the Mob having "no particular Enemies to encounter, but Cleanliness and good Manners, so nothing is more entertaining to them, than the dead Carcasses of Dogs and Cats, or, for want of them, Rags, and all Trompery that is capable of imbibing Dirt" (Mandeville 22). The distanced, upper-class "Observer," however, looks through the outward show of the felon's drunkenness and bravery, which is a kind of "Performance" meant to drown the fear of the approaching awful death. Henry Fielding, too, is aware of the perversions of public hangings as occasions of carnivalistic entertainment for the mob, and in his *An Enquiry into the Causes of the Late Increase of Robbers* (1751) he thinks about how to improve their effectiveness. His concept of solemnity refers to the theatrical character of law enforcement, especially of hangings, the ritual enactment of which is supposed to have the function of inculcating legal norms and values in the minds of the "mob." He therefore pleads for the absolute "Danger and Certainty of Destruction" for the criminal, "sacrificed to the Preservation of Thousands." The magistrate's business (as well as the poet's) is "to raise Terror," and executions should therefore be "in the highest degree solemn" (170).

Although the carnivalistic and riotous "ride to Tyburn" was ended in 1783 and the gallows were set up in the street outside Newgate, thus limiting the space available, huge crowds gathered to watch the hangings. Nevertheless, as the more than one hundred cant names for the

A Socio-Historical Perspective ❈ 39

gallows and the public hangings indicate, the euphemisms are a clear sign of tabooing (cf. McLynn 264). Public executions were still staged outside Newgate until the Private Execution Act was passed in 1868 and the condemned were hanged behind prison walls. When in 1836 J.S. Mill wrote in favor of capital punishment, he praised the "perfection of mechanical arrangements," thus "avoiding the presence not only of actual pain, but of whatever suggests offensive or disagreeable ideas, that a great part of refinement consists" of (Gatrell 589), thereby invoking the rules of middle class decorum and of silence—the main aspects of the taboo. When executions were thus concealed from public view, this was hailed as a "landmark in the more human treatment of criminals." Reporting the death of Alexander Mackay, the *Annual Register* remarked appropriately: "The sufferings of the murderer were dreadful, but on this we will not dwell" (ibid.).

We will, however, have in addition to analyze twentieth-century representations of death and the respective taboo, although death on the stage seems no longer to be a taboo (cf. Pankratz 2005). As is obvious from the history of crime literature and the Gothic novel, taboos related to murder, parricide, infanticide, or cannibalism have remained an inspiration for transgressive creative representation (for child murder and abuse, cf. Späth; Houswitschka). This is especially true with regard to cannibalism, the stigma being used as a weapon to accuse internal or colonial enemies of inhumanity. Whereas in Greek times, the so-called anthropophagy was associated with non-Hellenic barbarians, cannibalism was throughout English history used to define the dangerous "other" in Shakespeare's *The Tempest*, in Jonathan Swift's "A Modest Proposal," in Joseph Conrad's *Heart of Darkness*, evoking the "Unspeakable Rites," as well as in the popular accounts of the Scottish Sawney Beane family living in a cave by the sea in James VI's Scotland and robbing and murdering unwary travelers, or the lurid Barber of Fleet Street, Sweeney Todd, cropping up in Edward Lloyd's *The Spring of Pearls* (1840) and up to the present times reappearing on the stage, or the representations of the Irish Fenian as a monstrous Caliban, or the Irish revolutionary Charles Parnell as Frankenstein's monster (see the caricatures in *Punch*, 20 May 1882 and 19 Mar. 1870). Although the case of *Rex v. Dudley and Stephens* of 1884 may be called a modern common law defense of the necessity of cannibalism, it is still used as a means of stigmatizing, even in feminist stories such as Emma Tennant's short story "Philomela," based on one of Ovid's stories in *Metamorphoses*, as a means to attack a patriarchal society.

40 &&& *Uwe Böker*

c) Taboo in a Multicultural Society

Ever since Daniel Defoe's remarks about the "true-born Englishman"—"in speech an irony, in fact a fiction" (line 373)—immigrants have been welcomed to the British Isles, at least till the middle of the nineteenth century. The situation, however, changed with the debate about the health of the nation, and the 1905 Aliens Act (cf. Holmes 36ff.). Since then, there have been more and more occasions of minority, especially Jew, baiting, especially during the 1930s amid the influx of European Jews. As blasphemy protected only the Church of England, there were no blasphemy trials where Jewish taboos had been offended.

One the other hand, there have been successive waves of immigration from the former colonies. As a result, there are in present-day Britain many migrants with a culturally mixed identity and altogether different religious or social attitudes. Although in 2002, the Muslim population amounted only to 1.8 million (three percent of the total British population), the debates about the pros and cons of immigration led to a "racialisation of politics" (Solomos 3); the term race has in the meantime become a taboo-word itself.

Whereas one main result of modernization has been the separation "between the public realm of citizens and policies and the private realm of belief and worship" (Modood and Kastoryano 163), a similar differentiation of the religious and the profane spheres does not exist in Islam (cf. Khoury, Hagemann, and Heine 652). Thus, there is widespread criticism of the secular culture of European society amongst Muslims in present-day Britain and in addition, especially amongst the second or third generation of immigrants, the idea of a global, transnational community, a "re-imagined Ummah" (Kastoryano 65), which is the basis of a new "pride and self-respect." As Parekh notes: "While their parents would have said that they were Muslims, their offspring say that they have a Muslim or Islamic identity. The difference is deep and striking" (181). An essential aspect of this identity is the idea of living according to the fundamental religious tenets of Islam. This implies the observance of religious rites (cf. Khoury, Hagemann, and Heine 28off.), of dietary restrictions and taboos in respect to food, alcohol, fasting, clothing, bodily purity, sexual activities and gender roles etc., and especially the taboo of portraying the prophet Mohammed. These religious taboos have become, at least in present-day Britain, political taboos.

At the end of the 1980s, Salman Rushdie's *The Satanic Verses* came to be viewed as "the most serious challenge...to the legitimacy of certain brands of contemporary 'Islamic' politics" (Mufti 307) because of the author's disrespect for Islamic taboos. Although *The Satanic Verses* was not aimed at Muslim believers, it portrayed Mohammed as the orientalized Mahound. The reader is expressly made aware of the issue of blasphemy: "A man who sets out to make himself up is taking on the Creator's role, according to one way of seeing things; he's unnatural, a blasphemer, an abomination of abominations" (Rushdie 49). Thus, according to Williams and Khan, *The Satanic Verses* is indeed "blasphemous" because it draws on "a long line of literary opposition to the fictions favored by the state and church" (253). According to Rushdie's aesthetics, "no subjects...are off-limits and that includes God, includes prophets" (Ghosh-Schellhorn 214); he therefore writes "from the point of view of a secular person...provoking the imagination...to make people think" (ibid. 214 and 215). As Rushdie's novel embodies Western secular ideas, especially of free speech, it was bound to come into conflict with fundamentalist Muslim sensibilities. It was considered to be "a matter of satanically inspired blasphemy" (ibid. 215), even by those who never even read the text. "Many 'lapsed' and 'passive' Muslims (especially non-religious Muslims, for whom hitherto their Muslim background was not particularly important) (re)discovered a new sense of community identity" (Modood 2006, 42). Thus, the development of a transnational *Ummah* and the search for a political identity within a secular British society inevitably led to an awareness of the vulnerability of Islamic taboos, not only in the case of *The Satanic Verses*, but subsequently in connection with the 2006 BBC and ITV broadcasts of a set of cartoon drawings mocking the Islamic faith. They were then rerun in British papers, which maintained that the freedom of the press was more important than the protests and boycotts across the Arab world (cf. Marland and Bell).

Religious taboos are thus back on the agenda in present-day Britain. Above all they now serve as a means of creating new political identities, and they are as well an inspiration for literary creations that question individual attitudes and hegemonic power structures, encouraging creative writers to transcend the narrow boundaries of dogmas and fundamentalist absolutes. This is, to give one last example, the case with Hanif Kureishi's novel *The Black Album* (1995), which not only examines the state of the nation during the Thatcher years, but engages in the public debate following from the imposition

42 ☻ *Uwe Böker*

of the *fatwa* on Rushdie, challenging taboos on both sides. The same is true of Kureishi's short story "My Son the Fanatic," subsequently made into a play and a feature film (1997). The story dramatizes the conflict between Western and Islamic values within a family: the father is a westernized liberal, while his son discovers his Islamic faith, observing the traditional rituals and taboos. Here, we can see that taboos are not only important elements of identity construction and repression by a minority, but also, in the context of literary texts, a creative means of clarifying important religious and secular problems within a given society. Therefore, stories of 'how the world goes or should go' may indeed be the medium of a special kind of literary knowledge.

Works Cited

Ackroyd, Peter. *London: The Biography*. London: Vintage, 2001.

Adams, James Eli. "Victorian Sexualities." *A Companion to Victorian Literature & Culture*. Ed. Herbert F. Tucker. Oxford: Blackwell, 1999. 125–38.

Albright, Evelyn M. *Dramatic Publication in England, 1580–1640*. New York: D.C. Health, repr. 1971.

Altick, Robert. *The English Common Reader: A Social History of the Mass Reading Public 1800–1900*. Chicago: U of Chicago P, 1963.

Barber, C.L. *Shakespeare's Festive Comedy: A Study of Dramatic Form and Its Relation to Social Custom*. Princeton: Princeton UP, 1959.

Barroll, J. Leeds, et al., eds. *The Revels History. 1576–1613*. Vol. 3. London: Methuen, 1975.

Blackstone, Sir William. *Commentaries on the Laws of England*. Facsimile. Introd. Stanley N. Katz. 4 vols. Chicago: U of Chicago P, 1979.

Böker, Uwe. "Die Institutionalisierung literarischer Produktions- und Rezeptionsnormen: Überlegungen zur Erforschung der Unterhaltungsliteratur um 1800." *Unterhaltungsliteratur: Ziele und Methoden ihrer Erforschung*. Eds. Dieter Petzold and Eberhard Späth. Erlangen: Universitätsbibliothek, 1990. 139–60.

———. "'Speed the Printing Machine!' Die Industrialisierung der Literatur in der englischen, französischen und deutschen Diskussion zwischen 1830 und 1850." *Die Fürstliche Bibliothek Corvey: Ihre Bedeutung für eine neue Sicht der Literatur des frühen 19. Jahrhunderts*. Eds. Rainer Schöwerling and Hartmut Steinecke. Munich: Fink, 1992. 50–63.

———. "The Education of the Lower Orders, 1700 to 1850: Ridicule, Control, Investigation." *State, Science, and Modernization in England: From the Renaissance to the Present Time*. Ed. Jürgen Klein. Hildesheim: Olms, 1994. 287–320.

A Socio-Historical Perspective ✣ 43

Böker, Uwe. "Institutionalised Rules of Discourse and the Court Room as a Site of the Public Sphere." *Sites of Discourse—Public and Private Spheres—Legal Culture.* Eds. Uwe Böker and Julie Hibbard. Amsterdam: Rodopi, 2002. 35–66.

Bristol, Michael D. *Carnival and Theater: Plebeian Culture and the Structure of Authority in Renaissance England.* New York: Methuen, 1985.

Bristow, Edward J. *Vice and Vigilance: Purity Movements in Britain since 1700.* Dublin: Gill and Macmillan, 1977.

Caslon Analytics. "Blasphemy." January 2006. May 15, 2008 <http://www.caslon.com.au/blasphemyprofile.htm>.

Clare, Janet. "'Greater Themes for Insurrection's Arguing': Political Censorship of the Elizabethan and Jacobean Stage." *Review of English Studies* NS 38 (1987): 169–83.

Cohen, Ed. "Legislating the Norm: From Sodomy to Gross Indecency." *The South Atlantic Quarterly* 88 (1989): 181–217.

Cohen, S. *Visions of Social Control: Crime, Punishment and Classification.* Cambridge: Polity Press, 1985.

Connolly, Leonhard W. *The Censorship of English Drama, 1737–1826.* San Marino, CA: Huntington Library Press, 1976.

Defoe, Daniel. "The True-born Englishman." *Anthology of Poems on Affairs of State. Augustan Satirical Verse, 1660–1714.* Ed. George deF. Lord. New Haven: Yale UP, 1975. 624–50.

Dickson, Lovat. *H.G. Wells: His Turbulent Life and Times.* Harmondsworth: Penguin, 1972.

Egloff, Gerd. *Soziale Norm und literarische Form: Gesellschaftliche Bedingungen der Romanrezeption in England in den Jahren 1918–1930.* Meisenheim an der Glan: Hain, 1978.

Emsley, Clive. *The English Police: A Political and Social History.* 2nd ed. Harlow: Longman, 1996.

Farrell, Kirby. "Wilde on Trial: Psychic Injury, Exhibitionism, and the Law." *The Importance of Reinventing Oscar: Versions of Wilde during the Last 100 Years.* Eds. Uwe Böker, Richard Corballis, and Julie Hibbard. Amsterdam: Rodopi, 2002. 24–33.

Feather, John. *A History of British Publishing.* London: Croom Helm, 1988.

Fielding, Henry. *An Enquiry into the Causes of the Late Increase of Robbers and Related Writings.* Ed. Malvin R. Zirker. Oxford: Clarendon Press, 1988.

Foldy, Michael S. *The Trials of Oscar Wilde: Deviance, Morality, and Late-Victorian Society.* New Haven: Yale UP, 1997.

Foote, Stephanie. "Deviant Classics: Pulps and the Making of Lesbian Print Culture." *Signs: Journal of Women in Culture and Society* 31 (2005): 169–90.

Gatrell, V.A.C. *The Hanging Tree. Execution and the English People 1770–1868.* Oxford: Oxford UP, 1996.

Geraghty, Tony. "A Trip into Blair's Labyrinth." *Index on Censorship* 2 (1999): 15–18.

44 &&& *Uwe Böker*

Ghosh-Shellhorn, Martina. "*The Satanic Verses*: Salman Rushdie as Satanic Versifier?" *Traditionalism vs. Modernism*. Eds. Erhard Reckwitz, Lucia Vennarini, and Cornelia Wegener. Essen: Blaue Eule, 1994. 213–22.

Goldsmith, Netta Murray. *The Worst of Crimes: Homosexuality and the Law in Eighteenth-Century London*. Aldershot: Ashgate, 1998.

Griest, Guinevere L. *Mudie's Circulating Library and the Victorian Novel*. Bloomington: Indiana UP, 1970.

Holmes, Colin. *Anti-Semitism in British Society. 1876–1939*. London: Arnold, 1979.

Houswitschka, Christoph. "Family, Crime, and the Public Sphere: 'Incest' in Eighteenth-Century England." *Sites of Discourse—Public and Private Spheres—Legal Culture*. Eds. Uwe Böker and Julie Hibbard. Amsterdam: Rodopi, 2002. 167–78.

Hyde, H. Montgomery, ed. *Oscar Wilde*. Harmondsworth: Penguin, 1962.

Innes, Christopher. *Modern British Drama 1890–1990*. Cambridge: Cambridge UP, 1992.

Isaacs, Tina. "The Anglican Hierarchy and the Reformation of Manners 1688–1738." *Journal of Ecclesiastical History* 33 (1982): 391–411.

Johnston, John. *The Lord Chamberlain's Blue Pencil*. London: Hodder and Stoughton, 1990.

Kastoryano, Riva. "French Secularism and Islam: France's Headscarf Affair." *Multiculturalism, Muslims, and Citizenship: A European Approach*. Eds. Tariq Modood, Anna Triandafyllidou, and Ricard Zapata-Barrero. London: Routledge, 2006. 57–69.

Khoury, Adel Theodor, Ludwig Hagemann, and Peter Heine. *Islam-Lexikon*. 3 vols. Freiburg: Herder, 1991.

Kirchhofer, Anton. *Strategie und Wahrheit. Zum Einsatz von Wissen über Leidenschaften und Geschlecht im Roman der englischen Empfindsamkeit*. Munich: Fink, 1995.

Kühn, Thomas. "Die Fiktion des real existierenden Katholizismus in den Romanen von David Lodge." *Zwischen Dogma und säkularer Welt: Zur Erzählliteratur englischsprachiger katholischer Autoren im 20. Jahrhundert*. Eds. Bernd Engler and Franz Link. Paderborn: Schöningh, 1991. 55–66.

Liebenstein-Kurtz, Ruth von. *Das subventionierte englische Theater: Produktionsbedingungen und Auswirkungen auf das moderne englische Drama, 1956–1976*. Tübingen: Narr, 1981.

Loftis, John. *Comedy And Society From Congreve to Fielding*. Stanford, CA: Stanford UP, 1966.

Lowman, John, Robert J. Menzies, and T.S. Palys, eds. *Transcarceration: Essays in the Sociology of Social Control*. Aldershot: Gower, 1987.

Mandeville, Bernard. *An Enquiry into the Causes of the Frequent Executions at Tyburn*. Introd. Malvin R. Zirker, Jr. Los Angeles: Augustan Reprint Society, U of California, 1964.

Marland, Ian, and Susan Bell. "'Blasphemous' Cartoons Shown on British TV as Muslims Vent Outrage." First pub. *The Scotsman* February 3,

A Socio-Historical Perspective ▩ 45

2006. May 18, 2008 <http://news.scotsman.com/danishcartoonrow/
Blasphemous-cartoons-shown-on-British.2747643.jp>.

Marsh, Joss. *Word Crimes: Blasphemy, Culture and Literature in Nineteenth-Century England.* Chicago: U of Chicago P, 1998.

Maurer, Oscar. "'My Squeamish Public': Some Problems of Victorian Magazine Publishers and Editors." *Studies in Bibliography* 12 (1960): 21–40.

McLynn, Frank. *Crime and Punishment in Eighteenth Century England.* London: Routledge, 1989.

Meier, Franz. *Sexualität und Tod. Eine Themenverknüpfung in der englischen Schauer- und Sensationsliteratur und ihrem soziokulturellen Kontext (1764–1897).* Tübingen: Niemeyer, 2002.

Millgate, Michael. *Thomas Hardy. A Biography.* Oxford: Oxford UP, 1985.

Modood, Tariq. "British Muslims and the Politics of Multiculturalism." *Multiculturalism, Muslims, and Citizenship: A European Approach.* Eds. Tariq Modood, Anna Triandafyllidou, and Ricard Zapata-Barrero. London: Routledge, 2006. 37–56.

Modood, Tariq, and Riva Kastoryano. "Secularism and the Accommodation of Muslims in Europe." *Multiculturalism, Muslims, and Citizenship: A European Approach.* Eds. Tariq Modood, Anna Triandafyllidou, and Ricard Zapata-Barrero. London: Routledge, 2006. 162–78.

Modood, Tariq, Anna Triandafyllidou, and Ricard Zapata-Barrero, eds. *Multiculturalism, Muslims, and Citizenship: A European Approach.* London: Routledge, 2006.

Montague, Ashley. *The Anatomy of Swearing.* Philadelphia: U of Pennsylvania P, 1968.

Mufti, Aamir. "Reading the Rushdie Affair: 'Islam', Cultural Politics, Form." *The Administration of Aesthetics: Censorship, Political Criticism, and the Public Sphere.* Ed. Richard Burt. Minneapolis: U of Minnesota P, 1994. 307–39.

Norton, Rictor. *Mother Clap's Molly House: The Gay Subculture in England 1700–1830.* London: GMP Publishers, 1992.

——. "The Suppression of Lesbian and Gay History." February 12, 2005, updated June 12, 2008. March 22, 2009 <http://www.rictornorton.co.uk/suppress.htm>.

Outhwaite, R.B. *The Rise and Fall of the English Ecclesiastical Courts, 1500–1860.* Cambridge: Cambridge UP, 2006.

Pankratz, Annette. *Werterepertoires der Englischen Restaurationskomödie.* Essen: Blaue Eule, 1998.

——. *"Death Is... Not": Repräsentationen von Tod und Sterben im zeitgenössischen Drama.* Trier: WVT, 2005.

Parekh, Bhikhu. "Europe, Liberalism and the 'Muslim Question'." *Multiculturalism, Muslims, and Citizenship: A European Approach.* Eds. Tariq Modood, Anna Triandafyllidou, and Ricard Zapata-Barrero. London: Routledge, 2006. 179–203.

46   Uwe Böker

Perkin, Harold. *Origins of Modern English Society*. London: Routledge, 1969.

Perrin, Noel. *Dr. Bowdler's Legacy: A History of Expurgated Books in England and America*. London: Macmillan, 1969.

Price, Richard. *British Society, 1680–1880: Dynamism, Containment and Change*. Cambridge: Cambridge UP, 1999.

Radzinowicz, Leon. "Part I. Capital Punishment in the Eighteenth Century Criminal Law." *A History of English Criminal Law and Its Administration from 1750: The Movement for Reform*. Vol. 1. London: Stevens and Sons, 1948.

Rafetseder, Hermann. *Bücherverbrennungen: Die öffentliche Hinrichtung von Schriften im historischen Wandel*. Wien: Böhlau, 1988.

Roberts, M.J.D. *Making English Morals: Voluntary Association and Moral Reform in England, 1787–1886*. New York: Cambridge UP, 2004.

Robinson, J. *The Clergyman's Assistant; or, A Collection of Acts of Parliament, Forms and Ordinances, with Notes and References relating to the Rights, Duties, and Liabilities of the Clergy*. Oxford: Clarendon Press, 1828.

Roiphe, Katie. "Unhealthy Familiarity Breeds Contempt." *The Observer* November 19, 1995. Review section: 9.

Rolph, C.H., ed. *The Trial of Lady Chatterley: Regina v. Penguin Books Limited*. Baltimore: Penguin, 1961.

Rushdie, Salman. *The Satanic Verses*. Dover, DE: The Consortium, 1992.

Seale, Clive. *Constructing Death: The Sociology of Dying and Bereavement*. Cambridge: Cambridge UP, 1998.

Showalter, Elaine. "Subverting the Feminine Novel: Sensationalism and Feminine Protest." *A Literature of Their Own*. Princeton: Princeton UP, 1977. 153–81.

Sinfield, Alan. *Literature, Politics and Culture in Postwar Britain*. Oxford: Blackwell, 1989.

Solomos, John. *Race and Racism in Britain*. 2nd ed. Houndmills: Macmillan, 1995.

Späth, Eberhard. "Isaak, Iphigenia und andere: Zum Thema des Kindsopfers in der englischen Literatur." *Germanisch-Romanische Monatsschrift* 38 (1988): 291–303.

Stephen, Sir James Fitzjames. *A Digest of the Criminal Law (Crimes and Punishments)*. Eds. Sir H. Stephen and H. L. Stephen. 6th ed. London: Macmillan, 1904.

Stephens, John Russell. *The Censorship of English Drama, 1824–1901*. Cambridge: Cambridge UP, 1980.

Thomas, Donald. *A Long Time Burning: The History of Literary Censorship in England*. New York: Praeger, 1969.

Thomas, Keith. "The Double Standard." *Journal of the History of Ideas* 20 (1959): 195–216.

Warner, William B. "The Elevation of the Novel in England: Hegemony and Literary History." *Journal of English Literary History* 59 (1992): 577–96.

Williams, Mark, and G.I. Abdur Razzaq Khan. "Blasphemy and Cultural Sensitivity: Two Views of Rushdie's *Satanic Verses.*" *Landfall* 170.43 (1989): 252–59.

WrigleyClaimon.com. "Crime—1200–1799." May 17, 2008. May 18, 2008 <http://www.swarb.co.uk/lisc/Crime12001799.php>.

CHAPTER III

AGAINST CENSORSHIP: LITERATURE, TRANSGRESSION, AND TABOO FROM A DIACHRONIC PERSPECTIVE

Lars Heiler

There is a common-sense notion of censorship as being the repressive intervention of authorities trying to curb, control, and sanction the work of authors. In the past twenty years, however, censorship has been widely acknowledged as a more complex and differentiated phenomenon which is not necessarily the arch-enemy of artistic production but potentially its secret sharer. According to Neil Sammells this redefinition of censorship can partly be attributed to a move away from a Freudian view of censorship which envisages "the relationship between pleasure and power to be conflict-ual" (9) to a Foucauldian view which stresses "that power and pleasure are indivisible, that they are bound together in excitation and excite-ment" (7). Both views converge in the assumption that censorship can foster creativity and propel literary production rather than destroy it.

Critics such as Annabel Patterson foreground the collusion between literature and censorship rather than their collision in Early Modern England when she states that "it is to censorship that we in part owe our very concept of 'literature', as a kind of discourse with rules of its own" (16). South African writer J.M. Coetzee, on the other hand, is convinced that "[w]riting does not flourish under censorship" (11).

Obviously, it is difficult to generalize individual assessments on the negotiations between censorship and literature, because these negotiations are subject to historical change, as are the punishments and sanctions for transgressing sexual, religious, or political taboos.

50　　*Lars Heiler*

Therefore, an analysis of the writing strategies used by authors to transgress taboos (and to get away with it) must pay tribute to the specific historical and socio-cultural circumstances, that is, the taboos established by a society at a certain point in time.

A further challenge for such an analysis consists in identifying those texts which have not been censored by the authorities, such as the church or the state, but which have met with public criticism or even outrage, thereby providing evidence not only of their scandalous potential, but also of their successful camouflaging of "the subversive (the politically undesirable) and the repugnant (the morally undesirable)" (Coetzee vii). Alternatively, one would have to single out those texts which have not 'assaulted the eyes and ears' of the censors on publication but whose radical potential was exposed by literary critics much later.

Literary texts do not propound arguments or develop positions in an overtly monological, linear or even rational manner, they tend to stage, enact, and emplot conflicts and convictions usually without providing unequivocal opinions. Literary discourse is notorious for being potentially elusive, opaque, and unwilling to offer straightforward articulations of meaning. Therefore, it provides the ideal space for hosting subversive impulses which may permeate a text but may not be easily identified even by critical readers. Different approaches in literary theory have attempted to capture this protean quality of literature from different angles, in different terms and with different implications.[1] As diverse as these concepts might be in their basic premises, they all envisage literature as a form of discourse which cannot be reduced to one-dimensional value judgments and naïve representations of reality. The apparent detachment of literature from other discourses which ensues from such a view is its greatest asset in taking on the socio-cultural formations which it chooses to transform into imaginative spaces of critical dispute.

In the following chapters, I will discuss various dramatic and narrative texts in the force field between censorship and subversion by paying particular attention to the specific literary strategies each text employs in order not to be silenced. The selection of texts by Shakespeare, Swift, Thackeray, Stevenson, Wilde, Conrad, and McEwan is by no means definitive or exhaustive, but it does claim to be representative and paradigmatic. Despite, or rather because of the fact that they creatively transgress generic conventions, these works can be considered milestones in the development of their respective genres. All the texts were written in and reflect periods of change

Against Censorship 51

and transition in cultural and / or literary history and challenge received notions about the self-images and norms of these periods. That the respective authors manage to articulate forms of cultural critique and to break political, sexual, and religious taboos without provoking massive censorious reactions is due to their mastery of indirectness and the concomitant impartiality which seems to emanate from their works. As I would like to demonstrate, these effects are never achieved by one or two isolated literary strategies—such as allusion, parallel, or metaphor—but are in each case due to the interdependence of a whole network of transgressive maneuvers located on all discursive levels of the literary text. Rather than providing an abstract catalogue of transgressive techniques, the following analysis will therefore explore the workings of transgression in a series of canonical texts with a view to their respective socio-cultural contexts.

Shakespeare's English Histories

Shakespeare's history plays promise to be a good starting point for understanding the complex interaction between controlling authorities, subversive performance, and elusive meanings which characterize the relationship between literature and censorship in general, notwithstanding the historical evolution of both areas and the attendant changes in their multilayered interplay. First, the social position of the theater in Shakespeare's time is intriguing because it resists any straightforward attempts to be located either at the center or in the margins of Elizabethan society; rather, it floats precariously between the divergent expectations of the social classes and institutions (cf. Dollimore and Sinfield 211).

Second, Shakespeare's undisputed talent for dialectic structures, his preference for maintaining in his plays an admirable ideological openness instead of one-dimensional closure makes him "one of the most successful practitioners of something widespread in the Elizabethan and Jacobean theatre: a conformity to the letter of the law, precisely to express a corrosive intellectual curiosity about what compromises the spirit of the law" (Dollimore 2001, 128).

And finally, Shakespeare's English history plays provide an excellent example for the contesting forces of official historical myth-making and royal power versus transgressive enquiries into the nature, legitimacy, and fragility of this power, enquiries which penetrate taboo areas of royal authority and must have constantly risked

52 ■ *Lars Heiler*

alarming the censors. That these ideological enquiries are transmitted through the medium of theatrical representation only exacerbates the tension between the historical myth and its subversion, as Phyllis Rackin notes: "A deep contradiction, therefore, divides the subject of Shakespeare's English history plays from their medium, opposing the patriotic piety of historical mythmaking to the Machiavellian subversion of theatrical performance" (90).

In my analysis I will focus on Shakespeare's second tetralogy from *Richard II* to *Henry V*, and only briefly consider the first tetralogy (*Henry VI, 1–3* and *Richard III*) in order to illustrate the internal development of the cycles in terms of their structural differences and subversive potentials. As is well-known, the two cycles were not written in the chronological order from which a modern audience views them in retrospect: the first tetralogy covers the period which lies after the events in the second tetralogy, beginning with the death of Henry V in *1 Henry VI*.

The well-rehearsed arguments of Cultural Materialist and New Historicist critics assume a dialectical relationship in the history plays between subversion and containment which is played out in different nuances in the second tetralogy. In *Richard II*, the legitimacy of divine kingship is challenged by Richard's deposition and subsequent execution, acts precipitated by Henry Bolingbroke who is himself to become King Henry IV, a ruler who embraces Machiavellian strategies of theatricality and dissimulation in order to rise to power. The revolutionary potential of *Richard II* is reflected in the fact that the deposition scene is missing in the first editions of the play and only added to the 1608 quarto, for Janet Clare a clear indication of censorial intervention (cf. 47).

The bone of contention between Cultural Materialists and New Historicists is usually seen in the assessment of the respective weight of subversive and containing energies in the history plays (cf. Dollimore 1994, 2–17). Stephen Greenblatt and other New Historicists usually assume a full containment of the plays' subversive energies, whereas Cultural Materialists do acknowledge a more sustained and active effect of these energies. The centrifugal forces undermining royal authority become markedly stronger and more multi-faceted in *Henry IV, 1* and *2*, and in *Henry V*, a development which many critics have directly linked with Bolingbroke's 'fall from grace' in *Richard II*. Kiernan Ryan contends that "[t]he action contrived to clinch the exclusive legitimacy of Bolingbroke's claim to the throne breeds a multiplicity of sovereigns. The play disperses

Against Censorship ❧ 53

Henry's singularity and blatantly insinuates that to bear oneself like a monarch and don the roles of royalty may be all there is to being royal for real…" (2003, 158; cf. also Rackin 87). Royal power is in these plays involved in a game of subversion which might ultimately be more challenging to royal legitimacy than open rebellion.

The role of Falstaff as agent of carnivalesque transgression, as "Bakhtin's 'material bodily principle writ large'" (Holderness 1992, 154) has become a central topos in the readings of the *Henry IV* plays, particularly in connection with the *éducation carnivalesque* of Prince Hal. *1 Henry IV* depicts a prince under the apparent influence of the scoundrel Falstaff who is a master at bluffing, role playing and masquerading, techniques which Hal perfects in the Falstaff school. The most prominent example is the role play between Hal and Falstaff, in which the latter assumes the role of Hal, who in turn plays his father Henry IV and prefigures the constellation between authority and transgression at the end of Part Two, when the former prince discards Falstaff in order to become King Henry V. The question remains, however, whether Hal's soliloquy in *1 Henry IV* "Yet herein will I imitate the sun" (1.2.188–210) can be read as the early announcement of a process of "transformation, the discarding of an assumed disguise and the re-emergence of a hidden identity" (Holderness 2000, 163) or whether the "imitation" of the sun instead hints at Hal's proficiency in performing his monarchical role, thereby not abandoning the Machiavellian temptation of theatricality, but embracing it and allowing his rule to be guided by tabooed values of dissimulation and *realpolitik*: "…the clash between essentialist and performative notions of legitimacy that pervades the comic as well as the heroic scenes of Shakespeare's second tetralogy of English histories" (Montrose 96) becomes the pivotal aspect for the political implications of the plays and is taken to its logical conclusion in *Henry V*, the play which superficially purports the most explicit celebration of nationalist feeling and monarchical power. Nevertheless, modern critics agree that the (self-)fashioning of Henry as ideal monarch ultimately renders his rule doubly problematic. On one level, the play demonstrates that the creation of a powerful kingship necessarily foregrounds the subversive energies which threaten Henry's authority, laying bare the structural homology between protagonist and antagonists (cf. Dollimore and Sinfield 218). On another, the source of Henry's legitimacy is shown to be inextricably linked with the questionable and dubious qualities of theatrical representation, a connection which challenges Henry's legitimacy by reducing him to a mere actor (cf. Reinfandt 83).

54 ✍ *Lars Heiler*

Viewed in its entirety, the second tetralogy thus stages a gradually increasing number of moral and political transgressions which shatter the foundations of the early modern English monarchy, by subtly introducing Machiavellian assumptions about royal legitimacy. The deposition of *Richard II*, which did find fault with the Elizabethan censors, is only the most obvious form of taboo-breaking, and maybe not the most dangerous one—the Queen's fear of the scene serving as an 'insurrection manual' for her own opponents notwithstanding. Yet *Richard II* still adheres to a binary structure in which protagonist and antagonist represent forms of centralized power and opposition, whereas the following three plays of the second tetralogy disperse these powers and render their control ultimately impossible. Machiavelli is omnipresent in these plays and sides with all parties simultaneously, turning the dramatic universe of *1* and *2 Henry IV* and *Henry V* into an arena where the game is called 'survival of the slyest'. These plays foreground the instability of grand narratives as well as only seemingly solid power structures, thereby exposing the vulnerability and hypocrisy of the successful monarch whilst simultaneously purporting to establish his legitimacy, a strategy of semantic ambiguity which belies patriotic interpretations of the histories in the Tillyard tradition. Whether one places a larger emphasis on the containment or on the subversion factor in Shakespeare's English histories is not so important for my present purposes; the fact that these subversions are staged at all and that most of them did not fall prey to state censorship, is evidence of a largely successful circumvention of censorious restriction.

The internal development of the second tetralogy, with its proliferation of taboo-breaking instances, can be highlighted with a glance at the first tetralogy in order to show that the increasing corrosion of official Elizabethan values is paired with a development in Shakespeare's dramatic practice which involves a notable transgression of generic boundaries. As Tzvetan Todorov states, "each epoch has its own system of genres, which stands in some relation to the dominant ideology…Like any other institution, genres bring to light the constitutive features of the society to which they belong" (200). Todorov's claim can be directly applied to the evolution of Shakespeare's history plays, as the following quote by Phyllis Rackin shows:

> Character, in fact, emerges along with Machiavellianism as a motive force in Shakespeare's historical universe. In the providential universe

of the morality play, as in the paradigmatic expressions of universal rules of causality that Aristotle found in tragedy, character is subordinated to plot.... Character, however, becomes increasingly important in the increasingly secularized worlds of Elizabethan drama..., as human agency rather than transcendental teleology comes to motivate the action.

This opposition between providential plot and Machiavellian character can be seen in the first tetralogy, where the emblematic flatness of the characters who act in the name of God and country and the uniformity of their language contrast with the vivid particularity of the characters who oppose providential order to pursue their own agendas. In the later plays, however, they are no longer contained within the simple binary scheme that opposes character to plot and Machiavellian subversion to legitimate authority. (86f.)

Rackin's argument short-circuits ground-breaking Renaissance developments, above all the 'discovery' of individual character, with their impact on dramatic forms in general, and their consequences for Shakespeare's histories in particular, which gradually provide more privileged space for Machiavellian subversion as they transgress the laws of genre. When Todorov observes that "in order to exist as such, the transgression requires a law—precisely the one that is to be violated" (196), he could equally well be voicing a New Historicist argument about Shakespeare's English histories.

Jonathan Swift, *Gulliver's Travels*

Swift's satirical novel *Gulliver's Travels* (1726) is, like Shakespeare's histories, an excellent illustration of a subversive cultural critique which managed to pass the scrutiny of contemporary censors largely unnoticed. Moreover, it is a literary work that, like the history plays, is informed by and critically exposes the modernization process of its date of production and that also transgresses the boundaries of the literary genres it occupies.

The taboos that *Gulliver's Travels* breaks traverse whole areas of early eighteenth-century English society: the novel assails guiding principles of Enlightenment philosophy, absurdities of scientific progress, the rise of capitalism, Walpole's Whig government, party politics in general, religion, and the travel books that were fashionable at the time, but it does so in such oblique ways that eighteenth-century censors and modern critics alike are at a loss when trying to pin down the exact targets of the novel's satirical attacks. This is a

56 &ero; *Lars Heiler*

quality that *Gulliver's Travels* shares with all good satires and results mainly from the fact that 'satire' does not constitute a fixed literary genre, but is able to occupy any genre parasitically and use these genres as hosts which it eats up from within. Therefore, modern satire theory has recognized the futility of trying to establish the generic boundaries of satire, but views satire as a "mode" (Connery and Combe 9) of writing, a "frame of mind" (Knight 7) and "an 'open' form" (Griffin 186).

According to Melinda Rabb "[w]riters of satire employ unauthorized discourses, such as gossip, slander, libel, and secret history, that 'tell on' people.... Astute readers of satire—the group that Swift described as a few friends laughing in a corner—also become members of a conspiratorial cabal" (349). How is this satirical conspiracy realized in Swift's novel? There is a longstanding debate in Swift criticism about the use of general and particular satire in *Gulliver's Travels*, a debate that dates back to the novel's initial reception where readers sought to establish clear identifications between the book and existing persons. The issue centers on the particularity or universality of the novel, the points at which it has in its satirical purview specific contemporaneous individuals or events, and where it rails more generally against life's 'eternal' vices and follies. Interestingly, none of Swift's contemporaries felt personally attacked by the use of particular satire in the novel and located its satirical potential almost entirely in the realm of general satire. According to David Bywaters, Swift had to find new ways of generating double meanings and indeterminacy because the satirical machinery of his age had exhausted the "traditional uses of parallel" (718). At the same time, eighteenth-century readers were prone to suspect particular targets even in the most general allusions (cf. 726). The dilemma is clear: on the one hand a readership keen on spotting topical satire needed to be satisfied, on the other hand, Swift could not be too particular without waking too many sleeping (watch-)dogs. As Bywaters continues, Swift "chooses neither to surfeit nor to starve his reader's appetite for topical application, but rather to whet it with a series of partial parallels so delicately stated and so carefully placed that they suggest that far more is going on beneath the surface of the text than plainly appears" (727). Swift's masterstroke in order to negotiate between the Scylla of vague generalization and the Charybdis of blunt particularity was to merge both types of satire in such a way that they would both be constantly evoked by the text and that the reader would be unable to draw a neat line between them. Thus, Swift involves his

Against Censorship   57

readers in a satirical game of hide-and-seek in which they do not know exactly what to look for, or, if they have eventually found something are unable to tell if this was the object of their search in the first place. Equally, the censors were unable to tell if— or where—a transgression of taboos had happened: "Swift...provides, beneath an unequivocal sign of hidden meaning, an equivocal parallel" (732).

Apart from Swift's creative replenishment of the satirical parallel there are two further techniques employed which effectively insulate *Gulliver's Travels* against censorship or libel: the play of perspective and the position of Gulliver as unreliable narrator of his travels. In many instances both strategies are interrelated in the novel, as in the following example: during his stay in Brobdingnag—whose king dismisses the English as "the most pernicious race of little odious vermin that Nature ever suffered to crawl upon the surface of the earth" (*GT* 173) after having listened attentively to Gulliver's praise of England—Gulliver endeavors to instruct the king in the art of modern statesmanship and advises him to use gun powder against his enemies (cf. *GT* 174). When the king declines, horrified by Gulliver's callousness, the latter denounces him as backward and narrow-minded in front of his English readers, only to conclude:

> Neither do I say this with the least intention to detract from the many virtues of that excellent King, whose character I am sensible will on this account be very much lessened in the opinion of an English reader: but I take this effect among them to have risen from their ignorance, by not having hitherto reduced *politics* into a *science*, as the more acute wits of Europe have done. (*GT* 175f.)

Swift turns Gulliver into a jingoist who embraces notions of scientific progress and *realpolitik* and rejects the positive values of the king as old-fashioned. Judicious readers who might well have sided with the king's view of affairs are wooed by Gulliver who seeks their complicity, which they can hardly accept, but since Gulliver appeals to them as his (patriotic) English readers, they are put in a quandary regarding identification. Do they prefer Gulliver's Machiavellian hypocrisy and progressive zeal or the label of naïve backwardness? But the screw of refracted perspectives is turned once more: earlier Gulliver has presented himself as a pacifist who rejects gratuitous violence and declines to destroy the fleet of Blefuscu, against the king of Lilliput's orders. Since Gulliver's shifting value system and floating identity on his travels are neither coherent nor consistent,

58   *Lars Heiler*

the readers feel uneasy whenever Gulliver invokes any complicity between narrator and readers, because they can never be certain into what forms of identifications they are being lured this time. As narrator, Gulliver never directly attacks the targets of the novel's satire, and as often as not he himself becomes the target of his own narrative self-representation, yet the readers are unable to free themselves entirely from Gulliver's complicitous narratorial grasp.

In addition to breathing new life into the techniques of satirical writing, Swift exploits another genre that began to flourish in the early eighteenth century, the novel in the tradition of Daniel Defoe's *Robinson Crusoe*: "For Swift, the early novelistic experiments of the 1720s in England provided a tantalizing space for his satiric powers to run loose over new terrain. He distrusted virtually everything represented in the early novel…" (Seidel 73). Swift takes up the cues from Defoe's fictional travel book and begins to carnivalize the entire range of early eighteenth-century English (and European) optimism, self-complacency, and pride articulated therein, with Gulliver developing into a satirical and skeptical counter-model, an anti-Crusoe. The transgression of political, philosophical, and moral taboos in the novel is coupled with a subversion of the novelistic form, which, despite being in a state of infancy, is felt by Swift to represent the ideological quintessence of a new age that deserved all the suspicion he could muster. The narrative self-perfection of the autonomous liberal subject in a closed novelistic form encapsulates the convictions of the age, and it is exactly this kind of success story which *Gulliver's Travels* undermines (cf. Hunter 225). By "making encroachment, infiltration, possession, and subversion its central way of life" (225f.) the satirical force in *Gulliver's Travels* can be viewed as being directed against the philosophical and political presuppositions underpinning the emergent novel form. That "Swift's views stirred powerful reactions, resentments, and suspicions" (217) does not come as a surprise. But that the novel managed to avoid any major sanctions from a rigorous state censorship is remarkable indeed and was obviously not expected by Swift, who was eager to keep his authorship a secret and headed off to "Dublin immediately after arranging surreptitiously for the publication" (216)—obviously as a precautionary measure.

William Thackeray, *Vanity Fair*

Thackeray's notorious condemnation of the moral of Part IV of Swift's *Gulliver's Travels* as "horrible, shameful, unmanly, blasphemous"

(1853, 40) is all the more surprising, coming, as it does, from the greatest English satirist of the nineteenth century. Yet despite Thackeray's aversion to parts of *Gulliver's Travels*, his *Vanity Fair. A Novel without a Hero* (1847/48) shares many characteristic features with Swift's most popular work. Although both texts were successful with the majority of their respective audiences, they both met with hostile reactions on publication. While *Gulliver's Travels* "did have detractors, mostly on political grounds" (Hunter 217), many Victorian readers of *Vanity Fair* considered the novel to be "false and unwholesome teaching" (Lewes 756).

While Swift had to find new ways of creating satirical ambiguity and of voicing social and cultural critique by effacing the boundaries between general and particular satire, Thackeray saw himself confronted with the task of refining his "early satiric radicalism" (Palmeri 771f.) and of making it palatable to Victorian expectations of propriety and decency. As in the case of Swift, it is through a series of generic *and* moral transgressions that Thackeray probes the tolerance of his audience:

> If dividing his story between two focal characters was a technical innovation, Thackeray's decision to make those characters women— and especially to make one of them an unscrupulous and even immoral woman toward to whom the reader nonetheless responds sympathetically—was a remarkably bold step for a Victorian novelist to take. (Frazee 228)

The unscrupulous woman in question is Rebecca Sharp who can be considered the embodiment of moral transgression because she commits a plethora of misdemeanors and crimes: lying, blasphemy, adultery, neglect of her only child, and (very likely) murder. In spite of violating any taboo a Victorian 'angel in the house' can possibly trespass, Becky does not incur the wrath of a conventional poetic justice. What is more, her 'angelic' counterpart Amelia Sedley is exposed as a self-righteous hypocrite who subtly tyrannizes her environment through her pose of feminine weakness.

The intrusive authorial narrator of *Vanity Fair* goes out of his way to condemn Rebecca's misdeeds, but at the same time he defends his representation of her as observing the laws of propriety:

> I must pass over a part of Mrs. Rebecca Crawley's biography with that lightness and delicacy which the world demands—the moral world, that has, perhaps, no particular objection to vice, but an insuperable

repugnance to hearing vice called by its proper name.... In describing this siren... the author, with modest pride, asks his readers all round, has he once forgotten the laws of politeness, and showed the monster's hideous tail above water? No! Those who like may peep down under waves that are pretty transparent, and see it writhing and twirling, diabolically hideous and slimy, flapping amongst bones, or curling round corpses; but above the water-line, I ask, has not everything been proper, agreeable, and decorous...? (*VF* 638f.)

The narrator's claim to render the expurgated version of Becky's deeds and to take into account the moral sensitivity of his readers is a clever self-reflective maneuver through which he activates his reader's imagination more successfully than a blunt and moralizing foregrounding of Becky's crimes would have done. In a rhetorical countermovement he relocates Becky's monstrosity from a metaphorical onto a literal level on which he becomes very explicit about slime, corpses, and bones without having to talk about her social crimes. In this double movement of concealing and revealing, Becky's transgressions are coupled with the narrator's transgressive pleasure in saying more by saying less. Both are contained by the framework of representational discretion but continue their work in the murky waters of subtextuality (cf. Brontë 752).

Thackeray's rejection of Victorian narrative conventions goes far beyond the precarious treatment of Becky Sharp, the novel's true scandal lies in the depiction of an amoral and vain society without offering a positive counter-image. In fact, Becky's plots can only succeed because she uses her manipulative skills in a society which is only too susceptible to her attacks because it is built on vanity and the art of dissimulation (cf. Palmeri 770). Becky's oscillating position in the narrative between periphery and center is due to her double role as the scapegoat who must be expelled from the ranks of the respectable classes, and as the paradigm of a capitalist Victorian society who takes the premises of this society to its extreme but logical conclusions (cf. Miller 1049).

The dialectics of revealing and concealing in *Vanity Fair* is expanded through a distinctive feature which further destabilizes the narrative closure of the novel, namely through Thackeray's own illustrations, which are often not reproduced in modern editions of the text. As Christopher Coates argues, "[t]his other, pictorial narrative is not simply an amplification of what the written text offers," rather "... the pictorial text redefines and problematizes the written ones" (47 and 44). The term illustration is indeed misleading because it implies a pictorial imitation of the written text, but what Thackeray actually provides is a contrafactual relationship between text and image. The interplay between them constitutes another narrative diversionary tactics to disguise both Rebecca's actions and the narrator's role in misrepresenting them. Becky's role in the death of Jos Sedley is represented in the plate subtitled "Becky's second appearance in the character of Clytemnestra" (*VF* 686), invoking a mythical model for the murder plot which corroborates our worst suspicions without showing the actual murder. The final plate of the novel which shows Rebecca's transformation from femme fatale to a model of charity subtitled "Virtue rewarded. A booth in Vanity Fair" (*VF* 688) can be interpreted as yet another respectable pose of hers to find favor with society and exposes the whole extent of Rebecca's scandalous fictional fate, as Lisa Jadwin points out: "The final three illustrations of *Vanity Fair* are tableaux that insinuate visually what the narrator is unwilling to articulate: that Becky...has actually been substantially rewarded—by society—for her crimes" (48).

According to Jadwin, the feedback structure between text and image also "generates a theatrical effect: the novel increasingly seems less a series of narrated events than a series of theatrical spectacles, visual and verbal charades that the reader is called upon to interpret" (46). The theatricality of the representation has to be seen in conjunction with the novel's frame tale and the narrator's pose as puppet master who, in a variation of the *theatrum mundi* metaphor, sets the scene for the pervading theme of the novel, doubleness: "The narrator who describes himself in 'Before the Curtain' as 'Manager of the performance' admits with disarming frankness that he is 'double', not to be trusted" (39).

The narrator's elusive and theatrical presence makes *Vanity Fair* one of the few examples of unreliable authorial narration in the English novel. The traditional ideological complicity between authorial narrator and reader as well as the former's task of interpreting the world are replaced by epistemological uncertainty that radically redefines the conventions and practices of novelistic communication. This "hermeneutics of skepticism" (Fisher 114) has induced Wolfgang Iser to see *Vanity Fair* as paving the way for the modern novel, with its preference for—in Roland Barthes' sense—writerly over readerly properties:

> ...*Vanity Fair* marks a stage of transition between the traditional and what we now call the 'modern' novel....The author has not yet

withdrawn 'to pare his fingernails', but he has already entered into the shadows and holds his scissors at the ready. (2006, 776)

It is due to his formal and generic transgressions, his debunking of the tabooed omniscient narrator-God, that Thackeray manages to satirize the moral duplicity of the Victorian middle and upper classes. He is thus able to both confront his readers with the social monster Becky Sharp as their distorted alter ego and to steer clear of any censorious sanctions.

The *Doppelgänger* Text as Licensed Transgression: Stevenson, Wilde, Conrad

The *Doppelgänger* motif ideally lends itself to an analysis of transgression which is presented in more or less explicit terms, but which is—in its late Victorian articulations—contained by a moralistic narrative structure, be it through forms of poetic justice or the intervention of an intrusive narrator, and thereby achieves a form of decorum which guarantees its respectability.

A classic Victorian text which articulates transgression and its pleasures, but at the same time marks them as heinous crimes, is R.L. Stevenson's *Dr Jekyll and Mr Hyde* (1886). Its *Doppelgänger* constellation allows for a representation of Edward Hyde's sensual liberation as an ecstatic and pleasurable state. The interlocking narratives of Mr. Utterson, the lawyer, Jekyll's colleague Dr. Lanyon and finally Henry Jekyll's rendering of the case place the reader in an ever greater proximity with Jekyll's dark secret. By the time we learn about Jekyll's first transformation into Hyde from Jekyll's concluding intradiegetic narrative we are already accustomed to Hyde's portrayal as deformed monster. The actual transformation is rendered by Jekyll in terms of a Freudian 'oceanic feeling,' a liberation from social fetters and a quasi-mystical harmony, albeit without the quasi-paradisiacal purity and innocence conventionally associated with such a regressive state:

> There was something strange in my sensations, something indescribably new and, from its very novelty, incredibly sweet. I felt younger, lighter, happier in body; within I was conscious of a heady recklessness, a current of disordered sensual images running like a mill race in my fancy, a solution of the bonds of obligation, an unknown, but not an innocent freedom of the soul. (*Jekyll* 50)

Against Censorship 63

Jekyll's depiction of his transformation allows for the reader's temporary identification with the state of his alter ego even though Jekyll's further depiction of Hyde's physical and moral deformity revokes such an identification. The scientist's transgressive embrace of his darker and lighter side (which turns into addiction) is inscribed into a moral and theological framework from which he has to reject his dangerous experiment and his feelings of joy. Consequently, Hyde *and* Jekyll have to be punished, the former for his crimes, the latter for his hubris. Simultaneously, the novel indirectly deconstructs the ideal of the Victorian gentleman by showing the respectable lawyer Mr. Utterson to be a voyeuristic character who is fascinated and appalled by the crimes of his friend. Bearing in mind that Utterson is introduced as a character who "drank gin when he was alone, to mortify a taste for vintages" (*Jekyll* 7) the reader recognizes the neurotic potential of a late Victorian society which seems to breed either addiction (Jekyll) or abstention (Utterson) without granting a positive balance of pleasure. Since Utterson's perspective frames the intradiegetic narratives of Lanyon and Jekyll, Stevenson's novel seems to contain the transgression within the values of Victorian society, but at the same time it exposes their corrosion and decay.

Oscar Wilde's *The Picture of Dorian Gray* (1891) orchestrates the recognition of Victorian values and their simultaneous subversion in a similar way. Dorian has to face poetic justice for his crimes at the end of the novel, and his dream of freedom from the restraints of society is marked as a dangerous antisocial fantasy which cannot be integrated into the dominant cultural system. Nevertheless, Dorian's and Lord Henry Wotton's New Hedonist philosophy articulates a profound critique of this system:

> The aim of life is self-development. To realize one's nature perfectly—that is what each of us is here for. People are afraid of themselves, nowadays. They have forgotten the highest of all duties, the duty that one owes to oneself. Of course they are charitable. They feed the hungry, and clothe the beggar. But their own souls starve, and are naked.... The terror of society, which is the basis of morals, the terror of God, which is the secret of religion—these are the two things that govern us. (*DG* 41)

The subversion of culturally tabooed values such as Christian charity and conventional morality takes on a different quality in Lord Henry and in Dorian Gray. While Dorian indulges in lust, debauchery, and violence, Lord Henry, who "never say[s] a moral thing, and...never

64　⬦　*Lars Heiler*

do[es] a wrong thing" (*DG* 26), remains an armchair hedonist who observes social norms and values because he is too afraid of society's sanctions. Lord Henry's inner-fictional self-censorship parallels the self-censoriousness of the novel as a whole, which is punctuated by the pleasure of touching and breaking taboos, but abrogates the consummation of this pleasure as a self-defeating path and maintains its own literary respectability for contemporary readers.

Joseph Conrad's modernist short story "The Secret Sharer" (1910) takes up the *Doppelgänger* motif rather belatedly and with some decisive adjustments and changes to the narrative model practiced by Stevenson and Wilde. "The Secret Sharer" can also be perceived as a story about tabooed pleasures, but these are embedded in an initiation narrative and a—guardedly positive—process of self-development. The first-person narrator, a young captain at sea, manages to overcome a severe personal and professional crisis with the help of a secret visitor, Leggatt, the former chief mate of another ship, the *Sephora*, who killed a fellow seaman. Leggatt, who is arrested by his own captain, flees and is discovered by the narrator during his nightwatch. The captain who is uncertain of his own identity ("I was somewhat of a stranger to myself" [*TSS* 26]) conceives of Leggatt as his double in all respects. In contrast to Stevenson and Wilde, where the respective doubles exist either through scientific or artistic creation, the captain "constructs Leggatt for his own psychological purposes" (Schwarz 104). In a clear breach of marine law, he grants him refuge in his own cabin, hides him from the rest of the crew and helps him to leave the ship by undertaking a hazardous maneuver that might have endangered the ship and the lives of his crew, but ironically earns him the respect of his men and eventually establishes his authority as captain. Leggatt's impulsive manliness, which contrasts with the captain's diffidence and hesitancy, has helped the latter on his way to individual maturation. At the same time, he successfully resists the destructive side of Leggatt's character which is split off symbolically through Leggatt's final disappearance.

What sets Conrad's story apart from Stevenson and Wilde is the absence of a controlling voice of moral certainty which superficially at least contains the desire for transgression articulated in them. As James Phelan has shown, the captain is entangled in a whole web of problematic ethical questions which remain unanswered:

> Leggatt may be a murderer, and the captain's efforts to keep him hidden clearly interfere with the captain's performance of his primary responsibilities. In this way, hiding Leggatt's existence becomes the

captain's *guilty* secret, a guilt made all the more complicated by the captain's unspoken homosexual attraction. Indeed, Conrad is presenting us with a situation in which the two main internal "threats" to a company of sailors—homosexuality and murder—become located, albeit not clearly realized, in the captain's second self. (141)

These ethical questions are passed on to us as readers who "become the sharers of the captain's guilty secret, with the added burden of not being sure we can justify it to ourselves" (ibid.).

'Gay' readings of *Doppelgänger* texts are frequent because the form of the *Doppelgänger* text provides an opportunity to imply dissident sexuality within a broader scope of moral transgressions. According to Jeffrey Meyers "[h]omosexual novels are characteristically subtle, allusive and symbolic . . . and form a . . . kind of literary ambiguity. For the ambiguous expression of the repressed, the hidden and the sometimes secret theme suggests a moral ambiguity as well" (1f.).

Conrad's "The Secret Sharer" exploits the space of reflection and enunciation that the *Doppelgänger* motif engenders in analogous ways. The captain's secretive handling of Leggatt's presence on his ship combines questions of legal and ethical integrity with the underlying potentiality of homosexual attraction[2] which is communicated to the readers through the growing narcissistic identification between protagonist and double. That the captain undergoes a successful process of maturation and earns the respect of his crew through engaging in a homoerotic relationship with Leggatt, and that the latter manages to leave the ship without being arrested and probably convicted for his killing of a seaman constitutes a significant departure from the nineteenth-century model of the aforementioned *Doppelgänger* texts which do impose poetic justice on their protagonists. When Brian Richardson maintains that "'The Secret Sharer' is not a last, tired re-working of the by-then rather hackneyed theme of the *Doppelgänger*, but . . . a skeptical parody of this familiar Romantic topos" (317), he sees Conrad's short story as a text which undermines the generic expectations that the *Doppelgänger* genre raises, but also as a text which transgresses the moral boundaries set up by turn-of-the-century notions of sexual dissidence.

Censorship and Transgression in Contemporary Literature

In the first half of the twentieth century, representations of sexual and political dissidence seem to be the two central forms of transgressing

66　　*Lars Heiler*

cultural taboos. After the Second World War, the growing social and cultural differentiation and pluralization of British society makes an analysis of the interaction between taboo and transgression infinitely more difficult. The abolition of institutional censorship in 1968 is just one symptom of a new permissive society which seems to accept an ever-increasing amount of transgressive behavior and its depiction in literature, art, and film. The Holocaust seems to be one of the few remaining taboos which cannot be transgressed through denial or other forms of showing disrespect without provoking public outrage or legal consequences. In such a climate of almost general permissiveness the role of literature as taboo-breaking force seems to have faded away, literature seems like a dog that is still able to bark, but has lost its bite. In other words, literature may stage transgressions more overtly than ever, but without any noticeable effect.

If one proceeds, however, from the assumption brought forth in this volume that "temporally and geographically, the phenomena of taboo and transgression can be considered omnipresent, that is existent in all societies or cultures and at all times" (Horlacher, this volume), it seems that the erosion of traditional norms has not shaped a society which is free from taboos, but one that has rather erected new taboos and orthodoxies which are linked with concepts such as female and gay emancipation, multiculturality, religious tolerance, and political correctness (which has itself developed into a form of moral censorship). The power of these taboos can be gauged by the euphemisms, careful phrasing, and self-censorship that (democratic) politicians revert to when they talk about the issues in question, which represent discursive minefields for anyone who openly challenges their validity. Transgressions of these new cultural taboos are usually performed by reactionary, anti-democratic, or anti-emancipatory social forces which oppose one or more of the values established by an open society and sometimes propagate authoritarian and totalitarian views of the world and of social interaction.

Admittedly, the functions of literature in such a complex cultural force field are difficult to pin down. Does it side with the democratic forces against the transgression of liberal values? Or does it take the liberty of challenging the new orthodoxies and of provoking their advocates, or both? Ian McEwan's novel *The Comfort of Strangers* (1981) steers a precarious course between these two options by introducing a young English couple, Colin and Mary, who succumb to the fascination of an older couple, Robert and Caroline, during their holiday in a city resembling Venice. While Mary is characterized

Against Censorship ❧ 67

as a feminist and Colin as a man trying to come to terms with the demands of a new masculinity, the older couple lives according to a traditional division of gender roles: the enigmatic Robert is depicted as a patriarchal macho, the crippled Caroline as a model of feminine meekness. Toward the end of the novel Mary learns that Caroline's back was broken by Robert during a sadomasochistic sex game. Scandalously, Caroline not only finds excuses for Robert, but also admits the pleasure she feels in her role as victim: "He beat me with his fists as he made love to me. I was terrified, but the terror and the pleasure were all one.... I loved being punished" (*Comfort* 110).

The sexual thrills experienced by Robert and Caroline are contrasted with Mary's and Colin's shallow love-making which becomes temporarily more exciting after they have confessed their own destructive fantasies to each other. In the end, Colin is killed by Robert and Caroline with a razorblade, bled to death after a hypnotic and disturbing choreography of kisses and caresses while the helpless Mary, drugged by Caroline, can only watch the cruel and grotesque performance unfold before her eyes. When she awakes, Robert and Caroline have vanished like the phantoms from a bad dream.

What is so unsettling about *The Comfort of Strangers* apart from the graphic depiction of perversion and violence is the link that the novel establishes between sadomasochistic sexual practices and the patriarchal organization of gender relations, with both appearing to be more pleasurable and fulfilling than Mary's and Colin's supposedly emancipated form of companionship. It is true that the novel hastens to mark Robert's and Caroline's sphere as a nightmarish counter-world which brings about destruction, suffering, and death. By evoking disgust at their deeds the text reminds the reader that a radical regression from the contemporary state of gender relations can be no solution to the problems of performing postmodern gender roles. But the sheer power of the fantasies of domination and subjection which the novel unleashes can also be seen as a provocation for claims to equal rights and emancipation and a slap in the face of many feminist axioms. *The Comfort of Strangers* challenges received notions of feminine freedom and self-determination and probes the depths of repressed sources of pleasure in a politically incorrect way. In an interview with John Haffenden, Ian McEwan explained that in the novel he was interested in showing that sexual fantasies—sadistic or masochistic, in women or in men—should be acknowledged and admitted by everyone as part of their sexuality. He also reported how he was "attacked for providing a 'rapist's

68 ✥ *Lars Heiler*

charter' and for poaching on forbidden territory—women's experience" at a conference by "a broad coalition of socialists and femi-
nists" after stating that "true freedom would be for such women to
recognize their masochism and to understand how it had become
related to sexual pleasure" (Haffenden 178). The censorious reaction
of the conference audience proves that today there may be less formal, more dispersed forms of censorship, but they still indicate discursive boundaries which literature can transgress with some effect.
That the sanctions for such transgressions in contemporary Britain
are less serious than in previous centuries certainly means that texts
can articulate their outrageous potential more freely, but there may
be cases when a text remains impartial about the options it stages.
McEwan's (by now dated) reputation as *enfant terrible* of English literature and the taboo-like reticence of many literary critics to write
about his works in the early 1980s are certainly due to his penchant
for depicting shocking scenes of transgression without taking sides,
as Kiernan Ryan writes: "The idiom is deliberate, exact and impersonal, purged of emotive resonance and immune to empathy or agitation" (1999, 203). *The Comfort of Strangers* cannot be reduced to
enacting transgression for the sake of merely producing shock, but
the formulation of an enlightened, liberationist discourse about 'true
freedom' that McEwan provides in the above-mentioned interview
does not prevail either. The text is like a loose cannon that may roll
in all interpretive directions and cause massive destruction without
any chance of being controlled. According to Jonathan Dollimore:
"[t]o take art seriously—to recognize its potential—must be to recognize that there might be reasonable grounds for wanting to control
it.... We accord [art] the seriousness it deserves by trusting it less"
(2001, 97). There are not many contemporary texts which qualify for
such seriousness, but *The Comfort of Strangers* may be one of them.

Notes

1. Cf. deconstruction's insistence on the indeterminacy of the linguistic
   sign and the literary text (cf. de Man 17), the illimitable process
   of engendering meaning postulated by reader response theory
   (cf. Iser 1993, 235), or Bakhtin's writings on dialogism and polyphony
   (cf. Bakhtin 674).
2. According to Andrew Michael Roberts "homosexuality is neither
   definitely present nor definitely absent in Conrad's work, but figures
   as an occluded part of a homosocial structure, not as the key which
   undoes that structure" (9).

Works Cited

Bakhtin, Mikhail. "Discourse in the Novel." *Literary Theory: An Anthology.* Eds. Julie Rivkin and Michael Ryan. Oxford: Blackwell, 2004. 674–85.

Brontë, Charlotte. "To W.S. Williams." Qtd. after William Makepeace Thackeray. *Vanity Fair.* Ed. Peter Shillingsburg. New York: Norton, 1994. 752.

Bywaters, David. "*Gulliver's Travels* and the Mode of Political Parallel during Walpole's Administration." *Journal of English Literary History* 54.3 (1987): 717–40.

Clare, Janet. "*Art Made Tongue-tied by Authority.*" *Elizabethan and Jacobean Dramatic Censorship.* Manchester: Manchester UP, 1990.

Coates, Christopher. "Thackeray's Editors and the Dual Text of *Vanity Fair.*" *Word & Image: A Journal of Verbal/Visual Enquiry* 9.1 (1993): 39–50.

Coetzee, J.M. *Giving Offense: Essays on Censorship.* Chicago: U of Chicago P, 1996.

Connery, Brian A., and Kirk Combe, eds. *Theorizing Satire: Essays in Literary Criticism.* New York: St. Martin's Press, 1995.

De Man, Paul. *Allegories of Reading. Figural Language in Rousseau, Nietzsche, Rilke and Proust.* New Haven and London: Yale UP, 1979.

Dollimore, Jonathan. "Shakespeare, Cultural Materialism and the New Historicism." *Political Shakespeare. Essays in Cultural Materialism.* Eds. Jonathan Dollimore and Alan Sinfield. 2nd ed. Ithaca: Cornell UP, 1994.

———. *Sex, Literature and Censorship.* Cambridge: Polity Press, 2001.

Dollimore, Jonathan, and Alan Sinfield. "History and Ideology: The Instance of *Henry V.*" *Alternative Shakespeares (1).* Ed. John Drakakis. London: Routledge, 1985. 206–27.

Drakakis, John, ed. *Alternative Shakespeares (1).* London: Routledge, 1985.

Fisher, Judith L. "Ethical Narrative in Dickens and Thackeray." *Studies in the Novel* 29.1 (1997): 108–17.

Frazee, John P. "The Creation of Becky Sharp in *Vanity Fair.*" *Dickens Studies Annual: Essays on Victorian Fiction* 27 (1998): 227–44.

Griffin, Dustin. *Satire: A Critical Reintroduction.* Lexington: Kentucky UP, 1994.

Holderness, Graham. "Henry IV: Carnival and History." *Shakespeare's History Plays. "Richard II" to "Henry V."* Ed. Graham Holderness. Houndmills: Macmillan, 1992. 151–64.

———. *Shakespeare: The Histories.* Houndmills: Macmillan, 2000.

Hunter, J. Paul. "*Gulliver's Travels* and the Later Writings." *The Cambridge Companion to Jonathan Swift.* Ed. Christopher Fox. Cambridge: Cambridge UP, 2003. 216–40.

Hyland, Paul, and Neil Sammells. *Writing and Censorship in Britain.* London: Routledge, 1992.

70　❧❧❧　*Lars Heiler*

Iser, Wolfgang. *The Fictive and the Imaginary. Charting Literary Anthropology.* Baltimore: Johns Hopkins UP, 1993.

———. "The Implied Reader. The Reader as a Component Part of the Realistic Novel: Esthetic effects in *Vanity Fair.*" *The Novel: An Anthology of Criticism and Theory, 1900–2000.* Ed. and introd. Dorothy J. Hale. Malden, MA: Blackwell, 2006. 763–78.

Jadwin, Lisa. "Clytemnestra Rewarded: The Double Conclusion of *Vanity Fair.*" *Famous Last Words: Changes in Gender and Narrative Closure.* Ed. and introd. Alison Booth. Charlottesville: UP of Virginia, 1993. 35–61.

Knight, Charles A. *The Literature of Satire.* Cambridge: Cambridge UP, 2004.

Lewes, George Henry. Review in *Athenaeum.* August 12, 1848. Qtd. after William Makepeace Thackeray. *Vanity Fair.* Ed. Peter Shillingsburg. New York: Norton, 1994. 794–97.

McEwan, Ian. *The Comfort of Strangers.* New York: Vintage Books, 1994.

Meyers, Jeffrey. *Homosexuality and Literature 1890–1930.* London: Athlone Press, 1977.

Miller, Andrew. "*Vanity Fair* through Plate Glass." *PMLA* 105.5 (1990): 1042–54.

Montrose, Louis. *The Purpose of Playing. Shakespeare and the Cultural Politics of the Elizabethan Theatre.* Chicago: Chicago UP, 1996.

Palmeri, Frank. "Cruikshank, Thackeray, and the Victorian Eclipse of Satire." *SEL* 44.4 (2004): 753–77.

Patterson, Annabel. *Censorship and Interpretation. The Conditions of Writing and Reading in Early Modern England.* Madison: U of Wisconsin P, 1984.

Phelan, James. "Reading Secrets." *Joseph Conrad. The Secret Sharer.* Ed. Daniel R. Schwarz. Boston: Bedford/St. Martin's Press, 1997. 128–44.

Rabb, Melinda. "The Secret Memoirs of Lemuel Gulliver: Satire, Secrecy, and Swift." *Journal of English Literary History* 73.2 (2006): 325–54.

Rackin, Phyllis. "Stages of History: Ideological Conflict, Alternative Plots." *Shakespeare's History Plays.* Ed. R.J.C. Watt. London: Longman, 2002. 76–95.

Reinfandt, Christoph. "Reading Shakespeare Historically: 'Postmodern' Attitudes and the History Plays." *Historicizing/Contemporizing Shakespeare. Essays in Honour of Rudolf Böhm.* Eds. Christoph Bode and Wolfgang Klooss. Trier: WVT, 2000. 73–89.

Richardson, Brian. "Construing Conrad's 'The Secret Sharer': Suppressed Narratives, Subaltern Reception, and the Art of Interpretation." *Studies in the Novel* 33.3 (2001): 306–21.

Roberts, Andrew Michael. *Conrad and Masculinity.* Houndmills: Macmillan, 2000.

Ryan, Kiernan. "Sex, Violence and Complicity: Martin Amis and Ian McEwan." *An Introduction to Contemporary Fiction. International Writing in English Since 1970.* Ed. Rod Mengham. Cambridge: Polity Press, 1999. 203–18.

Ryan, Kiernan. "The Future of History: *1 and 2 Henry IV.*" *Shakespeare's History Plays*. Ed. R.J.C. Watt. London: Longman, 2003. 147–68.

Sammells, Neil. "Writing and Censorship: An Introduction." *Writing and Censorship in Britain*. Eds. Paul Hyland and Neil Sammells. London: Routledge, 1992. 1–13.

Schwarz, Daniel R. "'The Secret Sharer' as an Act of Memory." *Joseph Conrad: "The Secret Sharer."* Ed. Daniel R. Schwarz. Boston: Bedford/St. Martin's Press, 1997. 95–111.

Seidel, Michael. *"Gulliver's Travels* and the Contracts of Fiction." *The Cambridge Companion to the Eighteenth Century Novel*. Ed. John Richetti. Cambridge: Cambridge UP, 1996. 72–89.

Shakespeare, William. *Henry IV, Part 1*. Ed. A.R. Humphreys. London: Routledge, 1992.

Stevenson, Richard C. "The Problem of Judging Becky Sharp: Scene and Narrative Commentary in *Vanity Fair.*" *Victorians Institute Journal* 6 (1977): 1–8.

Stevenson, Robert Louis. *Dr Jekyll & Mr Hyde*. Ed. Katherine Linehan. New York: Norton, 2003.

Swift, Jonathan. *Gulliver's Travels*. Ed. Peter Dixon. Harmondsworth: Penguin, 1985.

Thackeray, William Makepeace. *English Humorists of the Eighteenth Century*. London: Smith, Elder and Co, 1853.

———. *Vanity Fair*. Ed. Peter Shillingsburg. New York: Norton, 1994.

Todorov, Tzvetan. "The Origin of Genres." *Modern Genre Theory*. Ed. David Duff. Harlow: Longman, 2000. 193–209.

Wilde, Oscar. *The Picture of Dorian Gray*. Ed. Peter Ackroyd. Harmondsworth: Penguin, 1985.

PART II

LITERARY ANALYSES

CHAPTER IV

HAMLET, MACBETH, AND 'SOVEREIGN PROCESS'

John Drakakis

> [t]he kingdome of Englande is farre more absolute than either the
> dukedome of Venice is, or the kingdome of the Lacedemonians was. In
> warre time and in the field the Prince hath also absolute power, so that
> his word is lawe, he may put to death, or to other bodilie punishment,
> whom he shall thinke so to deserve, without processe of lawe or forme
> of judgement.
>
> —*Smith, 44*

This passage from Book 2 Chapter 3 of *De Republica
Anglorum* is part of a larger discussion of the role "Of the
Monarch King or Queene of Englande," and it pinpoints
clearly occasions when 'absolute power'—because it is 'absolute'—can
justifiably depart from "processe of lawe or forme of judgement."
My concern in this paper is not to investigate what Smith implies is
a particularly violent departure from 'process', but rather to attempt
to analyze the deep structural connections between 'process' and
'violence' in Shakespeare's *Macbeth.* My cue for this lies in an earlier
Shakespeare play that is not normally closely associated with *Macbeth,*
where what becomes the tragedy of the later play is pre-figured and
contained. That play is *Hamlet,* and the precursor of the later protagonist is the player-king Claudius.

It is not until Act 3 that Claudius articulates the duplicitous practice through which he enacts the role of the sovereign. Following her
father's tutoring of Ophelia in the art of deception, Claudius 'pri-
vately' affirms Polonius's observation that "with devotion's visage /
And pious action we do sugar o'er / The devil himself" (3.1.45–49),[1]

76 ✸✸✸ *John Drakakis*

his is "The harlot's cheek, beautied with plast'ring art" that "Is not more ugly to the thing that helps it / Than is my deed to my most painted word. / O heavy burden!" (3.1.49–54)

Two scenes later, he is provoked into analyzing his predicament in more detail. Here his concern is with psychological turmoil that the collision between past, present and future has generated; he begins with a horrifyingly instrumental recognition of the operations of 'justice' and 'law' in a post-lapsarian world:

> In the corrupted currents of this world
> Offence's gilded hand may shove by justice,
> And oft 'tis seen the wicked prize itself
> Buys out the law. But 'tis not so above:
> There is no shuffling, there the action lies
> In his true nature, and we ourselves compell'd
> Even to the teeth and forehead of our faults
> To give in evidence. (3.3.58–64)

Here the player king *imagines* the legitimizing moment of sovereign authority, when he is compelled to articulate, as though in a court of law, an act of rebellion that is both a repetition and a cue for abandonment. Claudius has already identified with figures from an 'historical' past: there is the surreptitious identification with Cain (1.2.105), and there is the double repetition of the murder of Gonzago (3.2), which itself repeats Claudius's regicide. Gilles Deleuze's axiom that "Repetition is a condition of action before it is a concept of reflection" (90) could not have a more apposite demonstration. Claudius imagines a divine juridical process, and in doing so, recapitulates the originary moment of a politics in which the 'player' sovereign reverts to being a subject. In other words, Claudius will be forced to relinquish the sovereign role to which he has become accustomed, of being, in the words of Carl Schmitt, "he who decides on the exception" (5).

Horatio's initial narrative account of the confrontation between Old Hamlet and Old Fortinbras, two kings whose actions were "Well ratified by law and heraldry" (1.1.90), but who, by virtue of their sovereign power were possessed of the authority to make writing coincide with action, and, in the words of Giorgio Agamben, to "make sense coincide with denotation" (25), establishes a norm. Except that in Horatio's narrative of this event, which is an attempt to make sense of the appearance of the Ghost, it is difficult to decide whether the two sovereigns are presented and represented, represented but not presented; or presented but not represented (cf. Agamben qtd. in

Hamlet, Macbeth, *and 'Sovereign Process'* 77

Badiou 2). In what is, in effect, a gloss on Alain Badiou's tri-partite division of the possible types of membership of a mathematical set, Agamben observes:

> The sovereign exception is thus the figure in which singularity is represented as such, which is to say, insofar as it is unrepresentable. What cannot be included in any way is included in the form of the exception. In Badiou's scheme, the exception introduces a fourth figure, a threshold of indistinction between excrescence (representation without presentation) and singularity (presentation without representation), something like a paradoxical inclusion of membership itself. *The exception is what cannot be included in the whole of which it is a member and cannot be a member of the whole in which it is always already included.* What emerges in this limit figure is the radical crisis of every possibility of clearly distinguishing between membership and inclusion, between what is outside and what is inside, between exception and rule. (cf. 24f.)

In a further gloss Agamben extends this structural account into the sphere of the 'sovereign claim' of language, which achieves a stabilization of meaning by 'abandoning' its *denotata* and "withdrawing from them into a pure *langue* (the linguistic 'state of exception')." It is here that he finds a space for 'deconstruction' which posits "undecidables that are infinitely in excess of every possibility of signification" (25). This is what Agamben calls 'The logic of Sovereignty':

> The sovereign decision traces and from time to time renews this threshold of indistinction between outside and inside, inclusion and exclusion, *nomos* and *physis*, in which life is originarily excepted in law. Its decision is the position of an undecidable. (27)

This would suggest that 'the structure of sovereignty' is not 'an exclusively political concept', nor 'an exclusively juridical category', nor 'a power external to law' nor, indeed, simply that which fulfils the function of 'the supreme rule of the juridical order' (cf. 28). The modern gloss on 'exception' is 'emergency', although it is worth pointing out that both *Hamlet* and *Macbeth* begin in 'states of emergency.' It is, perhaps, no accident that the 'meaning' of the figure of the Ghost in *Hamlet,* or the Weird Sisters in *Macbeth,* is 'undecidable' in the manner suggested by Agamben's 'logic.' Each points in the direction of a dangerous energy that the structures of political power attempt to domesticate in different ways: the Ghost, located in the liminal

78 ✣ John Drakakis

space of Purgatory, and the Weird Sisters who are the 'irrational' transgressors of order. Collectively they represent different facets of a dangerous 'otherness' which art is attracted to even as it attempts to neutralize and to socialize it.

I want now to turn to a particular aspect of what is already becoming a complex configuration of concepts: the distinction between the originary violence that inaugurates law, and that which preserves law, that Claudius's private ruminations inadvertently uncovers. In Aristotle's *Politics*, a text that appeared in translation in 1598, the section on 'kingship' draws together the issues of 'force' and 'authority' in a manner that anticipates the connection between Walter Benjamin's distinction between creative violence and preservative violence:

> [I]s the intending king to have about him a force with which he will be able to impose his will on those who seek to resist his rule? How else is he to exercise his authority? For even if his sovereignty is such that he can act only in accordance with law, and do nothing of his own volition that is illegal, it will still be necessary for him to have sufficient armed force to give the laws protection. (224)

What frightens Claudius, I suggest, is the threat of a reversion to an originary structure of which the living Old Hamlet, present to himself, had been the entirely un-selfconscious, 'god-like' representative. His closing couplet in the prayer scene: "My words fly up, my thoughts remain below. / Words without thoughts never to heaven go" (3.3.97–98), reiterates the dilemma that arises when 'action' and 'language' are separated from each other, where representation is itself the question. Consequently, he posits a *difference* between the operation of divine justice, and the ruses available to him 'in this world.' What he fears most is not so much the 'application' of divine law to his case, as its consequence, final 'abandonment': a removal from the regimes of representation altogether. There he will be "at the mercy of *the* 'originary force of law'," and he fears an exclusion that the ending of the play will make permanent. However, in seeking 'freedom': "O limed soul, that struggling to be free / Art more engaged!" (3.3.68–69), we may wonder if he is expressing that 'daemonic desire' that Jonathan Dollimore has identified as an "untamed, unsocialized, and at heart non-human" energy, that in "[i]ts amoral core becomes the more potentially destructive of the human as a result of the human attempts to tame it" (73f.). The more

Hamlet, Macbeth, *and 'Sovereign Process'* 79

he struggles to free himself from the constraints of divine sovereignty, the more his own demonic 'sovereignty' is, paradoxically, compromised.

This momentary insight into what Agamben would call "the structure of the ban" (cf. 28f.) is superseded by Claudius's final soliloquy at the end of Act Four Scene Three that audaciously enlists the audience's support for a plan that both exposes his desire, while, at the same time, preserving his formal sovereignty. 'England' is asked to discharge "our sovereign process, which imports at full, / By letters congruing to that effect, / The present death of Hamlet" (4.3.66–68). Thus far the double signification of Claudius's language invites us to read the phrase "our sovereign process" ironically. What is Claudius protecting at this point? Is he protecting his 'crime?' Or is he protecting, in accordance with Aristotle's defense of force, 'the law?' Or is he acting above (or beneath the surface of) the law, as Smith would say: "without process of law or forme of judgement?" Or does this gesture reveal the sovereign who can act according to nothing that is "codified in the existing legal order," but who, in "a case of extreme peril, a danger to the existence of the state," has recourse to action that "cannot be circumscribed factually and made to conform to a pre-formed law" (Schmitt 6).

We may think that the answer to all these questions is obvious: here is a villain who wishes to neutralize a threat that could expose his crime of regicide, and in doing so is behaving in a manner that parodies sovereignty. But two scenes later Laertes enters at the head of what seems a popular rebellion. The imagery deployed by the anonymous Messenger is that of 'primal chaos', of a time immediately before the institution of the rule of law: "And as the world were now but to begin, / Antiquity forgot, custom not known—/ The ratifiers and props of every word—" (4.5.103–5). In *Hamlet* Law, it would appear, follows language, and informs a symbolic order that unites language and sovereignty. For Schmitt, "Sovereignty is the highest, legally independent, underived power" (17), whereas for Agamben, as we have seen, the *structure* of language and sovereignty are identical in that both are able to enact 'a state of exception.' Here, however, the 'rabble' that support Laertes do not revert to a formless 'life' (*zoë*), rather, they elect a 'king' (*bios*): "They cry, 'Choose we! Laertes shall be king'" (4.5.106). Laertes's 'rebellion' recapitulates a titanic struggle, but it also places him in a 'state of exception' and it threatens to repeat, in a different register, the regicide of Claudius. But Claudius forces further the comparison between his own and a divine

80 &ea *John Drakakis*

sovereignty through an appeal to the very metaphysical power that
authorizes sovereign process:

> Do not fear our person.
> There's such divinity doth hedge a king
> That treason can but peep to what it would,
> Acts little of his will. (4.5.122–25)

This audacious identification of his 'person' with the figure of the
'sovereign' is the 'satyric' (we might even say 'daemonic') version of
the figure of Old Hamlet ('Hyperion'), but in confronting his own
'rebellion' he reverts to a formulation that both invokes even as
it demystifies the ideology that sustains the institutions of sovereignty. Sovereign process in this play is not simply deciding upon
a 'state of exception' while at the same time evoking 'wonder';[2]
rather, it involves a repetition of the means whereby the 'sovereign'
comes into being as a means of structuring what would otherwise
be 'bare life." What emerges is a bio-politics whose features are
exposed, and in which accumulation figures as a primary motive.
In the case of Old Hamlet,—and also in the case of Duncan in
Macbeth—in the words of Georges Bataille, "We don't see the sovereign moment arrive" because in both cases "nothing counts but
the moment itself." In fact Bataille's definition of 'sovereignty' is
an enjoyment of "the present time without having anything else
in view but this present time" (199). When rebellion imitates sovereignty it 'looks' giant-like, but, as in the later case of Macbeth,
the incumbent is made to feel "his title / Hang loose about him
like a giant's robe / Upon a dwarfish thief" (*Macbeth* 5.3.20–22). No
matter how the play *Hamlet* resolves Denmark's crisis of authority,
the mystery of power to which Claudius appeals as part of 'sovereign process', is exposed as a political rhetoric that beautifies
"with plast'ring art" the harlot's cheek, a form of representation,
equally available to sovereign and regicide alike. This is an efficient demonstration, should one be required, of the way in which
"Offence's gilded hand may shove by justice" (3.3.58), and constitutes an important part of a fundamentally theatrical deception
that obscures the symbolic order that sovereign authority legitimates and sustains.

The play *Hamlet* makes very little drama out of Claudius's private
predicament, choosing to offer us only brief glimpses of the theatrical 'doubleness' that underpins his 'performance.' But in the

Hamlet, Macbeth, *and 'Sovereign Process'* 81

passage from *Hamlet* to *Macbeth* it gradually comes to assume a greater interest and a more complex form in Shakespeare's theatrical imagination.

Henry N. Paul's *The Royal Play of Macbeth* (1948) has long been accepted as the definitive account of the occasion of the play, but it rests on an invented conversation between Shakespeare and George Buc, the acting Master of the Revels some time during early September, 1605:

> He must have been at Oxford during the king's visit charged with some oversight of the plays; and it would have been quite in order for Buc to tell the dramatist of the King's Company that since the king did not seem to like the sorts of plays he had been shown at Oxford, it would be well for him to write a better play for his king, with suggestions as to subject matter, which sent him to the story of Macbeth as found in Holinshed. (24)

Paul concludes that it was Shakespeare's own awareness that "King James was to see the play" and that "as the dramatist sat at his desk and wrote, he was conscious of the face of the king looking straight at him," that shaped a language "to fit this expected audience" (401). I want to suggest that embedded in *Macbeth* is a critical view of 'sovereignty' that makes this a far less laudatory theatrical event than Paul would have us believe, and that, among other things, Shakespeare may well have had the unfinished business of *Hamlet* in mind.

Many of the features of *Hamlet* recur in *Macbeth*, to the extent that we might argue that it is the tragedy of *Hamlet* rewritten from the perspective of an exemplary hero whose lawful ambition transformed into unbridled desire, is turned against the sovereign power that nurtures it. But what has also changed between the two plays is tone. Claudius's Machiavellian confidence that can assert that "In the corrupted currents of this world / Offence's gilded hand may shove by justice" (3.3.57–58) is radically transformed into the fear of a secular justice, inscribed in the very 'bloody instructions' that comprise the actor's strategy:

> We still have judgement here; that we but teach
> Bloody instructions, which, being taught, return
> To plague th' inventor: this even-handed Justice
> Commends th' ingredience of our poison'd chalice
> To our own lips. (1.7.8–12)

82   John Drakakis

Power may succeed in *containing* the violence that it needs to sustain itself, but because it must expose its strategies, and what it teaches—the 'bloody instruction'—returns to its origins both as an 'even-handed Justice', *and* as a 'poison', reminiscent of the Derridean figure of the *pharmakon* (cf. Derrida 99). Power is desired, but the means necessary to attain and secure it, disclose, and render open to imitation what Agamben calls "the originary structure in which law refers to life and includes it in itself by suspending it" (28). The inner structure of this very Shakespearean expression of the *pharmakon*, compels Macbeth to traverse the space between the 'sovereign exception' and what Agamben calls 'the ban' that he later describes as "the originary exclusion through which the political dimension was first constituted" (83). What Macbeth brings together in this extraordinarily prescient utterance, is the identity of the sovereign both as he who decides on the 'exception', which is "the value or the non-value of life as such" (142), *and* who is placed "on the threshold in which life and law, outside and inside become indistinguishable" (28). The utterance is prescient precisely because Macbeth's own sovereignty will be eclipsed by the very status of 'bare' life, that is, life that is 'abandoned', and, in the play, ultimately reduced to animality: "They have tied me to a stake: I cannot fly, / But bear-like, I must fight the course" (5.7.1–2).

This is not unlike Claudius's fate, but it is also an acknowledgement of the 'violence' upon which both sovereign and regicide depend. It also indicates a movement away from the 'divine providence' that Hamlet comes to realize steers human history, and toward a 'Jacobean' perception of the secular tension between originary force and the unforeseen consequences of human action. It is this awareness of the deep structural connection between desire and political expediency that spurs Macbeth into further violations after he has become king: "To be thus is nothing, but to be safely thus" (3.1.47). But it succeeds only at great cost in that both he and Lady Macbeth register the *feeling* that such insecurity generates: "Nought's had, all's spent, / Where our desire is got without content: 'Tis safer to be that which we destroy, / Than by destruction dwell in doubtful joy" (3.2.4–7). In short, what Macbeth and his Lady have done is turn 'sovereignty', and the 'human', inside out, in such a way that its hitherto mystified structure is exposed, to reveal the explicit configuration of the originary moment of a Renaissance bio-politics. It is this that enables us to cast a critical glance at Duncan's 'sovereignty' and the violence (as well as the social structures) that sustain it, and

Hamlet, Macbeth, *and 'Sovereign Process'* 83

also at Malcolm's intended sovereignty, and particularly at that of the English king, who, as Derridean *pharmakeus*, is endowed with magical powers, but who may also be the bearer of 'poison.'

Desire and Excess

Macbeth and the Lady delude themselves into thinking that the fruition of true 'desire' will be safety and contentment. Theirs is a copy, a simulacrum, a 'mimetic desire', that is as incomplete as it is intense, and whose incompleteness is articulated as an 'excess' that always eludes their grasp. This logic of the supplement that is always to be found at the source (Malcolm, Banquo, Fleance, Macduff) infects the language of the play and is responsible for its 'equivocations', those excesses of meaning, that masquerade as stable and singular 'truths.' Macbeth's actions invert the natural flow of 'time' itself, and liberation from the resulting tyranny can only be guaranteed by an external power—one that in reality has already historically united the thrones of Scotland and England. It is a force that is external to the play that initiates the process of recuperating the regicide's mimetic violence and the slipperiness of language that it produces, for a sovereign power that itself, paradoxically, works through equivocation, thereby demystifying precisely what it sets out to rehabilitate. To align the rhetoric with the violence that binds the structure of sovereignty, and the feeling of 'wonder' that it generates is to suggest that the institution is, at one level, nothing more than the sum of its material supports, and that its bio-politics derive from an eradication of the distinction between 'violence' and 'law.' Following "the most ancient recorded formulation" of "the principle according to which sovereignty belongs to law," Agamben concludes that "the sovereign is the point of indistinction between violence and the law, the threshold on which violence passes over into law and law passes over into violence" (32). For Agamben, the 'state of nature' (external) and the 'state of exception' (internal) are two sides of a topological coin. He says:

> The state of exception is thus not so much a spatio-temporal suspension as a complex topological figure in which not only the exception and the rule but also the state of nature and law, outside and inside, pass through one another. It is precisely this topological zone of indistinction, which has to remain hidden from the eyes of justice, that we must try to fix under our gaze. (37)

84 ✎ *John Drakakis*

He is concerned to investigate the modern forms that the category of 'bare life' assumes as a consequence of an unpicking of the limited juridical concept of sovereignty. Central to my argument is that in some respects *Macbeth* anticipates Agamben's enquiry and that it is precisely its reconstitution of 'sovereignty' through repetition, and hence, the exposure of its inner structure, that allows us to read the play against the grain.

King Duncan

Ostensibly Macbeth's transgression and its consequence constitutes the central action of the play, although the problem extends far beyond the act of regicide itself. One of Shakespeare's main 'sources' for *Macbeth* was Holinshed's *Chronicles of Scotland*, in which Duncan is portrayed as a weak and ineffectual king, who is reluctant to punish wrongdoers, and it is left to Macbeth and Banquo to compensate for the king's lenient treatment of rebels. In the play, Duncan is presented differently, even though some directors have chosen to follow the line that has its origins in Holinshed. There is some textual evidence to support this portrayal in Macbeth's soliloquy at 1.7.16–20:

> Besides, this Duncan
> Hath borne his faculties so meek, hath been
> So clear in his great office, that his virtues
> Will plead like angels, trumpet-tongued, against
> The deep damnation of his taking off;

This is a much more condensed, and apparently less militaristic, version of features that Horatio attributes to Old Hamlet, and the phrase 'so clear in his great office' indicates a sovereign subject *"as he appears to himself from within"* (Bataille 237). What Macbeth fails to internalize, and what Banquo retains is "a bosom franchis'd, and allegiance **clear**" (2.1.27–28), the complimentary facets of the *divinity* of sovereign power that "concentrates the virtues of a miraculous presence" (211). It is this capacity to perform 'miracles', projected onto the 'English' king, that will be re-asserted at the end, but not before the content of its charisma has been exposed.

Shakespeare's revision of Holinshed's narrative is telling in this respect. Instead of accepting a narrative of permanent regicide that begins with the provocation leading to MacDonwald's murder

Hamlet, Macbeth, *and 'Sovereign Process'* ⬧⬧⬧ 85

of King Duff, Shakespeare casts the Thane of Cawdor, and then Macbeth, as loyal subjects who begin by following the dictates of sovereign Law, but who fall from grace, and are then designated *exceptions*. In the figure of Macbeth both the decision concerning the 'exception' and the 'state of exception' are combined in a spatio-temporal framework that passes from 'revolution', through the semblance of sovereignty, finally to 'bare life' as the life that can be killed with impunity. Macbeth, like Claudius, and like Cawdor before him, must be 'abandoned' before he can be killed.

At the outset it is Macbeth, "Bellona's bridegroom, lapp'd in proof," whose active allegiance guarantees sovereign power. But unlike in the case of Laertes's rebellion, and Claudius's unwitting identification of himself with Cain, *Macbeth* emphasizes that the primal trauma will replay Satan's rebellion that is the pre-history of the Fall of man. This locates the originary moment of the politics of sovereignty in the mystery of 'divine right.' In undertaking to 'represent' his king, Macbeth simply imitates the violent sovereign process that lies at the origin of the order over which Duncan presides. Duncan's is the sovereign violence that brings the Law into being *and* that maintains its efficacy, but in the secular world, the king occupies a position on the threshold between an originary and constitutive violence and the 'life' whose exclusion the Law is called upon to mediate. It is this threshold position that gives to sovereignty a 'sacred' value. It incorporates a 'bare life' that can be killed but not sacrificed—in other words, its death can have no meaning as part of any ritual practice undertaken to reinforce social order. The metaphysical upheavals that accompany regicide are all part of the moral structure of prohibition that functions to obscure the content of sovereignty. The sovereign violence that initiates Law also engenders a *politics*: the regulation of competing interests with the specific objective of instituting, stabilizing and harmonizing of social life.

Duncan fulfils precisely the function that Agamben asserts in his theoretical account of 'the logic of sovereignty', when he says that "[t]he exception does not only confirm the rule; the rule as such lives off the exception alone" (16). It is that capacity to determine the complex dialectic of "rule" and "exception": in other words, to socialize desire, that those who aspire to sovereign power covet. Agamben goes on to tease out the inexplicable paradox that resides at the heart of sovereign power in the observation that "what is excluded in the exception maintains itself in relation to the rule in the form of the rule's suspension" (17f.). He aims to rethink Ernst

86 ⬧ *John Drakakis*

Kantorowicz's account of 'political theology' in *The King's Two Bodies* (1957), in which the permanence of the 'corpus mysticum' of the sovereign is shown to compensate for the mutability of his physical body, but in which 'politics' is downplayed in favor of 'theology.' But in a recognizably Derridean move, he also seeks to counter the structuralist claim, and that of Carl Schmitt, that the state of exception is "the chaos that precedes order" arguing rather that the position of the sovereign is "*taken outside (ex-capere)*, and not simply excluded" (18). His concern is to map the metaphysical process whereby the originary violence that inaugurates 'the political dimension' of sovereignty collapses the distinction between the realms of the 'religious' and the 'profane.' He argues that what he calls "the sphere of sovereign decision" is one in which the Law is suspended "in the state of exception" so that it "implicates bare life within it" (83). By 'bare life' he means 'life' outside and prior to all of those politically motivated ritual practices and institutions that give it meaning. He puts the matter in this way:

> The political sphere of sovereignty was thus constituted through a double exclusion, as an excrescence of the profane in the religious and of the religious in the profane, which takes the form of a zone of indistinction between sacrifice and homicide. *The sovereign sphere is the sphere in which it is permitted to kill without committing homicide and without celebrating a sacrifice, and sacred life—that is, life that may be killed but not sacrificed—is the life that has been captured in this sphere.* (ibid.)

This is a difficult point, but it explains the distinction in the play between 'lawful ambition' that the sovereign authorizes and legitimates, and that inhabits the political institutions it brings into existence, and unlawful or proscribed ambition (transgressive desire) that imitates the originary act of sovereign violence, but that cannot be wholly divorced from it. This explanation helps to position Duncan—and, indeed, the figure of the sovereign generally—on the threshold, as Agamben would say, between the 'inside' and the 'outside', thus making "the validity of the juridical order possible" (19). Macbeth's "[v]ulting ambition" (1.7.27) that is compelled to "o'erleap" (1.4.49) any obstacle that is placed in his way, challenges the authorized limits of sovereign law. He recognizes, however, that in placing himself beyond *the* limit, beyond *all ethical* limits, his ambition only "o'erleaps itself / And falls on th'other" (1.7.27–28). In this instance "th' other" is 'bare life' cut adrift from the structures that

Hamlet, Macbeth, *and 'Sovereign Process'* &&& 87

incorporate, and seek to control it. Whereas Duncan's sovereign power embodies both the 'norm' and the 'exception', Macbeth's repetition of Cawdor's treachery is a starkly reductive imitation of what is in reality the inexplicable paradox that resides at the heart of the institution of sovereignty itself. It is for this reason that under the guise of sovereign power he commits acts that are unlawful, and that in general challenge the basis upon which "the juridical order, and what is excluded from it, acquire their meaning" (19). It is also why none of the social rituals that he enacts once he becomes king, have any authoritative or restorative meaning. The mimetic energy of the regicide is here seen confronting its nemesis, producing a fracturing of the self that undoes the political logic of the sovereign power that Duncan represents in its most obscured form.

Duncan's confidence in the originary violence that inaugurates and sustains sovereign power allows him to remain detached from Cawdor's treachery to the point where he can generalize authoritatively upon human behavior and upon the paradox of representation:

> There's no art
> To find the mind's construction in the face:
> He was a gentleman on whom I built
> An absolute trust—(1.4.11–14)

In a play in which meaning is radically unstable from the outset, Duncan's legislative aphorism is open to two mutually opposed interpretations: (a) that the human mind is unrepresentable or, (b) that no *art* is necessary to represent the mind since its machinations are 'naturally' and transparently figured in the face. This doubleness finds a surprising but profound gloss in Malcolm's exchange with Macduff at 4.3., in that it treats precisely of the discrepancy between thought and deed, motive and action, origin and representation. Malcolm observes aphoristically that "A good and virtuous nature may recoil / In an imperial charge" (4.3.18–20), but there is something deeply paradoxical about this formulation: power may corrupt, but in a post-lapsarian world 'good' cannot easily be distinguished from the 'evil' that seeks to imitate it, and moreover, it has no defense:

> Angels are bright still, though the brightest fell:
> All things foul would wear the brows of grace,
> Yet Grace must still look so. (4.3.22–24)

88 &&& *John Drakakis*

In this important scene, sometimes savagely cut in performance, Malcolm incorporates into himself all that sovereign power necessarily *excludes* or 'abandons', as ethically unacceptable, but that is symbolically central to its operation. He would "cut off the nobles for their lands; / Desire his jewels, and this other's house" (4.3.79–80), in short, indulge an 'avarice' that is without limit and that involves an outright rejection of all "the king-becoming graces":

> As Justice, Verity, Temp'rance, Stableness,
> Bounty, Perseverance, Mercy, Lowliness,
> Devotion, Patience, Courage, Fortitude,
> I have no relish of them; but abound
> In the division of each several crime,
> Acting in many ways. Nay, had I power, I should
> Pour the sweet milk of concord into Hell,
> Uproar the universal peace, confound
> All unity on earth. (4.3.92–100)

Of course, Macbeth has already used his 'power' to "pour the sweet milk of concord into Hell," but Malcolm's description of 'bare life' through whose aegis he formulates sovereign power negatively serves to consolidate its place on the *threshold* where the constitutive process of inclusion and exclusion operates: the space, in short, where politics begins. Agamben describes precisely this situation:

> The 'sovereign' structure of the law, its peculiar and original 'force' has the form of a state of exception in which fact and law are indistinguishable (yet must, nevertheless, be decided on). Life which is thus obliged, can in the last instance be implicated in the sphere of law only through the supposition of its inclusive exclusion, only in an *exceptio*. There is a limit-figure of life, a threshold in which life is both inside and outside the juridical order, and this threshold is the place of sovereignty. (27)

In this scene Malcolm demonstrates precisely *why* he is Duncan's legitimate heir.

The Language of *Macbeth*

The central concern of *Macbeth* is rebellion, cast in archetypal terms, but geographically located in the margins of the realm—Scotland. The play's immediate historical background was the Catholic

Hamlet, Macbeth, *and 'Sovereign Process'* 89

terrorist conspiracy to assassinate the king and his parliament, on 5 November 1605. Two years earlier James I's accession to the throne had united England and Scotland, and the Gunpowder plot had sought to undermine that unity. But, of course, evidence of disunity and disorder is present from the beginning, *well before* Duncan's murder. They embody a propensity for dissolution that provokes a counter-violence through which sovereign power establishes itself. They are part of that dialectic of inclusion/exclusion that resides in this play at the heart of 'Nature.'

In his essay "Critique of Violence," Walter Benjamin noted "a dialectical rising and falling in the law-making and law-preserving formation of violence," and he went on:

The law governing their oscillation rests on the circumstance that all law-preserving violence, in its duration, indirectly weakens the law-making violence represented by it, through the suppression of hostile counter-violence.... This lasts until either new forces or those earlier suppressed triumph over the hitherto lawmaking violence and thus found a new law, destined in its turn to decay. (300)

This is a perception that Macduff's young son grasps briefly just before he is murdered. Benjamin opposes as 'pernicious' "all mythical law-making violence, which we may call executive" and "the law-preserving administrative violence that serves it," but he insists that "Divine violence, which is the sign and seal but never the means of sacred execution, may be called sovereign violence" (ibid.). This helps us to understand the various forms of violence that appear in *Macbeth*: 'sovereign' violence represented by Duncan; the violence of resistance encouraged by the Weird Sisters and furthered by Macbeth; and the sovereign 'counter-violence' that, in process, reveals the precarious basis of its own authority.

Just as *Hamlet* brings the motif of 'madness' into the orbit of the feminine, so *Macbeth* locates the subversive force of 'equivocation' in the sphere of the 'feminine', and it is the Lady (Macbeth) who augments the activities of the Weird Sisters. Macbeth himself echoes the grammatical formulations of the Weird Sisters even before he has met them: "So foul and fair a day I have not seen" (1.3.38). At the end of the play, however, he comes to realize the linguistic duplicity that they embody: "And be these juggling fiends no more believed, / That palter with us in a double sense; / That keep the word of promise to our ear, / And break it to our hope" (5.8.19–22).

90 ◦◦◦ *John Drakakis*

The Weird Sisters represent linguistically, and visually what happens when sovereign power, that prescribes and legitimizes meaning, and that authorizes representation, is laid bare; they invert reality, but in doing so they expose the mystery of patriarchal power for the ideology that it is. In addition to making the Weird Sisters the heroines of the play, Terry Eagleton has claimed that "the witches figure as the 'unconscious' of the drama, that which must be exiled and repressed as dangerous but which is always likely to return with a vengeance" (2). He goes on to argue that "[t]he unconscious is a discourse in which meaning falters and slides, in which firm definitions are dissolved and binary oppositions eroded: fair is foul and foul is fair, nothing is but what is not" (ibid.).

This is partly true, but the Freudian account of 'repression' is not at issue in the play, or at least, not in any straightforward sense. For example, while criticism has always focused upon the violence that Macbeth engages in: killing the king, then Banquo, then engineering the murdering of Lady Macduff and her children, little is made of the violence that is endemic in Duncan's own rule. Duncan fertilizes his kingdom, the garden he tends, with human blood. He 'plants' Macbeth "and will labour / To make [him] full of growing." He implies the same for Banquo, although here the rewards are less tangible: "Noble Banquo, / That hast no less deserv'd, nor must be known / No less to have done so" (1.4.28–31). The king is 'indebted' to his vassals, in that his regal obligations in rewarding them are a condition of his being included in a relation from which he is, as sovereign, excluded. As the origin of Law he is excluded from its quotidian operations, an issue that had perplexed state theorists for over half a century, and to which Marlowe had, in part, addressed his play *Edward II*. Agamben notes the sense of 'being-in-debt' as an originary sense of the term 'guilt', a form of recompense for the act of violence that inaugurates sovereignty. But the play *Macbeth* also explores two other crucial meanings of 'guilt' that both position the hero while at the same time testifying to a growing inability of sovereign power to legislate meaning. 'Guilt' is the term used to distinguish between the licit and the illicit, that the subject of power internalizes as the operation of 'conscience', a mechanism for regulating behavior. The homophone 'gilt', on the other hand, richly theatrical in its suggestiveness, transforms obligation into a market transaction, in which self-esteem, and the ethics that sustain it can be bought like a theatrical costume, thus allowing Macbeth to buy "golden opinions from all sorts of people, / Which would be worn now in their newest gloss, / Not cast aside so

Hamlet, Macbeth, *and 'Sovereign Process'* ❦ 91

soon" (1.7.33–35). This leads to the Lady's cynical manipulation of all these meanings in a reference to Duncan's 'golden' blood, that undermines radically the originary language of sovereign power: "If he do bleed / I'll gild the faces of the grooms withal, / For it must seem their guilt" (2.2.55–56). This is not 'repression' in the Freudian sense of the term, so much as plenitude: as a plenitude that undermines hierarchies of meaning, and the very process of representation itself.

Macbeth's consciousness is too full and too inclusive to allow us to talk about 'repression.' It is true that "The Golden round" that the Lady thinks that "fate and metaphysical aid doth seem / To have thee crown'd withal" (1.5.28–30) requires an act that Macbeth is reluctant to perform, because it carries with it a high moral price: 'guilt.' It is also true that she is willing to suppress her matriarchal feelings as a means of encouraging her husband, just as Macbeth himself must forget the etiquette surrounding Duncan's rewards for his loyalty. Indeed, in this play the dramatic characters appear to have no (Freudian) unconscious, and Macbeth's "way of life…fall'n into the sere, the yellow leaf" (5.3.22–23) and the "Tomorrow and tomorrow" speech (cf. 5.5.19–20) indicate a knowing, if retrospectively realized collapse into 'bare life.' However, as auditors, we recognize these variations in meaning as 'slips of the tongue' or as parapraxes. They inaugurate a logic in which initial success leads to disaster for Macbeth and the Lady, and ultimately to a restitution of the very political order that regicide has temporarily inverted; although, as we have seen, not before exposing the vulnerability of the ideological materials that shape that order. Eagleton's point is that it is the 'text' not the characters that has an 'unconscious' but is he right? What we need, perhaps, is a more historical (maybe even less rational) understanding of the 'unconscious' that the play sketches out.

In the early part of the play it is the Lady who usurps the masculine active role, although if we look a little more closely at it, then we realize that it is a reduced masculinity,—an inhumanity even—that she encourages. Her invocation to those "Spirits / That tend on mortal thoughts" to "unsex me here, / And fill me, from the crown to the toe, top-full / Of direst cruelty!" (1.5.40–43) is a plea to evade 'guilt' itself by stopping up "the access and passage to remorse" (1.5.44). It is also a plea to keep "the compunctious visitings of Nature" (1.5.45) at bay, where "compunctious" (a word that for Shakespeare is unique to the text of *Macbeth*) is a quality of Nature itself and refers to "the pricking or stinging of the conscience or heart…consequent upon sin or wrong-doing" (*OED* 1a). It is precisely this debate that

92 ❊❊❊ *John Drakakis*

Macbeth conducts with himself from his first soliloquy at 1.3 onward. The moral and ethical implications that Lady Macbeth seeks to *suppress* (rather than repress) are precisely elements of "that suggestion / Whose horrid image doth unfix my hair, / And make my seated heart knock at my ribs, / Against the use of nature" (1.3.134–37) that Macbeth feels once he considers submitting himself to the logic of events inaugurated by the Weird Sisters' prophesy. The horrid image whose suggestion he contemplates unfixes much more than his hair. In precisely the same way that meanings of words like 'guilt' are unfixed, so Macbeth seeks to deny the inexorable logic that 'assassination' calls into being: "if th' assassination / Could trammel up the consequence, and catch / With his *surcease success*" (1.7.2–4). 'Surcease' refers here to the act of 'desisting': it means both "ceasing from some action" (*OED* 1a) and "to come to an end, or to discontinue," (*OED* 3a) but it is also "to give up or resign a position of office." (*OED* 3†b) The impersonal nature of Macbeth's language here serves to align the act of regicide with a voluntary resignation of power that will absolve him from guilt, and elides two semantically opposed words together that are imperfectly homophonic. As the play progresses, these 'equivocations' (or disturbances of linguistic hierarchy) multiply, and in the final stages the action turns upon how these linguistic signs are interpreted.

The nature of Nature

It is clear that Macbeth and the Lady regard Nature as an enemy. It is part of the play's ideology that Nature *naturalizes* sovereign power. But sovereign power, as I suggested earlier, places the king in a precarious position, since he is both *inside* and *outside* the order of Law (cf. Agamben 27): the source of the originary act of violence that brings Law into being, and is above the Law, but that incorporates into its sphere 'bare life.' We can see what happens when a figure like Hamlet is forced to confront this threshold position; he begins to question the nature of 'being' itself. We can also see what happens when in *King Lear* the sovereign exception is stripped of all that makes him different from the 'life' over which he exerts power: Lear confronts the 'bare life' in himself. It is the secret of sovereign power that Macbeth glimpses in a much starker form as his actions systematically sever his ties with 'Nature', to the point where he becomes a 'player' king, and finally an 'idiot' whose tale 'full of sound and fury' signifies *nothing*. His is the 'bare life' against which a hierarchical

Hamlet, Macbeth, *and 'Sovereign Process'* 93

Nature concentrates its powers, transforming the figure of 'the player king' into "a poor player, / That struts and frets his hour upon the stage" (5.5.24–25), that signifies 'nothing', and thence into an animal.

But there is something peculiar about 'the nature of Nature' in the play. Elsewhere in Shakespeare the forces that seek to undermine order are usually potentially anarchic (possibly libidinal, and almost certainly chaotic) energies. In *Hamlet* Claudius's lust for power is perceived by Hamlet to involve a reprehensibly demonic sexual energy that comes to be focused on his mother and on Ophelia; in *Othello* the figure of the 'Moor' that Shakespeare had begun to experiment with in a minor way in *The Merchant of Venice*, becomes the site of competing forces in which a series of masculine Venetian values require to be defended against a barbaric 'otherness.' In *Macbeth* the agency of subversion is the Weird Sisters. The initial evaluation of the Weird Sisters comes from Banquo; Macbeth is too caught up in musing on the future that they map out for him. For Banquo they melt into Nature: "The earth hath bubbles, as the water has, / And these are of them" (1.3.79–80), and Macbeth notes that "what seem'd corporal, / Melted as breath into the wind" (1.3.81–82). But they also lead Banquo to question their corporeal reality, through the deployment of a metaphor that draws attention to Nature's capacity to pervert nourishment and subvert 'reason': "Were such things here, as we do speak about, / Or have we eaten on the insane root, / That takes the reason prisoner?" (1.3.83–85) Perhaps another way of putting this is to say that the linguistic stability that the sovereign process of naming initiates, is a means of ordering and socializing the existence of particular situations (cf. Badiou 81). It is significant that the Weird Sisters, like Macbeth himself later in the play, either cannot, or will not, name what they do. The 'truth' of monarchy that Macbeth is encouraged to replicate in such a way that his rule becomes a 'simulacrum', a theatrical representation of an institution, is shown to be dependent upon (or at least intertwined with) a demonic force that they embody. And it is Banquo who sees this: "And oftentimes, to win us to our harm, / The instruments of Darkness tell us truths; / Win us with honest trifles, to betray's / In deepest consequence" (1.3.123–26). He acknowledges the evil that is secreted at the very heart of 'truth' itself, and that Alain Badiou identifies in another context as, "that Evil which it recognizes as the underside, or dark side, of these very truths" (91).

Indeed, the play's antithetical logic shapes Nature as the space where opposed forces compete openly for supremacy, to the point

94   John Drakakis

that we might say that of all Shakespeare's plays *Macbeth* is unusually 'conscious' of its own 'unconscious.' In a play where all that nourishes life can easily be transformed into its opposite, Banquo registers the effects of the resulting conflict, though he arrives at conclusions diametrically opposed to those of Macbeth. At the beginning of Act 2, at Inverness castle, he feels the urge to sleep but cannot:

> Hold, **take my Sword:**
> There's Husbandry in Heauen,
> Their Candles are all out: take thee that too.
> A heauie Summons lyes like Lead vpon me,
> And yet I would not sleep:
> **Mercifull Powers**, restraine in me the cursed thoughts
> That **Nature** giues way to in repose.
> *Enter Macbeth and a Seruant with a Torch.*
> **Giue me my Sword**: who's there? (*Folio*, 135–36: 725–26)

This is the Folio reading and it prompts a series of questions. Is Banquo saying that it is 'human nature' that is *his* 'nature' that yields to 'cursed thoughts' once he is asleep? Or is he saying that on those occasions when 'Nature' suspends its task of ordering 'reality', then its dark side, the 'cursed thoughts', rise to the surface? The Folio lineation, metrically imperfect though it appears to be, is poetically and dramatically very powerful in directing our attention. As Banquo relaxes, giving up his sword, so the embodiment of those 'cursed thoughts' (in the representational guise of Duncan's vassal) enters. We know that Macbeth has already begun to "yield to that suggestion / Whose horrid image doth unfix my hair, / And make my seated heart knock at my ribs, / Against the use of nature?" (1.3.134–37) This involves a rebellion of the physical 'body', a perversion of its use that the sovereign power of Nature has authorized. The 'event' that generates this mental anguish—the meeting with the Weird Sisters—produces opposite reactions in Banquo and Macbeth. What for both are 'cursed thoughts', obscures what for Macbeth is a 'political sequence': if he leaves matters to 'chance' then he deprives himself of the power to effect his desire, but if he *acts* then he replicates but only at the level of a *simulacrum*, the originary violence that constitutes sovereignty. These are the 'cursed thoughts'—the descent into a secular politics that would separate sovereignty from the mystery of its own origins—that Banquo fears when the ordering power that he ascribes to Nature relaxes her control. Much later in the play, we will see the obverse of the situation that Banquo here experiences

Hamlet, Macbeth, *and 'Sovereign Process'* 95

and describes, when the sleep-walking Lady will be unable to eliminate from her dreams (as she manages to do effectively from her waking life) the regulating mechanism of 'conscience' and the force of the 'human' that she has hitherto suppressed. In a world where the pursuit of secular political goals has become the norm, the 'good' in Nature disrupts its own regenerative mechanism, sleep, to take on the role of a subversive 'other' that resists control. 'Fair is foul and foul is fair' indeed. In the intoxicated Hell of Macbeth's castle, for whom the Porter stands gatekeeper, there develops a gulf between 'desire' and 'performance.' Alcohol is to sexual performance, what criminal accomplishment, and the mimetic strategies it deploys, is to the transgressive mechanics of desire.

That disturbance signals the decline of sovereignty into the nightmare realm of a secular politics. Indeed, the play stages the dilemma of early modern sovereignty: if there is no 'divinity' that can protect the sovereign from regicide, and if 'conscience' cannot be relied upon to regulate the behavior of subjects, in what does sovereign authority, and its hierarchical system of representations, reside? Moreover, if sovereignty can be rendered vulnerable, imitated, deprived of its mystery, reduced to 'process' and to theatrical performance, what is there that can prevent it from declining into tyranny, or from being overthrown? In the brief comments on 'dreams' that we find in Timothy Bright's *A Treatise of Melancholie* (1586), a book that Shakespeare was thought to have consulted in relation to *Hamlet*, dreams become a matrix. They are "sensible actions of the minde" that cannot be regarded as 'false':

> because it seeth in dreames things past as present: for so it doth also future things sometimes: which rather may argue, that both past, and to come are both present vnto the mind, of such things as fall into the capacitie of her consideration. If anie man thinke it much to aduance the mind so high, let him remember from whom it proceeded, & the maner howe it was created, and the most excellent estate thereof before the fall, and no doubt it will sufficiently aunswer that difficultie, and confirme that which I haue said. (119)

Macbeth's tragedy lies in a conflict that folds a politically-realized fantasy of power into the struggle between pre-lapsarian order and post-lapsarian desire. Banquo's 'cursed thoughts' are the excesses, reversions to undifferentiated similitude, that a waking political existence regiments and contains. Macbeth's *actions* reject the controlling imperatives of Nature, and catapult him into a world of

96 &&& *John Drakakis*

nightmare in which human desire that is the dark side of a sovereign politics, is doomed never to be satisfied. In the play, politics, like 'history', inaugurate the desire of the desiring subject. This suggests a different account of the play from that offered by H.N. Paul, when, during his discussion of the *Basilicon Doron* of James I, he suggests that Shakespeare "shows us in his royal play a good and kindly king cut off by the treason of an unnatural subject" (136). What Paul omits is an issue that the play fudges: the origins of the prophecies of Macbeth's success. In *Basilicon Doron* James asserted that "Prophecie proceedeth onelie from GOD: and the Devill hath no knowledge of things to come," but he then goes on:

> And that the Diuel is permitted at som-times to put himself in the liknes of the Saintes, it is plaine in the Scriptures, where it is said, that Sathan can trans-forme himselfe into an Angell *of Light*. Neither could that bring any inconvenient with it to the visiones of the Prophets, since it is most certaine, that God will not permit him to deceiue his own: but only such, as first wilfully deceiues them-selues, by running vnto him, whome God then suffers to fall in their owne snares, and justly permittes them to be illuded with great efficacy of deceit, because they would not beleeue the trueth (as *Paul* sayeth). (Craigie 1982, 2f.)

In this passage James projects onto 'God' the determination of the 'exception', but in Shakespeare's play it is Duncan who inadvertently confirms the Weird Sisters' prophecy, and by doing so 'traces' and 'renews' a "threshold of indistinction between outside and inside, inclusion and exclusion, *nomos* and *physis*, in which life is originarily excepted in law" (Agamben 27). We can now see why Shakespeare should have discarded Holinshed's narrative of Macbeth's successful years as ruler. To have followed this strand would have been to capitulate to a pragmatic politics in which the yardstick of practical efficiency could be used to measure sovereign authority and legitimacy. The Anglo-Scottish royal presence, which hovers just outside the boundaries of the play, and which would appear to sanction the recuperation of the 'equivocations' of the Weird Sisters for a benign, but mysterious sovereignty, cannot quite contain those excesses—of language, of political action, of desire—that Nature itself periodically releases into human society, and of whose warring forces he is, himself, the regal embodiment. Indeed, what the play invites us to observe is the returning of a disputed ground of politics to Nature, and once the mechanics of that ideological operation are laid open for display—as on a stage—then what they lose is their mystery and mystique.

Notes

1. All Shakespearean references in this chapter are taken from *The Arden Shakespeare Complete Works*.
2. Cf. Bataille 280 where he defines 'sovereignty' as the preference "for an unproductive use of wealth" compared to "the preference of the bourgeois world" for "*accumulation*."

Works Cited

Agamben, Giorgio. *Homo Sacer: Sovereign Power and Bare Life*. Stanford: Stanford UP, 1998.

Aristotle. *The Politics*. Harmondsworth: Penguin, 1992.

Bataille, Georges. *The Accursed Share*. Vols. 2 and 3. New York: Zone Books, 1993.

Benjamin, Walter. *Reflections*. New York: Schocken Books, 1986.

Bright, Timothy. *A Treatise on Melancholie*. London: Windet, 1586.

Craigie, James, ed. *Minor Prose Works of James VI and I*. Edinburgh: Scottish Text Society, 1982.

Deleuze, Gilles. *Difference and Repetition*. London: Athlone Press, 1994.

Derrida, Jacques. "The Pharmakon." *Dissemination*. Chicago: U of Chicago P, 1981.

Dollimore, Jonathan. *Sex, Literature and Censorship*. Oxford: Polity Press, 2001.

Kantorowicz, Ernst. *The King's Two Bodies*. Princeton: Princeton UP, 1957.

Paul, Henry N. *The Royal Play of Macbeth*. New York: Octagon, 1971.

Schmitt, Carl. *Political Theology. Four Chapters on the Concept of Sovereignty*. Cambridge, MA: MIT Press, 1985.

Shakespeare, William. *The Arden Shakespeare Complete Works*. Ed. Richard Proudfoot, Ann Thompson, and David Scott Kastan. Walton-on-Thames: Thomas Nelson and Son Ltd, 1998.

———. *Macbeth*. Folio ed., 1623.

Smith, Sir Thomas. *De Republica Anglorum: De Republica Anglorum: The Maner of Government or Policie of the Realme of England*. 1583.

CHAPTER V

THE TABOO OF REVOLUTIONARY THOUGHT AFTER 1660 AND STRATEGIES OF SUBVERSION IN MILTON'S *PARADISE LOST* AND BUNYAN'S *THE HOLY WAR*

Jens Martin Gurr

The Restoration, Censorship, and the Submerged Tradition of Radicalism

In a period rich in paradoxical situations, surprising connections and unexpected alliances, it is one of the supreme if subtle ironies to find the much-hated chief censor, royalist pamphleteer and persecutor of nonconformists, Sir Roger L'Estrange (1616–1704), on the printed list of subscribers to the fourth edition of Milton's *Paradise Lost* in 1688 (cf. Parker 1: 662f.). Focusing on Milton and Bunyan as the crucial figures in late-seventeenth-century religious and political dissent, this essay will explore the intricate interplay between political taboos, censorship, and subversive literary strategies in the period after 1660.[1] This context calls for a specific reconceptualization of the notion of "taboo" as not so much a ban on forbidden and socially repressed acts or practices—incest, cannibalism, certain sexual practices, irreligious behavior—that violate societal and individual norms of decency and acceptability. Rather, this essay studies what can quite literally be viewed as a ban on thought, a form of suppressing a set of political ideas and their utterance by means of censorship and other forms of political and legal repression.

The unique subversive strategies of political writing in this period can only be understood in the context of the political climate and the legal situation in the years after 1660. As David Ogg observed in his classic study *England in the Reign of Charles II*, Charles's return in May 1660 appears to have occurred "on the crest of a great wave," triumphantly sweeping away "every vestige of republicanism or political experiment" (1: 139).[2] But as Christopher Hill and others have shown, a tradition of radical republicanism survived despite wide-spread enthusiasm for the Restoration (cf. 1976, 10–15 *et passim*).[3] Such radical thinking, however, was forced underground by the 'Clarendon Code', the umbrella term given to restrictive post-Restoration legislation such as the *Corporation Act* (1661), the *Act for the Preservation of the King* (1661), the *Act of Uniformity* (1662) or the *Conventicle Act* (1664). Thus, while the overtly millenarian enthusiasm of the 1640s and early 1650s had already been considerably dampened by the Protectorate, the vigorous pamphlet wars and the free expression of largely republican radical political thought came to end in the years after 1660 with the new licensing and censorship regulations enforced especially by the notorious *Licensing Act*. This *Act for Preventing the Frequent Abuses in Printing Seditious, Treasonable and Unlicensed Books and Pamphlets, and for Regulating of Printing and Printing Presses*, as it was officially titled, came into effect in June 1662 and lapsed in 1679, only to be renewed in 1685 (cf. Keeble 96ff.). Even more explicitly, the 1661 *Act for the Preservation of the King* drew attention to the connection between republican thought, subversive writing and danger to the monarchy by declaring the regicide of 1649 and the ensuing Commonwealth period to have been the direct consequence of subversive writing: "the late troubles and disorders did in a very great measure proceed from the multitude of seditious sermons, pamphlets and speeches daily preached, printed and published." Henceforth, it was to be considered an act of treason to "incite or stir up the people to hatred or dislike of the person of his Majesty or the established government" (Rpt. in Browning 63, 65). The laws against religious nonconformity and political radicalism as well as the repressive measures against dissenting writers and printers frequently proceeded from the assumption, as Lord Halifax was to write in 1687, that "it is impossible for a dissenter not to be a rebel" (Keeble 29). In this vein, research on the period, for instance Greaves's excellent book on the broad tradition of radicalism and nonconformism between 1664 and 1677, has shown that religious nonconformism and political radicalism cannot be studied in isolation from one another.

The Taboo of Revolutionary Thought ▩ 101

In addition to repressive legislation, there was virtually a discursive taboo on republican thought after the traumatic experience of two decades of civil war, military dictatorship and political chaos. Throughout the Restoration, "[s]corched historical memories" (Harris 2001, 252) of the 1640s and 1650s were used roundly to discredit republican thought. Thus, during the exclusion crisis of 1679–1681[4], it was a central Tory strategy to compare the Whigs to the Presbyterians and Independents of the early 1640s and to insist on the regicide and Cromwell's dictatorial government as direct consequences of such rebellious behavior, in other words constantly to invoke the threat of yet another civil war in order to silence political dissent. With insistent references to the events of the 1640s and 1650s, the Whigs were thus branded as "nonconformists, factious, king killers, mob rousers, tyrants, and hostile to the Church of England" (Harris 1987, 139). There was thus effectively a taboo on radical thinking, especially on republicanism, after the Restoration.

In trying to understand subversive strategies of political writing in this repressive climate after the Restoration, it is vital to bear in mind the central role of censorship: For authors such as Milton, notorious republican and defender of the regicide, or Bunyan, dissenting lay preacher, the Restoration brought the threat of death and both were imprisoned—Milton only briefly late in 1660, Bunyan for some twelve years from 1661 to 1672. This naturally also meant that their publications would be scrutinized by the censor—if they were not published illegally, without a license, as most of Bunyan's works indeed were.[5] Thus, although there was inevitably much unlicensed printing, a number of the period's key texts such as *Paradise Lost* were in fact submitted for a license.

Given this ubiquity of the censor, texts of this period must, as Christopher Hill insisted, be read as "cryptograms to be decoded" (Hill 1977, 65; cf. also Wittreich). Hill, Keeble (*passim*) and others have therefore drawn attention to the extent to which subversive writing of the period had to rely on ambiguity, *double entendre*, multiple allegorical levels, oblique allusiveness, intertextual pointers, hints at anachronistic recontextualization and other strategies of encoding (cf. for instance Hill 1977, *passim*, and Hill 1991, 2f.). Such strategies of evasion are crucial in the negotiation of political taboos, and it is the use of such strategies in *Paradise Lost* and *The Holy War* that I will be concerned with in this essay.

102 &&& *Jens Martin Gurr*

Coded Republicanism in *Paradise Lost*

That *Paradise Lost* can on one level be read as engaging with the English Revolution has long been established.[6] Thus, it cannot be the aim of my essay to attempt another political reading of Milton's opus magnum. What is of particular interest here, however, are the subversive and anti-monarchical tendencies of the epic, more precisely, the subversive strategies which allow Milton to voice revolutionary thoughts after 1660, when such thoughts were tabooed and suppressed by rigid censorship. How, in other words, does the text announce and carry out its transgressive maneuvers?

A passage from the invocation *"in persona auctoris"* (Fowler's note on VII, 1–50) early in book VII will serve as a point of departure. As has long been established, it refers to Milton's own precarious situation after the Restoration and to his "unchanged" political convictions. Fearing imprisonment or even death in these "evil days," slandered by "evil tongues"—not least that of Sir Roger L'Estrange in his vicious pamphlet *No Blinde Guides* of April 1660—the blind poet "in darkness" perseveres with his ambitious work, invoking Urania's help in the endeavor to find readers "fit...though few" willing and able to decode its complexities:

> More safe I sing with mortal voice, unchanged
> To hoarse or mute, though fallen on evil days,
> On evil days though fallen, and evil tongues;
> In darkness, and with dangers compassed round,
> And solitude; yet not alone, while thou
> Visitst my slumbers nightly, or when morn
> Purples the east: still govern thou my song,
> Urania, and fit audience find, though few. (*PL* VII, 24–31)

Such topical references to the time of writing, while also part and parcel of the epic tradition, suggest that the subject matter may not be all that far removed from present or recent realities and thus point toward a topical reading (cf. also *PL* V, 897–907; VI, 29–32 and VI, 145–48).[7]

A further strategy suggesting that *Paradise Lost* might be read as relating very concretely to recent events in England is apparent in a number of passages which function as 'bridges', as it were, between the cosmic events on the literal level of the text and events on earth. Several passages invite one to see heaven as a stand-in for earth and the war in heaven as a coded rendering of the recent English Civil

The Taboo of Revolutionary Thought 103

War. In this vein, Raphael's remark to Adam that the war in heaven, which "surmounts the reach / Of human sense" (*PL* V, 571f.), must be described in earthly terms so as to make it comprehensible to humans, can be read as indicating a close connection between events on earth and in heaven, suggesting that Raphael's description, rather than being a didacticized version of a super-human war in heaven, may indeed be a coded reference to an all-too-human and very recent war on earth:

> ...what if earth
> Be but the shadow of heav'n, and things therein
> Each to other like, more than on earth is thought? (*PL* V, 574–76)

Similarly, Raphael refers to the war in heaven as an "[i]ntestine war" (*PL* VI, 259), that is, a *bellum intestinum*, a civil war—a Latinism the topicality of which is hardly accidental.[8] Raphael further points to the analogy between heaven and earth when he states "earth now / Seemed like to heaven" (*PL* VII, 328f.). In very similar terms, Satan, too, confirms the likeness: "O earth, how like to Heav'n" (*PL* IX, 99).[9]

Thus attuned to potentially subversive topical references and *double entendres*, the careful reader stumbles upon a number of jarring anachronisms, telling parallels and analogies to contemporary political developments and other suggestions of topical referentiality, all of which constitute further strategies of transgressing political taboos. Arguably the most astonishing and certainly the most controversial such strategy lies in the attribution of strong anti-monarchical sentiments to Satan. As Steven Jablonski ("Embodied All in One" and "Freely we serve") and others have long demonstrated, Satan and his rebel angels are clearly republicans, who, in books I, II and especially V, speak a language and use anti-monarchical arguments that must have reminded any contemporary reader of recent republican rhetoric against monarchy in England. Satan's republicanism is remarkably close to Milton's own. Thus, the historian Blair Worden has remarked on "how close is Satan's republicanism, which is accorded its most ample documentation in Book V, to the language of [Milton's] *The Ready and Easy Way to Establish A Free Commonwealth* early in 1660, the year when...Milton is likely, during the succeeding months, to have written Book V" (235; cf. also Jablonski 1994, 118 *et passim*). In Satan's rousing speech to the rebel angels, his anti-monarchical rhetorical question, which seeks to undermine the

104 ❦ *Jens Martin Gurr*

legitimacy of Christ's headship of the angels, is indeed remarkably apt also for earthly monarchy:

> Who can in reason then or right assume
> Monarchy over such as live by right
> His equals, if in power and splendour less,
> In freedom equal? (*PL* V, 794–97)[10]

By describing God's rule in terms of earthly regimes, Milton opens up the political reading. In the purely theological realm, he may well have been concerned to "justify the ways of God to men" (*PL* I, 26), but where the tyranny, cruelty and injustice of God go beyond what can be found in the Bible, we should be disposed to look for political parallels in Milton's own day. As Herbert Grierson wryly remarked, suggesting further parallels between heaven and earth: "[I]f the third part of a school or college or nation broke into a rebellion, we should be driven, or strongly disposed, to suspect some mismanagement by the supreme powers" (116).[11] Seen in this light, even the non-chronological structure of *Paradise Lost*, though clearly also a nod to the epic tradition of beginning *in medias res*, can be understood as a strategy of foregrounding. Keeble comments on the structure as follows: "[The] structural design makes a thematic point. The chronologically prior war in heaven is subordinated to man's story.... From potentially an epic tale in its own right it is reduced to a parenthetical episode in the history of humankind" (206). Though I follow Keeble's reading of the structure, I would propose a slightly different emphasis: By firmly situating Satan's republicanism in book V inside the human story, it is structurally suggested that the political rhetoric as well as the battles of allegedly far removed celestial or infernal powers may be quite human and bitingly topical after all.

In his 1997 essay "'Freely we serve': *Paradise Lost* and the Paradoxes of Political Liberty," Steven Jablonski restates part of the problem as a "paradox that has long puzzled readers of *Paradise Lost*." He asks: "[H]ow could Milton, an Arminian, be both a professed enemy of earthly kings and a proponent of liberty and yet represent God in his greatest work as a king and Satan as a proponent of liberty?" (117) That part of the conflict concerned with the seeming contradiction between Milton's advocacy of worldly disobedience and divine obedience is easily resolved: Milton evidently thought of heavenly and earthly hierarchies as dichotomous and followed the Old Testament

The Taboo of Revolutionary Thought   105

understanding that false kings and prophets who have usurped divine authority must be removed. Political rebellion on earth may therefore even serve to reinforce divine hierarchies. Jablonski himself in an earlier essay ("Embodied All in One") very perceptively pointed out Milton's appropriation of the body politic metaphor generally used by royalists to defend the king as 'head' of the state, with the citizens serving him as limbs or members. He then shows how Milton in the passage on the Son's election as "Head" of the angels (*PL* V, 600–15) consciously echoes the headship argument usually employed by worldly rulers, but at the same time makes clear the difference between them. While Christ's headship of the angels and his incarnation are signs of humility, the royal presumption to headship is a form of arrogation and self-aggrandizement. Divine rule and political rule on earth thus emerge as incommensurable fields (cf. also Smith 263 and Hill 1977, 367). The "principle of reversal" (Smith 254f.) in attributing his own republican sentiments to Satan and the rebel angels can thus by no means be read as encoding Milton's acquiescence to the monarchy and a retraction of his radicalism during the Revolution. This would be seriously to underestimate the complexity of the text and would entail overlooking a good number of radically if obliquely anti-monarchical passages.

Furthermore, it is important to point out that the "principle of reversal" in marking Satan as a republican must not be taken to imply a simplistic identification of God with Charles I and of Satan with Cromwell, suggestive as that constellation might be: *Paradise Lost* is not, after all, an *épopée à clef.* Satan is not only cast in the role of the indomitable republican, he also bears traits of the avarice and ambition of many revolutionary leaders and of the blasphemous speculations of some of the more radical sects who had divided and discredited the supporters of the revolutionary cause—just as the fallen angels also bear many royalist traits. In this vein, Satan is associated with royalty:

> At length into the limits of the North
> They came, and Satan to his royal seat
> High on a hill…. (*PL* V, 755–57)

The reference to Satan's throne as the "royal seat" by implication identifies Satan with a monarch. This is further enhanced by the reference to "the North" as the origin of evil: Although the association is biblical already (cf. for instance Jer. 1.14), this may well be taken as

106 ❧ *Jens Martin Gurr*

a hint at the treachery of the Scots, who broke the Solemn League and Covenant of 1643 and changed sides in 1648 to support Charles I against the revolutionary army. In his 1648 sonnet to Fairfax, Milton had explicitly referred to Scotland as "the false North" (1992, 188).[12]

A further subversive strategy is surely the use of fairly precise political and religious key terms which occasionally sound curiously anachronistic in contexts such as the war in heaven or Adam and Eve's expulsion from Eden. What, for instance, are we to make of a passage such as the following in Michael's prophecy to Adam about the future of mankind?

> ...one shall rise
> Of proud ambitious heart, who not content
> With fair equality, fraternal state,
> Will arrogate dominion undeserved
> Over his brethren, and quite dispossess
> Concord and law of nature from the earth,...
> From heaven claiming second sovereignty.... (*PL* XII, 24–37)

Though such passages can always be given an 'innocent' theological reading—in this case, the overt reference is to the Old Testament figure of Nimrod (Gen. 10.8–10)—they also function as pointers to a subversive subtext. It is hard not to read this passage in the light of Milton's frequent pronouncements on the evils of monarchy in a number of his prose texts. Throughout his political writings from the 1640s to the eve of the Restoration in 1660, Milton had expressly stated that the very idea of kingship, the very idea of raising one human being above the others was contrary to the teachings of Christ himself. Thus, shortly before the Restoration, in a last-ditch attempt to plead against the restoration of the Stuart monarchy, he wrote in *A Ready and Easy Way to Establish a Free Commonwealth*: "All Protestants hold that Christ in his church hath left no viceregent of his power, but himself, without deputie, is the only head thereof, governing it from heaven: how then can any Christian-man derive his kingship from Christ?" (Milton 1953–1982, 7:429; cf. also Jablonski 1994, 116). In his 1649 *The Tenure of Kings and Magistrates*, there is a passage that is even closer to the thoughts expressed here: "[N]o Christian Prince...would arrogate unreasonably above human condition, or derogate so basely from a whole Nation of men his Brethren" (Milton 1953, 3:204). In order to do justice to the complexity of Milton's poetry both in this passage and elsewhere, it is necessary to point out that an entirely different reading is also possible: Given Milton's repeated reference to Cromwell's ambition, and given Cromwell's constant invocation of divine authority—worthy of a Stuart monarch—, the implication may also lead to Cromwell. In addition, the arrogation of dominion over one's "brethren" (*PL* XII, 28) is also resonant when taken to refer to a Puritan republican as ruling over his brethren equals.[13] The predominant implication, however, is anti-monarchical, especially if we consider remarkably similar passages in a number of Milton's previous prose works. Finally, the anti-monarchical impetus of this passage is confirmed in Adam's response to Michael a few lines later:

> …man over men
> [God] made not lord; such title to himself
> Reserving, human left from human free.
> (*PL* XII, 69–71; cf. the entire passage 64–78)

As many commentators have noted, the entire vision of the future of mankind in Books XI and XII is decidedly republican (cf. for instance Smith 262).

Arguably the most condensed and one of the most seditious political passages of the entire epic is a description of Satan, who, even after the Fall, has not entirely lost his original splendor:

> …his form had yet not lost
> All her original brightness, nor appeared
> Less then archangel ruined, and the excess
> Of glory obscured: As when the Sun new ris'n
> Looks through the horizontal misty air
> Shorn of his beams, or from behind the moon
> In dim eclipse disastrous twilight sheds
> On half the nations, and with fear of change
> Perplexes monarchs. (*PL* I, 591–99)[14]

This, incidentally, is the only passage which the censor with his otherwise fortunately limited gift for subversive exegesis apparently found objectionable in the process of licensing *Paradise Lost* for publication. The multilayered metaphorical intricacy of this passage combines many of the strategies discussed above: The comparison of Satan to the misty morning sun, by means of the established association of the sun as a symbol of royalty, identifies Satan with the monarch. On the other hand, the solar eclipse, by means of the same association, functions as an image presaging doom to the monarchy: The

108 ❧ *Jens Martin Gurr*

eclipsed sun "sheds…disastrous twilight…and with fear of change /
Perplexes monarchs." These notions are held together by the image
of the rising sun as an established symbol of revolution.

Thus, even if the text as a whole as well as individual passages are
remarkably double-edged and can also be read as rather scathingly
critical of the revolutionary leaders, the predominant impression
yielded by any sensitive decryption of these passages is one of strong
republicanism. Achinstein goes so far as to state that "Milton's literary mode in *Paradise Lost* may have been an allegory for king-killing
politics" (160). A multiplicity of ambiguities in individual passages,
subtle intertextual ploys, and oblique allusions in *Paradise Lost* thus
constitute an intriguingly complex arsenal of transgressive strategies
to circumvent a taboo on republican radicalism enforced not least by
a system of censorship under the notorious *Licensing Act*.

Bunyan, *The Holy War*, and the Stuart Monarchy in the Early 1680s

Like many others during the heady 1640s and 1650s, Bunyan had
believed the Millennium to be imminent. Such hopes were dashed
after 1660, but this did little to make radicals like Bunyan accept
the status quo; it did, however, force them to encode their religious
and political dissent and to voice millenarian hopes more obliquely
(cf. Hill 1989, 151f.). Several of Bunyan's works such as *The Holy City*
of 1665 and *The Holy War* of 1682 are evidence of this submerged
millenarianism and coded political critique. Of these, the allegorical prose epic *The Holy War, made by Shaddai upon Diabolus, For the
Regaining of the Metropolis of the World, or The Losing and Taking Again
of the Town of Mansoul*, published after the Licensing Act had lapsed
in 1679, is more outspoken in its indictment of the restored Stuart
monarchy—if only on one of several allegorical levels—than any of
Bunyan's previous works could be.

The Holy War is a complex allegorical epic in the basic form of the
classic *psychomachia* (cf. Gurr 2003a, 118ff.): As with *Paradise Lost*, it
makes the human soul the site of a struggle between God and Satan,
here called "Shaddai"—a Hebrew name for God, especially in Job and
Revelation—and "Diabolus." It narrates the history of the "Town of
Mansoul" from its foundation through several swings of fortune in
the wars of Diabolus against King Shaddai and his son Emanuel, in
which Mansoul is the object of contention, to its ultimate liberation
from Diabolus by Emanuel, who leaves the town in a precarious but

hopeful balance, with a promise to return for an ultimate period of long and glorious rule.

Similar to *Paradise Lost*, the story begins with the fall of Diabolus and the rebel angels from heaven, their council of war, and their decision to take revenge on King Shaddai by corrupting the crowning achievement of his creation, the Town of Mansoul. Diabolus succeeds in his attempt to have the citizens fall under his sway, and in taking control of Mansoul, he remodels the corporation by replacing officials loyal to Shaddai with his own men. Shaddai then sends the Captains Boanerges ["Son of Thunder," or "Powerful Preaching"],[15] Conviction, Judgement and Execution to liberate the town. But it is only Emanuel who is finally capable of defeating Diabolus and of redeeming Mansoul. The city, however, relapses into its old evil ways, Emanuel withdraws himself to his Father's court, and Diabolus can recapture the town, but not the citadel—glossed as "The heart." After a period of anguished civil war between the Mansoulians and the Diabolonians, after the moral reformation of Mansoul and much petitioning for Emanuel's pity, Diabolus is finally chased out and the army of Bloodmen and Doubters he raised for his last stand is defeated. Most of the Diabolonians are executed, but the Lords Unbelief and Carnal Sense survive and continue to lurk in Mansoul as a constant threat.

This epic of some 250 pages operates on three, occasionally four, allegorical levels and thus encodes its subversive politics behind several layers of religious allegory. The first of these levels corresponds to the individual life of the Christian soul—the town of Mansoul here represents the individual Christian soul. This is the most sustained and consistently present of the allegorical planes. On the second level, the story of the Town of Mansoul recounts Christian world history from pre-lapsarian innocence via the Fall, Christ's redemption, falling away from early Christian faith, the rise of papacy and the reformation to Bunyan's own time. On the third, less consistently present level, many of the events in *The Holy War* can be read as a Nonconformist commentary on the contemporary politics of Bunyan's time, with the English Revolution, the Restoration and the persecution of dissenters to the very time of composition in the early 1680s (for a succinct account of the political context and a brief reading of *The Holy War* cf. Greaves 2001 and Hill 1989, 240). This is the level I am mainly concerned with here. On a fourth level of interpretation only occasionally present, the events might be read in terms of the Millenarianism of the biblical book of Revelation. This will

110 ❦ *Jens Martin Gurr*

only be of marginal interest to my reading. Behind these four levels, of course, lies the traditional fourfold interpretation of scripture, although the further levels here do not neatly correspond to the traditional *sensus allegoricus, sensus tropologicus* and *sensus anagogicus.*[16]

In his rhymed preface to *The Holy War,* Bunyan hints at a topical relevance of the epic by stating that his are not "vain stories":

> But, Readers, I have somewhat else to do,
> Than with vain stories thus to trouble you;
> What here I say, some men do know so well,
> They can with tears and joy the story tell. (*HW*, 1)

The first taking of Mansoul by Diabolus and the ensuing events, for instance, can be read on all three relevant levels. Diabolus remodels the town by replacing the Lord Mayor, Lord Understanding, with Lord Lustings, and the Recorder, Mr. Conscience, with Mr. Forget-good (cf. *HW* 18, 25), and, having corrupted Mr. Wilbewill, standing for the much-contested free will, makes him "*Captain* of the *Castle,* Governour of the *Wall,* and keeper of the Gates of *Mansoul*" (*HW* 22). Diabolus encourages "*the lusts of the flesh, the lusts of the eyes, and the pride of life*" (*HW* 24) to further alienate the town and its citizens from King Shaddai. On the level of individual Christian spiritual history, Diabolus' successful temptation of Mansoul, his ensuing debauching of its former Recorder, Mr. Conscience, and the dissolution of all order and reasonable conduct in the town correspond to phases of sin and temptation in an individual Christian's life. In the eschatological terms of Christian world history, it corresponds to the Fall and the following moral corruption of the human soul, while on the level of political commentary, the tyrannical "new King" (*HW* 28) Diabolus bears traits of Charles II, and the Diabolonian maltreatment of the righteous inhabitants of Mansoul recalls the persecution of Nonconformists after the Restoration. Here and elsewhere throughout the text, the eschatological level is telescoped into the level of contemporary politics: the veiled references to the persecution of Nonconformists under the Stuarts in the continued attacks of the Diabolonians from outside and within the town after the second liberation of Mansoul by Emanuel can simultaneously be read as standing for the continuing threat to 'true Christianity' posed by unbelief, papacy and persecution.

All in all, there is a fairly sustained level of political commentary: The remodeling of the town by Diabolus on his first taking it

The Taboo of Revolutionary Thought ❦ III

recalls the remodeling of corporations in the last years of Charles II in order to gain control of the boroughs and to curb the influence of Whigs and dissenters. The royal party sought to make corporations yield their old charters and urged acceptance of new ones. The new burgesses and aldermen installed by Diabolus under the Mayor Lord Lustings and the Recorder Forget-good must have seemed to Bunyan's contemporaries "caricatures of the Tory-Anglicans" taking office as a result of Charles II's remodeling of the corporations (cf. Greaves 1989, 150). Though Bunyan's Bedford only received its new charter in 1684, the process was well under way; the outcome was plain for all to see from the late 1670s and early 1680s onward and required no divinatory powers on Bunyan's part to portray in 1682 (cf. Sharrock and Forrest xx–xxv, xxxiii–xxxv, and 256n, as well as Greaves 1989, 149 *et passim*).

But Bunyan's indictment of the Stuart monarchy is even more drastic in the strong hints of an equation of Charles II with Diabolus: under "the new King or rather rebellious Tyrant" (*HW* 28), Bloodmen persecute the righteous citizens of Mansoul, which brings to mind the persecution of Nonconformists after 1660. Among the army of Bloodmen (*HW* 228) Diabolus launches against Mansoul in his last stand are Captain Nimrod and Captain Pope, who may be taken as references to the Stuart monarch and to the fear of a resurgence of Catholicism under James II during the Exclusion Crisis of 1679–1681.

Even the ending, the ultimate defeat of Diabolus, and Emanuel's concluding exhortation "hold fast till I come," though apparently no longer having a parallel in the dire political climate of the early 1680s, may be read as expressing a political hope: "[W]as Bunyan expressing hope that the Protestant prince, Monmouth, would soon save Mansoul?" (Greaves 2001, 282) The reference would then be to the hope for a successful rebellion of Charles II's illegitimate son, the Duke of Monmouth, a rebellion that did indeed occur in 1685 but failed dismally.

In his essay on Bunyan and the Stuart state, Richard L. Greaves has perceptively drawn attention to a curious contrast in Bunyan's political thought: Bunyan aggressively indicts the Stuart monarchy and, at the same time, advocates political quietism and meek suffering under worldly authorities, a position he explicitly derives from Romans 13.1 with its famous support for earthly rulers: "Let every soul be subject unto the higher powers. For there is no power but of God: the powers that be are ordained of God." Greaves harmonizes

112   *Jens Martin Gurr*

this contrast as a "constant...advocacy of passive disobedience" and speaks of Bunyan's "militancy of the spirit, not the sword" (Greaves 1989, 160). This, as Hill and Achinstein have shown, underestimates the radicalism of Bunyan's antagonism to the Stuarts and, I believe, explains away the inconsistencies in Bunyan's views on monarchy and kingship. Invoking parallels from Bunyan's other writings of the period, Hill persuasively argues that Bunyan did espouse—albeit in the circuitously indirect manner enforced by censorship and the continuing threat of further imprisonment—the overthrow of the Stuart regime. Hill draws attention to the parallels with *Antichrist and his Ruin*, which Bunyan in all likelihood wrote early in the 1680s but which was impossible to publish under the prevailing conditions of censorship. In *Antichrist and his Ruin*, "Bunyan insisted that Antichrist—like Diabolus in *The Holy War*—has set up his own church government, officers and discipline....He did not say that this government must be overthrown, but the conclusion was inescapable" (Hill 1989, 153, cf. Achinstein 101–7). Liberation from oppression, it is clear through all allegorical levels of Bunyan's epic, can only be effected by means of military power and violence.

To conclude: The literature of dissent after the Restoration of 1660, with Milton and Bunyan as its two most important figures, who both wrote at a time during which the taboo on radical political thought was enforced by means of rigid censorship and political oppression, provided generations of subversive writers throughout the later seventeenth and the eighteenth centuries all the way until the Reform Bill Period of the 1830s with inspiration and with techniques for the circumvention of censorship (for this tradition cf. for instance Thompson, as well as Achinstein 243–55). One such technique, as we have seen, is to suggest that events or characters in a text seemingly unrelated to contemporary politics—whether an account of the expulsion from Eden or of a battle for Mansoul—might be read as being highly topical after all. Given my key concern in this essay—the relationship between political taboo, censorship and Milton's and Bunyan's ingenious techniques of subversion—, a final instance of this technique in *The Holy War* brings me back full circle to the opening of the essay: Upon his first taking of the Town of Mansoul, Diabolus hires one "Mr. Filth" to encourage the publication of filthy literature, to suppress more worthy writing, and to "give licence" to sin and indulgence (*HW* 31f.). Many contemporaries would have recognized "Mr. Filth" as a satirical indictment of none other than Sir Roger L'Estrange, royalist pamphleteer of the

The Taboo of Revolutionary Thought 113

coarser kind and licenser of the press who made life difficult for Nonconformist writers and printers throughout the Restoration (Sharrock and Forrest xxxiii and 257)—and who, in 1688, the year in which the Glorious Revolution finally cost him his job, was to subscribe to a special edition of *Paradise Lost*.

Notes

1. For the radicalism of Milton and Bunyan after the Restoration cf. especially Hill 1977, 1989 and 1991; Meller.
2. For accounts of the Restoration and the consequences of the Restoration Settlement cf. for instance Hutton 157; Harris; Houston and Pincus; for the situation in London cf. Gassenmeier 11–21 *et passim*.
3. Radicalism and non-conformism after 1660 have been widely discussed and still generate a lot of interest. Cf. especially Keeble, surely still the best book on the subject; cf. also Jose; Hutton; Greaves 1990; Hirst and Strier; Morton and Smith; for the role of the English Revolution and the later seventeenth century for eighteenth-century radicalism cf. Nünning 142–61 *et passim*. For the tradition of radicalism—including praise of the 1649 regicide—preached from the dissenting pulpits in the eighteenth century, cf. Bradley 146ff.
4. For the exclusion crisis cf. especially Knights; Harris 1987, 96–188; for Tory propaganda cf. ibid. 133–55.
5. For censorship cf. for instance Keeble 110–20 *et passim*; Hill 1991, 2f.; Quint.
6. Like anyone attempting a political reading of *Paradise Lost*, I am indebted to Christopher Hill's scholarship. Cf. Hill 1977, 370ff. for a related reading of a number of the following parallels. For a brief survey of previous readings all the way from the later seventeenth century via the Romantics to key positions in the twentieth century, cf. Gurr 2003b.
7. Cf. Achinstein 121ff. and Smith 256f.
8. Cf. also VI, 667f., in the context of the war in heaven: "Infernal noise; war seemed a civil game / To this uproar."
9. Cf. also VII, 617: "this new-made world, another heaven."
10. Cf. the entire passage V, 772–802; for anti-monarchical images in *Paradise Lost* cf. also Davies and Bennett.
11. Cf. also his remark that "Heaven [in *Paradise Lost*] is a totalitarian state" (117).
12. For the North as the seat of evil cf. also the "Argument" to book V and V, 688–90.
13. For different readings of this passage cf. for instance Hill 1991, 3; Smith 262; for a survey of previous comments cf. Fowler's note on this passage.

114   *Jens Martin Gurr*

14. For censorship of this passage and a compelling subversive reading cf. Meller 531f. Cf. also Keeble 118f. and Fowler's note on lines 596ff. in his edition of *Paradise Lost*.
15. The name derives from Mark, 3.16f.
16. For the Bible as an inspiring source for subversive typological reading and writing in Bunyan's case cf. Achinstein, 101–7.

Works Cited

Achinstein, Sharon. *Literature and Dissent in Milton's England*. Cambridge: Cambridge UP, 2003.

Bennett, Joan S. "God, Satan, and King Charles: Milton's Royal Portraits." *PMLA* 92 (1977): 441–57.

Bradley, James E. *Religion, Revolution and English Radicalism: Nonconformity in 18th-Century Politics and Society*. Cambridge: Cambridge UP, 1990.

Browning, Andrew, ed. *English Historical Documents 1660-1714*. London: Eyre and Spottiswoode, 1966.

Bunyan, John. *The Holy War, Made by Shaddai upon Diabolus, For the Regaining of the Metropolis of the World, or The Losing and Taking Again of the Town of Mansoul*. Eds. Roger Sharrock and James F. Forrest. Oxford: Clarendon Press, 1980.

Davies, Stevie. *Images of Kingship in Paradise Lost*. Columbia: Missouri UP, 1983.

Gassenmeier, Michael. *Londondichtung als Politik: Texte und Kontexte der City Poetry von der Restauration bis zum Ende der Walpole-Ära*. Tübingen: Niemeyer, 1989.

Greaves, Richard L. "The Spirit and the Sword: Bunyan and the Stuart State." *Bunyan in Our Time*. Ed. Robert G. Collmer. Kent, OH: Kent State UP, 1989. 138–60.

———. *Enemies Under His Feet: Radicals and Nonconformists in Britain, 1664–1677*. Stanford: Stanford UP, 1990.

———. "Bunyan and the Holy War." *The Cambridge Companion to Writing of the English Revolution*. Ed. N.H. Keeble. Cambridge: Cambridge UP, 2001. 268–85.

Grierson, Herbert J.C. *Milton and Wordsworth, Poets and Prophets: A Study of Their Reactions to Political Events*. London: Chatto and Windus, 1963.

Gurr, Jens Martin. "Bunyan, Psychomachia and the Dissolution of Calvinism through Allegory: *Grace Abounding, Pilgrim's Progress*, and *The Holy War*." *The Human Soul as Battleground: Variations on Dualism and the Self in English Literature*. Heidelberg: Winter, 2003a. 105–29.

———. "'When Upstart Passions Catch the Government': Political and Mental Hierarchies in Paradise Lost." *The Human Soul as Battleground: Variations on Dualism and the Self in English Literature*. Heidelberg: Winter, 2003b. 81–103.

The Taboo of Revolutionary Thought   115

Harris, Tim. *London Crowds in the Reign of Charles II: Propaganda and Politics from the Restoration until the Exclusion Crisis.* Cambridge: Cambridge UP, 1987.

——. "Understanding Popular Politics in Restoration Britain." *A Nation Transformed: England after the Restoration.* Eds. Alan Houston and Steve Pincus. Cambridge: Cambridge UP, 2001. 125–53.

Hill, Christopher. *Some Intellectual Consequences of the English Revolution.* Madison: U of Wisconsin P, 1976.

——. *Milton and the English Revolution.* London: Faber and Faber, 1977.

——. *A Tinker and Poor Man: John Bunyan and His Church, 1628–1688.* New York: Knopf, 1989.

——. "Milton, Bunyan and the Literature of Defeat." *Mosaic* 24.1 (1991): 1–12.

Hirst, Derek, and Richard Strier, eds. *Writing and Political Engagement in Seventeenth-Century England.* Cambridge: Cambridge UP, 1999.

Houston, Alan, and Steve Pincus, eds. *A Nation Transformed: England after the Restoration.* Cambridge: Cambridge UP, 2001.

Hutton, Ronald. *The Restoration: A Political and Religious History of England and Wales 1658–1667.* Oxford: Clarendon Press, 1985.

Jablonski, Steven. "'Under Thir [*sic*] Head Embodied All in One': Milton's Reinterpretation of the Organic Analogy in *Paradise Lost.*" *Spokesperson Milton: Voices in Contemporary Criticism.* Eds. Charles W. Durham and Kristin Pruitt McColgan. Selinsgrove: Susquehanna UP, 1994. 113–25.

——. "'Freely We Serve': *Paradise Lost* and the Paradoxes of Political Liberty." *Arenas of Conflict: Milton and the Unfettered Mind.* Eds. Kristin Pruitt McColgan and Charles W. Durham. Selinsgrove: Susquehanna UP, 1997. 107–19.

Jose, Nicholas. *Ideas of the Restoration in English Literature, 1660–71.* London: Macmillan, 1984.

Keeble, Neil. *The Literary Culture of Nonconformity in Later Seventeenth-Century England.* Leicester: Leicester UP, 1987.

Knights, Mark. *Politics and Opinion in Crisis, 1678–1681.* Cambridge: Cambridge UP, 1994.

Meller, Horst. "Der Nationalepiker als Ireniker: John Miltons Themenwahl für sein *Verlorenes Paradies* im Kontext der konfessionspolitischen Bürgerkriege." *Nation und Literatur im Europa der frühen Neuzeit: Akten des I. Internationalen Osnabrücker Kongresses zur Kulturgeschichte der frühen Neuzeit.* Ed. Klaus Garber. Tübingen: Niemeyer, 1989. 516–53.

Milton, John. "The Tenure of Kings and Magistrates." *Complete Prose Works of John Milton.* Gen. Ed. Don M. Wolfe. Vol. 3. New Haven: Yale UP, 1953. 184–258.

——. *Complete Prose Works of John Milton.* Gen. Ed. Don M. Wolfe. 8 vols. New Haven: Yale UP, 1953–1982.

——. *Poetical Works.* Ed. Douglas Bush. 13th ed. Oxford: Oxford UP, 1992.

——. *Paradise Lost.* Ed. Alastair Fowler. 2nd ed. London: Longman, 1998.

116 &&& *Jens Martin Gurr*

Morton, Timothy, and Nigel Smith, eds. *Radicalism in British Literary Culture 1650–1830: From Revolution to Revolution.* Cambridge: Cambridge UP, 2002.

Nünning, Vera. *"A Revolution in Sentiments, Manners, and Moral Opinions": Catherine Macaulay und die politische Kultur des englischen Radikalismus, 1760–1790.* Heidelberg: Winter, 1998.

Ogg, David. *England in the Reign of Charles II.* 2 vols. Oxford: Clarendon Press, 1934.

Parker, William Riley. *Milton: A Biography.* 2 vols. Oxford: Clarendon Press, 1968.

Sharrock, Roger, and James F. Forrest. "Introduction." *The Holy War.* By John Bunyan. Eds. Roger Sharrock and James F. Forrest. Oxford: Clarendon Press, 1980. ix–xxxix.

Smith, Nigel. *"Paradise Lost* from Civil War to Restoration." *The Cambridge Companion to Writing of the English Revolution.* Ed. Neil Keeble. Cambridge: Cambridge UP, 2001. 251–67.

Thompson, Edward P. *The Making of the English Working Class.* Harmondsworth: Penguin, repr. 1977.

Wittreich, Joseph. "'He Ever Was a Dissenter': Milton's Transgressive Maneuvers in *Paradise Lost." Arenas of Conflict: Milton and the Unfettered Mind.* Eds. Kristin Pruitt McColgan, and Charles W. Durham. Selinsgrove: Susquehanna UP, 1997. 21–40.

Worden, Blair. "Milton's Republicanism and the Tyranny of Heaven." *Macchiavelli and Republicanism.* Eds. Gisela Bock, Quentin Skinner, and Maurizio Viroli. Cambridge: Cambridge UP, 1990. 225–46.

CHAPTER VI

WORSHIPPING CLOACINA IN THE EIGHTEENTH CENTURY: FUNCTIONS OF SCATOLOGY IN SWIFT, POPE, GAY, AND STERNE

Jens Martin Gurr

Nothing deflates human pretensions to grandeur more quickly . . . than the satirist's insistence upon biological processes.

—*Frontein, 301*

The Taboo of Excretion in the Eighteenth Century

At one point in Nick Hornby's 2005 novel *A Long Way Down*, a number of characters debate taboos in film and, by implication, in literature:

> "It's all part of life, isn't it?"
> "People always say that about unpleasant things. . . . I'll tell you what else is all part of life: going for a crap. No one ever wants to see that, do they? No one ever puts that in a film. Let's go and watch people take a dump this evening."
> "Who'd let us? . . . People lock the door." (253)

While it is certainly true that excretion has been a taboo in films, literature and virtually all other media—people generally do "lock the door"—, one period in Anglophone literature conspicuously throws open the doors to afford more or less detailed views of precisely those moments

[When] gentle goddess Cloacine[1]
Receives all offerings at her shrine.

118 ❧ *Jens Martin Gurr*

> In separate cells, the he's and she's,
> Here pay their vows on bended knees.... (Swift "Panegyric," ll. 205–8)

This is not to say that the eighteenth century miraculously lifted the taboo—it certainly did not, as is apparent from the air of transgression that accompanies many of these instances. But it appears as though the insistence upon the baser animal nature of humans served a specific function in this period: Out of sixty-eight entries for the keywords "scatology" or "scatological" for English and Irish literature in the MLA database since 1963, twenty-seven are related to the eighteenth century, with significantly fewer than ten entries each for the Middle Ages, the sixteenth, seventeenth, and nineteenth centuries; even for the twentieth century, there are only twenty-three entries. Although, strictly speaking, this only proves a greater scholarly interest in scatology in this period, one can reasonably assume that it also reflects the frequency of scatological themes in eighteenth-century literature. This observation raises a number of important questions: Why this high incidence of scatology in the eighteenth century? How does one say the unsayable, and why bother saying it in the first place? More precisely, what purpose is fulfilled by the taboo of excretion and what is the function of the transgressive insistence upon such bodily functions in a given cultural environment, here the cultural context of the Enlightenment in the British Isles? This essay thus follows a largely functional approach to the study of taboo in the period in question by attempting a contextual reading of selected texts by Alexander Pope, John Gay, Laurence Sterne and, most importantly, Jonathan Swift. This list might easily have been complemented by numerous other early eighteenth-century writers and texts, but for reasons of space, I shall confine my discussion to a number of key examples which will furnish enough material to make my point.

I will argue that, in addition to a number of more specific functions in individual cases, the blunt insistence on humans' inescapably excremental physiology with Swift and his contemporaries served as a drastic counter-image to the overly optimistic assessments of human moral and intellectual capabilities expounded in the philosophical and literary writings of the early Enlightenment. This is not meant to contradict the findings of Norbert Elias and others on the changing habits concerning such matters through the centuries as documented by Elias from conduct books and other sources (for matters scatological cf. Elias 1: 174–94). What I mean to add is a more specific

Worshipping Cloacina ❄ 119

contextualization for the surge of scatological references in the eighteenth century. Before discussing previous attempts to account for the ubiquity of scatological references in the period, however, one must ask why excretion is tabooed in the first place—historically in general and in the eighteenth century specifically.

Generally speaking, the taboo on excretion as well as a number of related taboos can be conceptualized in terms of Kristeva's notion of "abjection": "The abject confronts us, on the one hand, with those fragile states where man strays on the territories of *animal*. Thus, by way of abjection, primitive societies have marked out a precise area of their culture in order to remove it from the threatening world of animals or animalism" (Kristeva 12f.). Seen in this way, it is the taboo on excretion which separates humans from animals. Thus, a transgression of the taboo is regarded as a threat to human society and becomes a mark of social instability. A related explanation for the taboo nature of excretion and feces is provided by Mary Douglas's exploration of the connection between taboo, the human body and the social order as well as her view that excrements suggest the transgression of bodily boundaries as well as a threat to the social order (cf. 35, 115–21 *et passim*). Douglas here draws on Sartre's analysis of the symbolism of stickiness in *L'être et le néant* (1943, *Being and Nothingness*, 1956) and argues that purity comes to be virtually synonymous with order, while impurity represents disorder, instability, chaos (cf. also Persels and Ganim xiv). Given this close link between the body and society and the symbolic connection between physical purity and social stability, which has also been explored by Stallybrass and White (cf. 192 *et passim*), the specific form in which the taboo on excretion is negotiated is of significant diagnostic value in understanding a given culture: "Paying close attention to this [taboo], understanding the treatment of impurity and its concomitant 'danger' within a given society's conceptualization of its own nature, becomes critical to a full and accurate appreciation of that society" (Persels and Ganim xiv). Taking their cue from Foucault's notions of "censorship," "denial," and "repressive hypotheses" in the *History of Sexuality*, Persels and Ganim speak of a specific "aesthetic and linguistic code" that originates in the "social desire to silence literary and artistic representations of [the scatological]" (xv).

To complicate matters further, in studying the relationship between society and taboo, we have to bear in mind the inextricable connection between taboo and transgression and the fact that transgression is even constitutive of the taboo, as classically set

120 ❧ *Jens Martin Gurr*

out in Bataille's *L'érotisme* (1957). It is in the very moment of transgression that the taboo is once more made explicit. Eggert appropriately points out: "As a consequence of the ambivalence of taboo and transgression, one can observe an ambivalence of a ban on representation and representation which nonetheless occurs—a taboo, after all, must be publicly marked as a taboo" (22, my transl.). It is the very act of transgression explicitly and deliberately marked as such which draws renewed attention to the taboo. Thus, in the period in question, too, circuitous euphemisms, dashes substituted for letters and the particularly drastic language used in cases when the texts *do* become explicit, in a good number of instances draw attention to the taboo nature of urination and excretion. A case in point is the famous dash in the notorious final couplets of "Cassinus and Peter," when horrified Cassinus entrusts to his friend Peter the shocking secret of how he has been disillusioned about the angelic nature of his beloved Cælia:[2]

> And yet, I dare confide in you;
> So take my Secret, and adieu.
> Nor wonder how I lost my Wits;
> Oh! Cælia, Cælia, Cælia sh—(ll. 115–18)

Similarly, in "The Lady's Dressing Room," though it does talk about "excremental smell" in rather unflattering detail, the reference to feces as "[t]hings, which must not be exprest" (l. 109) only highlights the taboo. Finally, a further variation of this reference to the taboo nature of excretion in the very moment of transgression is to be found in characteristic euphemisms such as "to pluck a rose." This euphemism is employed for Chloe in "Strephon and Chloe," for instance, when we learn that "None ever saw her pluck a Rose" (540, l. 16).[3] Thus, in the very act of transgressing the taboo on excretion, these texts recall and thus paradoxically reinforce the taboo.

This intricate relationship between taboo and transgression and the multiplicity of strategies in representing both are also addressed by Eggert when he states that

> [t]aboos are always connected to problems of representation and their negotiation: taboos have a genuinely aesthetic component ranging from the non-verbal symbolizations to a regulation of aesthetics.... Any research on taboos [therefore] has to attend to strategies and contents of symbolization; it cannot merely conceive of taboos as a

Worshipping Cloacina ❧ 121

social phenomenon, but must also consider aesthetic traditions. (22, my transl.)

Seen in this light, the specifically transgressive nature of texts dealing with excretion manifests itself not only in content, but also in generic transgression: thus, Swift's scatological poems can also be seen as transgressive of established poetic conventions and sub-genres. In this vein, "Cassinus and Peter" has been regarded as a "burlesque elegy" (Aden 26), "Strephon and Chloe" can be seen as a "mock epithalamion" (Davis 195), while Pope's *Dunciad* is the archetype of the mock-heroic epic (for such transgressive variations of established genres cf. also Zimmerman 133).

Madness, Misogyny, or Misanthropy?—Potential Functions of Scatology in Swift and Others

Swift's engagement with scatology alone, as a recent commentator states, has "engendered, and continues to maintain, a critical industry....Few topics in Swift have been revisited as often" (Child 83). Aldous Huxley (93–106) was probably the first to draw attention to the centrality of excremental imagery in Swift, but he began the tradition of attributing this—in a vulgarization of Freudian criticism—to a perversion on the part of the author. Fortunately, this simplistic and reductionist branch of pseudo-Freudian criticism with its tendency to condemn the author and his pieces as "so perverse, so unnatural, so mentally diseased, so humanly wrong" (Murry 440) largely came to an end with the more subtle readings of later critics. A far more balanced psychological account of Swift's scatological pieces, for instance, is provided by Ehrenpreis (cf. 3: 688–95), though he, too, does not see them in the context of eighteenth-century philosophy.

Similarly, the superficially plausible reading of these texts as being misogynist has also long been shown to be untenable: In his classic 1959 essay "The Excremental Vision," Norman O. Brown already deplored a critical distortion in the tendency "to transform Swift's misanthropy into misogyny" (613). These poems, Brown argued, are not misogynist, but rather mock the attitude of those who naively raise women to the status of incorporeal angels. In a related vein, Ellen Pollak, for instance, understands them as attacks upon idealizations of women, speaking of "mock-petrarchan features of the poems" (181; cf. also Gilmore 33; Brown 617; Siebert 21). The

122 ❧ *Jens Martin Gurr*

disillusioning effect of an insistence upon bodily functions is especially clear in "Strephon and Chloe," where Strephon is drastically brought to his senses when his idealized, angelicized beloved turns out to be all-too-human after all during the wedding night:

> In Bed we left the married Pair:
> 'Tis Time to shew how Things went there....
> The Nymph opprest before, behind,
> As Ships are toss't by Waves and Wind,
> Steals out her Hand, by Nature led,
> And brings a Vessel into Bed....
> *Strephon* who heard the fuming Rill
> As from a mossy Cliff distill;
> Cry'd out, Ye Gods, what Sound is this?
> Can *Chloe*, heav'nly *Chloe*—?
> But, when he smelt a noysom Steam
> Which oft' attends that luke-warm Stream;...
> And though contriv'd, we may suppose,
> To slip his Ears, yet struck his Nose:
> He found her, while the Scent increas'd,
> As *mortal* as himself at least. ("Strephon and Chloe," ll. 145–86)

This deflation of idealized conceptions of femininity also appears to be the function of the notorious "The Rose, Paris" chapter in Sterne's 1768 *Sentimental Journey*, prominently placed at the very end of vol. I. On an outing in the countryside, Madame de Rambouilet, "the most correct...of all women," desires to leave the coach:

> I ask'd her if she wanted any thing—*Rien que pisser*, said Madame de Rambouilet—Grieve not, gentle traveller, to let Madame de Rambouilet p-ss on—And, ye fair mystic nymphs! go each one *pluck your rose*, and scatter them in your path—for Madame de Rambouilet did no more—I handed [her] out of the coach; and had I been the priest of the chaste Castalia, I could not have served at her fountain with a more respectful decorum. (63)

Here, the *frisson* of discussing in euphemisms and *double entendres* the act of urination and—by implication—defecation of a respectable woman surely also serves to deflate allegedly disembodied female beauty and propriety.[4]

However, even if it is agreed that these texts are not misogynist but that they deflate the idealization of women, it seems to me an insufficiently specific contextualization to read them exclusively

Worshipping Cloacina 123

as anti-Petrarchan. What might account for the emergence of anti-Petrarchan poetry in the eighteenth-century? Zimmerman appropriately argues that these texts are "rendered more rational if the values they enforce are ungendered, the female body then standing for the human condition" (142). These poems—and the same is true of *Gulliver's Travels*, for instance—are just as unflattering and scathing about the male body: Strephon in "Strephon and Chloe" urinates and breaks wind, too (ll. 187–92), and Cassinus in "Cassinus and Peter" is as unkempt, greasy and unwashed as any female.

Thus, although simplistic readings of Swift's poems and other scatological pieces in the eighteenth century as expressions of their authors' diseased minds or of their misogyny have been discarded, many previous readings are devoid of any concrete contextualization, and most commentators remain curiously vague about just *what* might more convincingly be identified as the immediate target of their satire. Why, in other words, this outburst of scatology in the eighteenth century?

In the sense of the ancient reminder, often mistakenly attributed to St. Augustine, that "inter urinam et faeces nascimur," the insistence on man's animal nature in any age of course effectively deflates grand human pretensions, and the coupling of a concept, person or place with feces is easily recognizable as a form of denigration. The connection of unpleasant or hostile characters with excrement to express dislike, for instance, seems timeless and common across many cultures.

A case in point of this function of scatology as a form of denigration is the cloacal vision of London as one great sewer of material, intellectual and moral filth in Swift's "Description of a City Shower" (1710), Gay's *Trivia* (1716, enl. 1730) or Pope's *Dunciad* (1728, enl. 1743). In this vein, Swift's "Description of a City Shower" represents London as an infernally dirty and smelly sewer overflowing with excremental filth. As Gassenmeier has shown in a detailed contextual reading (261–78), this image of excremental London serves to counter contemporary celebrations of the city as a shining model of liberty, commerce and progress. A similarly cloacal image of London is to be found in the passage of Gay's *Trivia* concerned with the Goddess of the sewers, "*Cloacina*," "[w]hose sable Streams beneath the City glide" (II, ll. 115f.; for a reading cf. Meller 164f.). A final text indulging in the cloacal imagination of excremental London is Pope's *Dunciad*. Pope's satirical targets, the hack writers, poetasters, critics and cultural functionaries of contemporary London, are

124 ❧ *Jens Martin Gurr*

here made to engage in degrading contests of tickling, noise-making and sewer-diving in "Fleet-ditch" (II, l. 259). Diving and splashing about in the excrement-filled sewer, the dunces are courted by "Mud-nymphs" (II, l. 308) and "Merdamante brown" (II, 310). This deployment of scatological imagery clearly serves drastically to denigrate opponents, suggesting their bestiality by associating them with filth (for a brief discussion of the *Dunciad* in this vein cf. Gassenmeier 282ff.).

Generalizing the purpose of such more specific attacks, Brown in his discussion of Swift's "excremental vision" regards "scatological imagery" as Swift's "decisive weapon in his assault on the pretensions, the pride, even the self-respect of mankind" (611). In his reading of *Gulliver's Travels*, for instance, "[t]he Yahoos represent the raw core of human bestiality" (620). But much as Brown rightly rejects the simplistic psychoanalytical reading of Swiftian scatology as being an expression of the satirist's diseased mind, his reading of the poems as "anticipations of Freudian theorems about anality, about sublimation, and about the universal neurosis of mankind" (617) remains remarkably vague and devoid of any reasonable contextualization. Similarly, even Irving Ehrenpreis, who in his magisterial three-volume study of Swift reads *Gulliver's Travels* as "a radical comical criticism of human nature" (3: 455), merely regards the emphasis on bodily functions as a general rather than specific counter-balance to human intellectual pride: "On the one hand, the body is the spirit's tragedy; on the other, it is the spirit's farce. *Gulliver's Travels* [like the 'unprintable poems'] is designed to keep both these attitudes in sight at once, and to destroy the dignity of man in all his shapes by their constant juxtaposition." (3: 464) Thus, a survey of Swift criticism reveals that what Bakhtin calls "grotesque realism" (*passim*), the general tendency to privilege bodily excess and the lower regions of the body including its waste products over the spiritual and intellectual, has frequently been explored (cf. for instance Stallybrass and White). The specific way in which much eighteenth-century writing uses the physical to deflate the claims of the spiritual and intellectual side of humankind, however, deserves further consideration. Rawson gestures toward a more directly contextual reading when he comments on Swift's scatology as follows:

> Swift's scatology is undoubtedly aggressive [but the aggression may] be less against the bowels or the sexual parts than against that highly personalized representative of mankind, the reader: against his

Worshipping Cloacina 125

squeamishness, his complacent normality, his shoddy idealisms and self-deceptions, his attachment to the human form divine, and his belief in the rationality of the human mind....(Rawson 82)

But what, the question remains, is the immediate occasion?

Carole Fabricant, J. Paul Hunter and recently Paul W. Child have drawn attention to more concrete contexts. Far from being evidence of Swift's perverse mind, references to feces and the related olfactory sensations must be understood as unremarkable in an age when "travellers toward London consistently reported that they could smell it before they could see it—not because of the industrialization which historically lay just ahead but because of the primitive plumbing and open sewers that could only inadequately serve the physical needs of the teeming city" (Hunter 230). Further, this ubiquity of excrement and horrendous stench was by no means confined to London: Carole Fabricant, who has an entire chapter titled "Excremental Vision vs. Excremental Reality" (24–42), has pointed to Swift's more immediate local context, St. Patrick's Cathedral in Dublin and its particularly nasty and smelly surroundings: "Excrement, then, was very much a fact of life for Swift; his landscape was literally as well as linguistically full of it" (30). Such facts of life, we are apt to forget, were very much inescapable in early eighteenth-century life and must have been overpoweringly present to all senses. Finally, in a recent essay on scatology in Swift, Child takes issue with a dominant strand in the criticism of these texts, which he summarizes as follows: "...Swift levels our proud pretensions, reminding us, in dark Augustinian fashion, that we resemble ordure more than we do angels. Mankind, mired in original sin, is 'excrementally filthy'" (84). In contrast to this rather vague reading of Swiftian scatology as being a general reminder of human baseness and animality, Child persuasively traces Swift's fecal imagery to the very concrete medical "fact that faeces was tool-in-trade of diagnostic and...*therapeutic* medicine" (93). He further argues that such excremental medical practices ideally lent themselves to "satirizing the medical profession, one of [Swift's] favourite targets" and that they provided "a narrative structure for his various attacks on modern projecting madness" (85).

The mere presence of an "excremental reality" as diagnosed by Fabricant, Hunter, and Child, however, hardly distinguishes the early eighteenth century from other periods similarly marked by such unpleasant facts of life. The question remains what function the insistence on the scatological might have played in early

126 ❧ *Jens Martin Gurr*

eighteenth-century literature and culture. Why, again, this outburst of scatology specifically in the early eighteenth century?

Concrete Contexts: The Intellectual and Moral Pretensions of Enlightened Anthropological Optimism

This is not the place for a survey of conceptions of human rationality and moral philosophy during the English Enlightenment.[5] A few remarks on some key notions from early eighteenth-century treatises on moral philosophy and on the role of reason in this context, however, will be sufficient to recontextualize eighteenth-century scatology. There can be little doubt that late-seventeenth and early-eighteenth-century thinkers were more optimistic about the intellectual and moral capabilities of humans—both collectively and individually—than most previous generations. In his short account of *The Enlightenment Tradition*, Robert Anchor speaks of "the autonomy of man, the secularisation of knowledge and thought, the natural goodness and perfectibility of human nature, and belief in reason and experience, science and progress" as "the credo of the Enlightenment" (69f.).

It is true, of course, that rationality had for centuries been regarded as the distinct characteristic which elevates humans above animals. This distinction is again made as late as 1690 in Locke's *Essay Concerning Human Understanding*, where "reason" is defined as "that faculty whereby man is supposed to be distinguished from beasts, and wherein it is evident he much surpasses them" (394, IV, xvii, 1). The belief in rationality as the distinguishing feature of humanity and in the general capacity of humans productively to make use of it, was hardly ever more prominent than in the period in question, and though the entire tradition of regarding man as the "animal rationale" may be considered to be Swift's target, it seems reasonable to assume this current vogue of optimistic assessments of human nature and human rationality as the more concrete and more immediate target. Thus, in a much-cited letter to Pope, Swift wrote about *Gulliver's Travels*: "I have got Materials Towards a Treatis proving the falsity of that Definition *animal rationale*; and to show it should only be *rationis capax*. Upon this great foundation of Misanthropy…the whole building of my Travells is erected" (Swift, "Letter to Pope, 29 Sept. 1725," 585). In a later letter to Pope dated November 26, 1725, he writes: "I do not hate Mankind, it is vous autres who hate them because you would have them reasonable Animals, and are Angry for being disappointed" (586).

Worshipping Cloacina ✤ 127

That especially book III of *Gulliver's Travels* is directed against the "New Sciences" inspired by Bacon and particularly practiced by the Royal Society, has long been established (cf. Real and Vienken 86 *et passim* and Nate 299). The rampant scientific enthusiasm of the early English enlightenment is documented in texts such as William Wotton's *Reflections upon Ancient and Modern Learning*, published in 1694, of which Swift is known to have possessed the second edition of 1697 (cf. Real and Vienken 174n). Wotton here enthuses: "Such Swarms of Great Men in every Part of Natural and Mathematical Knowledge have within these few Years appeared, that it may, perhaps, without Vanity, be believed, that...the next Age will not find very much Work of this Kind [left] to do" (qtd. in ibid. 89). In this vein, *Gulliver's Travels* satirically lampoons human pretensions to intellectual respectability, rationality, perfectibility, and progress (cf. ibid. 110 *et passim*). It is hardly a coincidence that book III, with the Academy at Lagado (III, v and vi, 152–64) as the satirical representation of the Royal Society (cf. Real and Vienken 90; Nate 300), is particularly scatological in nature. The academy is closely associated with feces in the description of various experiments such as the attempt "to reduce human Excrement to its original Food," for which the filthy scientist receives "a weekly Allowance from the Society, of a Vessel filled with human Ordure" (III, v, 153) or the experiment of the "great Physician" who attempts to cure trapped winds by means of "a large Pair of Bellows...conveyed eight Inches up the Anus, and drawing in the Wind" or by "[discharging] the Bellows full of Wind...into the Body of the Patient" (III, v, 154f.; cf. also *Battle of the Books* vii, 338 or ix, 354). Finally, a letter to Sheridan dated September 11, 1725, explicitly connects the bestial nature of the Yahoos in the particularly unflattering book IV of *Gulliver's Travels* with overly optimistic assessments of human nature: "[E]xpect no more from Man than such an Animal is capable of, and you will every day find my Description of Yahoes [*sic*] more resembling" (583f.).

As far as early-eighteenth-century moral philosophy is concerned, a representative work in the tradition of enlightened enthusiasm about human nature is Francis Hutcheson's influential *Inquiry into the Original of Our Ideas of Beauty*, first published in 1725. That many of Hutcheson's ideas were already current at the time of publication is already apparent from the title page of the *Inquiry*, where it is announced as a work "in which the Principles of the Late Earl of Shaftesbury are Explain'd and Defended against the Author of the *Fable of the Bees*." The reference is of course to Shaftesbury's 1711

128 ❦ *Jens Martin Gurr*

Characteristics of Men, Manners, Opinions, Times, which—despite fore-runners in Latitudinarian theology and the Cambridge Platonists—is generally regarded as the founding text of the "moral sense" school with its anthropological optimism (cf. Gurr 29–50). Following Shaftesbury, Hutcheson maintains that humans naturally have a moral sense, which unerringly helps them to tell good from evil—and Hutcheson is Platonist enough to assume that to know the good is to will it:

> [A]s the Author of *Nature* has determin'd us to receive, by our *external Senses*, pleasant or disagreeable Ideas of Objects, according as they are useful or hurtful to our Bodies; and to receive from *uniform Objects* the Pleasures of *Beauty* and *Harmony*...so he has given us a Moral Sense, to direct our Actions, and to give us still *nobler Pleasures*; so that while we are only intending the *Good* of Others, we undesignedly promote our own greatest *private Good*. (123f.)

In keeping with his belief that "there is a *universal Determination* to *Benevolence* in *Mankind*, even towards the most distant parts of the Species" (195, cf. also 215f.), he assumes that humans will generally act benevolently and altruistically: "It is plain that we have some *secret Sense* which determines our Approbation [of an action or thought] without regard to *Self-Interest*; otherwise we should always favor the fortunate Side without regard to *Virtue*" (112). Yet more optimistically, he maintains without much qualification that "The *human Nature* is a lovely Form" (131) and even goes so far as to claim that "a *natural, kind Instinct*, to see Objects of *Compassion*" (217) was the cause which induced Romans to attend gory gladiatorial contests and which made crowds flock to see public executions (cf. 217f.). His views are representative of the new moral optimism when he states: "I see no harm in supposing, that Men are *naturally* dispos'd to *Virtue*" (176).

The drastic insistence on human's fecal nature in *Gulliver's Travels* and the other scatological pieces of the period considerably gains in specificity of purpose if regarded as a reaction against such idealistic pretensions. In this vein, *Gulliver's Travels* (1726)—which, as we have seen, drastically undermines faith in humankind as an *animal rationale*—just as fundamentally questions the belief in humans as amiable, benevolent, and altruistic. There is good reason, therefore, to regard it as not least a response to the cultural climate which produced Hutcheson's idealistic *Inquiry* published only a year before (cf. also Wedel 23, who merely mentions Hutcheson, however). Though

Worshipping Cloacina 129

substantially finished before Hutcheson's *Inquiry* appeared in 1725, *Gulliver's Travels* can be seen as a reaction against the current of optimistic moral philosophy of which Hutcheson is merely one of the more prominent exponents.

In his comprehensive study of Swift, Ehrenpreis briefly outlines the satirist's view of the contemporary doctrine of natural benevolence as taught by Shaftesbury and others: "Swift believed that human nature had room for a moderate striving toward moral integrity, though sin and ignorance constantly drove this tendency back....Swift distrusted the psychology of natural benevolence taught by Latitudinarian preachers, and he hastened to disown Shaftesbury's 'free Whiggish'[6] *Letter concerning Enthusiasm*" (2: 288). As an adherent of the moral scepticism of his idols Montaigne, Pascal or La Rochefoucauld (cf. the resp. entries in Passmann and Vienken), Swift had no patience for the Whiggish liberalism implied in the beliefs of the moral sense school of Shaftesbury and his followers. Ehrenpreis does not, however, read Swift's satire in the scatological pieces in this context.

In a 1926 essay that is still worth reading, T.O. Wedel identifies "a revolution in ethical thought" (24) and describes as follows the new faith in human nature, in human reason and natural goodness, which had superseded the anthropological pessimism of the older Christian tradition: "The pessimism of Pascal has given way to the optimism of Leibnitz [*sic*]; the theory of self-love of La Rochefoucauld to the theory of benevolence of Hutcheson and Hume; the scepticism of Montaigne to the rationalism of Locke, Toland and Clarke" (ibid.). Thus, at a time when "Locke and the Deists had given man a new trust in Reason [and] the Cambridge Platonists and Shaftesbury were discovering in him a moral sense" (27), "Swift seems to have seen clearly enough that in assaulting man's pride in reason, he was attacking the new optimism at its very root" (31). Neither Wedel nor later critics, however, have consistently attempted to read the early eighteenth century's preoccupation with feces, excretion and other such drastic facts of life as a specific strategy in the demolition of this optimism.

Conclusion

In sum, what *Gulliver's Travels*, Swift's scatological poems, Pope's rendering of a diving-contest in the excrement-filled London sewer, Gay's emphasis on cloacal London, and Sterne's Madame de Rambouilet and her need to "p-ss" have in common is their insistent focus on the flip-side of the period's virtually disembodied emphasis on human rationality and sentimentality. The insistence upon anality, excrement, human stench, and bestiality can thus be read as a direct response drastically countering the period's ideal of humans as remarkably non-corporeal, purely intellectual or purely sentimental beings. Whether we look at human nature as envisaged by the moral sense school of Shaftesbury or Hutcheson, the "man of sympathy" of Adam Smith and David Hume or the novelists' "man of feeling," or whether we consider the period's widespread belief in mankind as an *animal rationale*—it is the seemingly boundless anthropological optimism in some quarters of eighteenth-century British philosophy and literature that can plausibly be regarded as the foil for Swift's, Pope's, Gay's and Sterne's insistence on the less than flattering physical nature of humanity. Such lofty pretensions of human rationality on the one hand and of human benevolence and moral perfectibility on the other hand, one can argue, are most effectively 'deflated' in the drastically literal sense of 'letting out' what really puffs up the human frame: trapped winds and excrements. By violating the taboo on excretion in their emphasis on such creaturely processes as defecation and urination, Swift and others blur the sacred boundary between human and animal and acutely point out the all-too-animal nature of humans. The implications of this drastic shift of emphasis for the period's lofty intellectual and moral pretensions are rather akin to those of Mandeville's insistence on egoism as the driving force of all human actions for the benevolist idealism of the moral sense school in the wake of Shaftesbury:

> [These] notions, I confess are generous and refined: They are a high Compliment to Human-kind, and capable by the help of a little Enthusiasm of inspiring us with the most Noble Sentiments concerning the Dignity of our exalted Nature: What Pity it is that they are not true. (Mandeville 1: 324)

Some fifty years ago, John Traugott stated: "One of the complications of literary history is that the modern term 'Enlightenment' is applied to a period that produced so many satirists whose principal study was to denigrate the human reason" (17). This "complication" upon closer inspection ceases to be one: It is precisely the frequently excessive optimism in enlightened conceptions of human rationality and morality which, as a countermovement, provoked the

Worshipping Cloacina ✱ 131

taboo-breaking denigrations of human reason and morality by Swift and Company.

Notes

1. Cloacine or Cloacina, "Goddess of common Sewers," also features prominently in Gay's "Trivia," cf. Gay II: 115ff., and in Pope's *Dunciad*, cf. II, 89ff. and *Dunciad Variorium* II, 93ff. Cf. my discussion in this chapter.
2. Cf. also "Strephon and Chloe" (1731), ll. 77–78, 161f. and 175–78; or "A Beautiful Young Nymph Going to Bed" (1731), where the vowel in the word "pist" [pissed] is replaced by hyphens (l. 62).
3. Cf. also "A Panegyric on the Dean," l. 216, and the passage in Sterne's *Sentimental Journey* quoted below.
4. Cf. also the nauseating survey of Swift's "The Lady's Dressing Room," which also appears to counter naïve idealizations of non-corporeal feminine beauty.
5. For a review of such optimistic assessments of human reason and moral capabilities cf. Gurr 19–50.
6. The reference is to Swift's "Letter to Ambrose Philips, 14 Sept. 1708," 206f.

Works Cited

Aden, John M. "Those Gaudy Tulips: Swift's 'Unprintables.'" *Quick Springs of Sense: Studies in the Eighteenth Century.* Ed. Larry S. Champion. Athens: U of Georgia P, 1974. 15–32.

Anchor, Robert. *The Enlightenment Tradition.* Berkeley: U of California P, 1967.

Bakhtin, Michail M. *Rabelais and His World.* Cambridge, MA: MIT Press, 1968.

Bataille, Georges. *L'érotisme.* Paris: Éd. de Minuit, 2001.

Brown, Norman O. "The Excremental Vision." *Life against Death: The Psychoanalytical Meaning of History.* London: Routledge and Kegan Paul, 1960.

Child, Paul W. "Once More into the Breech: Jonathan Swift and Excremental Medicine." *Swift Studies* 20 (2005): 82–101.

Davis, Herbert. *Jonathan Swift: Essays on His Satire and Other Studies.* Oxford: Oxford UP, 1964.

Douglas, Mary. *Purity and Danger: An Analysis of Concepts of Pollution and Taboo.* London: Routledge and Kegan Paul, 1966.

Eggert, Hartmut. "Säkuläre Tabus und die Probleme ihrer Darstellung: Thesen zur Eröffnung der Diskussion. " *Tabu und Tabubruch: Literarische*

132 ❦ *Jens Martin Gurr*

und sprachliche Strategien im 20. Jahrhundert. Eds. Hartmut Eggert and Janusz Golec. Stuttgart: Metzler, 2002. 15–24.

Ehrenpreis, Irvin. *Swift: The Man, his Works, and the Age.* Vol. 3. Cambridge, MA: Harvard UP, 1962–1982. 3 vols.

Elias, Norbert. *Über den Prozeß der Zivilisation: Soziogenetische und psychogenetische Untersuchungen.* Vol. 1. Frankfurt am Main: Suhrkamp, 1993.

Fabricant, Carole. *Swift's Landscape.* Baltimore: Johns Hopkins UP, 1982.

Frontain, Raymond-Jean. "Scatology in the Sophomore Survey; or, Teaching Swift as a Christian Satirist." *Critical Approaches to Teaching Swift.* Ed. Peter J. Schakel. New York: AMS Press, 1992. 297–305.

Gassenmeier, Michael. *Londondichtung als Politik: Texte und Kontexte der City Poetry von der Restauration bis zum Ende der Walpole-Ära.* Tübingen: Niemeyer, 1989.

Gay, John. "Trivia: Or, The Art of Walking the Streets of London." *Poetry and Prose.* Ed. Vinton A. Dearing. Oxford: Oxford UP, 1974. 1, 134–81.

Gilmore Jr., Thomas B. "The Comedy of Swift's Scatological Poems." *PMLA* 91.1 (1976): 33–43.

Gurr, Jens Martin. *Tristram Shandy and the Dialectic of Enlightenment.* Heidelberg: Winter, 1999.

Hornby, Nick. *A Long Way Down.* London: Viking, 2005.

Hunter, J. Paul. "*Gulliver's Travels* and the Later Writings." *The Cambridge Companion to Jonathan Swift.* Ed. Christopher Fox. Cambridge: Cambridge UP, 2003. 216–40.

Hutcheson, Francis. *An Inquiry into the Original of our Ideas of Beauty and Virtue. The Collected Works of Francis Hutcheson.* Facsim. Ed. Bernhard Fabian. Vol. 1. Hildesheim: Georg Olms, 1971.

Huxley, Aldous. *Do What You Will.* London: Chatto and Windus, 1970. 93–106.

Kristeva, Julia. *Powers of Horror: An Essay on Abjection.* New York: Columbia UP, 1982.

Locke, John. *An Essay Concerning Human Understanding.* Ed. Peter H. Nidditch. Oxford: Clarendon, 1975.

Mandeville, Bernard. *The Fable of the Bees: Or, Private Vices, Publick Benefits.* Ed. F.B. Kaye. Vol. 1. Oxford: Clarendon, 1924. 2 vols.

Meller, Horst. "Swifts Stadtsatiren und Gays Ursprungsmythos des Vierten Standes." *Irland: Gesellschaft und Kultur.* Ed. Dorothea Siegmund-Schultze. 4 vols. Halle an der Saale: Martin-Luther-Universität, 1985. 160–69.

Murry, John Middleton. *Jonathan Swift: A Critical Biography.* London: Jonathan Cape, 1954.

Nate, Richard. *Wissenschaft und Literatur im England der frühen Neuzeit.* Munich: Fink, 2001.

Passmann, Dirk F., and Heinz J. Vienken. *The Library and Reading of Jonathan Swift: A Bio-Bibliographical Handbook.* 4 vols. Frankfurt am Main: Lang, 2003.

Persels, Jeff, and Russel J. Ganim. "Scatology, the Last Taboo." *Fecal Matters in Early Modern Literature and Art: Studies in Scatology*. Eds. Jeff Persels and Russel J. Ganim. Aldershot: Ashgate, 2004.

Pollak, Ellen. "'Things, Which Must Not Be Exprest': Teaching Swift's Scatological Poems about Women." *Teaching Eighteenth-Century Poetry*. Ed. Christopher Fox. New York: AMS Press, 1990. 177–86.

Pope, Alexander. "The Dunciad Variorium." *The Poems of Alexander Pope: A One-Volume Edition of the Twickenham Text*. Ed. John Butt. London: Routledge, 1963a. 317–457.

———. "The Dunciad in Four Books." *The Poems of Alexander Pope: A One-Volume Edition of the Twickenham Text*. Ed. John Butt. London: Routledge, 1963b. 709–805.

Rawson, Claude J. "The Nightmares of Strephon: Nymphs of the City in the Poems of Swift, Baudelaire and Eliot." *English Literature in the Age of Disguise*. Ed. Maximillian E. Novak. Berkeley: U of California P, 1977. 57–99.

Real, Hermann J., and Heinz J. Vienken. *Jonathan Swift: Gulliver's Travels*. Munich: Fink, 1984.

Shaftesbury, Anthony Ashley Cooper, 3rd Earl of. *Characteristics of Men, Manners, Opinions, Times*. Ed. John M. Robertson. Introd. Stanley Grean. Indianapolis: Bobbs-Merrill, 1964.

Siebert, Donald T. "Swift's *Fiat Odor*: The Excremental Re-Vision." *Eighteenth-Century Studies* 19.1 (1985): 21–38.

Stallybrass, Peter, and Allon White. *The Politics and Poetics of Transgression*. London: Methuen, 1986.

Sterne, Laurence. *A Sentimental Journey through France and Italy*. Ed. Ian Jack. Oxford: Oxford UP, 1968.

Swift, Jonathan. "A Description of a City Shower." *The Writings of Jonathan Swift*. Eds. Robert A. Greenberg and William B. Piper. London, New York: Norton, 1973. 518–20.

———. "Letter to Sheridan, 11 September 1725." *The Writings of Jonathan Swift*. Eds. Robert A. Greenberg and William B. Piper. London, New York: Norton, 1973. 583–84.

———. "Letter to Pope, 29 September 1725." *The Writings of Jonathan Swift*. Eds. Robert A. Greenberg and William B. Piper. London, New York: Norton, 1973. 584–85.

———. "Letter to Pope, 26 November 1725." *The Writings of Jonathan Swift*. Eds. Robert A. Greenberg and William B. Piper. London, New York: Norton, 1973. 585–86.

———. *Gulliver's Travels*. *The Writings of Jonathan Swift*. Eds. Robert A. Greenberg and William B. Piper. London, New York: Norton, 1973. xi–260.

———. "The Lady's Dressing Room." *The Writings of Jonathan Swift*. Eds. Robert A. Greenberg and William B. Piper. London, New York: Norton, 1973. 535–38.

134 ❧ *Jens Martin Gurr*

Swift, Jonathan. "A Beautiful Young Nymph Going to Bed." *The Writings of Jonathan Swift*. Eds. Robert A. Greenberg and William B. Piper. London, New York: Norton, 1973. 538–40.

———. "Strephon and Chloe." *The Writings of Jonathan Swift*. Eds. Robert A. Greenberg and William B. Piper. London, New York: Norton, 1973. 540–47.

———. "Cassinus and Peter: A Tragical Elegy." *The Writings of Jonathan Swift*. Eds. Robert A. Greenberg and William B. Piper. London, New York: Norton, 1973. 547–50.

———. "A Panegyric on the Dean, in the Person of a Lady in the North." *The Complete Poems*. Ed. Pat Rogers. Harmondsworth: Penguin, 1983. 436–44.

———. "Letter to Ambrose Philips, 14 September 1708." *The Correspondence of Jonathan Swift, D.D.* Ed. David Woolley. 4 vols. Frankfurt am Main: Lang, 1999–2001. I, 206–7.

Traugott, John. *Tristram Shandy's World: Sterne's Philosophical Rhetoric*. Berkeley: U of California P, 1954.

Wedel, T.O. "On the Philosophical Background of *Gulliver's Travels*." *Studies in Philology* 23 (1926): 434–50.

Zimmerman, Everett. "Swift's Scatological Poetry: A Praise of Folly." *Modern Language Quarterly* 48.2 (1987): 124–44.

CHAPTER VII

THE ORGANIC UNCANNY: TABOO, SEXUALITY, AND DEATH IN BRITISH GOTHIC NOVELS

Stella Butter and Matthias Eitelmann

Gothic thrives on transgression: incest, rape, perversion, crime, insanity, and death are prominent themes within the Gothic tradition, which embodies an obsession with the darker side of human life. The recurrent violation of taboos represented in Gothic fiction is closely tied to its primary strategy of evoking terror and fear in the recipient. While one of the fundamental functions of taboos is to create a sense of security and social stability by means of excluding phenomena felt to be threatening along the axes of the sacred and profane and the pure and impure, the dialectical moment of transgression is at the same time constitutive for taboos (cf. Bataille). This paradoxical structure inherent to taboos helps to explain why we have the tendency to react with emotional ambivalence where taboos have been violated: we oscillate between fear and fascination, between "attraction and repulsion, worship and condemnation" (Punter 1996b, 190 with reference to Sigmund Freud), or, expressed in Gothic terms, we experience 'dreadful pleasure'. It is due to its pronounced focus on taboo areas of socio-psychological life that the Gothic imagination tends to realize "[o]ur 'psychological' fears...in very physical terms" (Morgan 6). The sheer endless tropes of bodily deviance and victimization in Gothic fictions cannot solely be seen as a "metaphorical reference to cultural situations" (92); instead, the represented "physicality is a medium of significance in and of itself" (ibid.). As Jack Morgan succinctly puts it, Gothic texts "expose taboo aspects of the fleshly reality we inhabit" (91).

136 &&& *Stella Butter and Matthias Eitelmann*

It is in the wake of the return of this repressed 'fleshly reality' with its attendant abject qualities that the organic is rendered uncanny (cf. 109). The interrelation of the uncanny with taboo was highlighted by Freud when he elaborated its Janus-faced quality: on the one hand, taboos demarcate both the realm of the holy and sacred; on the other hand, taboos signal danger, impurity and the uncanny (*unheimlich*) (cf. Freud 311). The feeling of the uncanny

> is perhaps inseparable from an apprehension...of something that should have remained secret and hidden but has come to light.... The uncanny has to do with a strangeness of framing and borders, an experience of liminality.... It may thus be construed as a foreign body within oneself, even the experience of oneself *as* a foreign body.... It would appear to be indissociably bound up with...the return of the repressed.... (Royle 2)

The uncanny points to 'our own foreignness' and it is this foreignness that is brought home in Gothic's exploration and invocation of a "biological plenum that defies rational mapping" (Morgan 3). If Gothic texts seek to address taboo-areas of life, especially deep-seated cultural anxieties regarding the uncanny dimension of physicality (cf. ibid.), then the predominance of themes related to sexuality and death in Gothic works comes as no surprise, since both can be considered as the two fundamental taboos in cultures and societies throughout the ages (cf. Bataille 52).

Since Gothic fiction deals with an array of culturally and historically specific taboos regarding sexuality and death, a reading of Gothic novels provides valuable insights into the changing literary (re)negotiations of threatening and thus tabooed physicality. The following analysis of selected Gothic novels will take as its point of departure works from the first heyday of Gothic writing (1764–1820). Although Gothic works from this age display stock characteristics, they are far from sharing the same value system regarding taboo areas, as close readings of works from the two most prominent Gothic writers during the late eighteenth century, Ann Radcliffe and Matthew Gregory Lewis, will show. Due to the fact that Radcliffe and Lewis have come to be associated with two different 'schools of Gothic'—the 'school of terror' and the 'school of horror' respectively—, a focus on the novels of these two authors serves to highlight two distinct approaches within eighteenth-century Gothic's exploration of tabooed physicality. The analyses will concentrate on Lewis's *The Monk* (1796) and Ann Radcliffe's *The Italian* (1797), the latter of which was written in response to the aesthetic challenge that *The Monk* presented to Radcliffe's previous Gothic fiction. In order to provide at least a brief insight into Gothic's still ongoing transmutations and (re)negotiation of the organic uncanny, this chapter will close with a look at New Gothic's treatment of taboo by drawing on Angela Carter's *The Magic Toyshop* (1967) as an illustrative example.

The School of Horror: Lewis's Visceral Gothic

The rise of the Gothic novel, which dominated the literary market during the 1790s, may be seen as a literary response to and reworking of social changes and political turmoil (first and foremost the French Revolution) that arose at the end of the eighteenth century in Europe (cf. MacLachlan xxi–xxii). This was also a period that was marked by important changes in the history of sexuality and death. The century's close brought with it a proliferation of sexual discourses as "[t]he flesh was brought down to the level of the organism" (Foucault 117) in the wake of a new "'technology' of sex" (90), which comprised the interrogation of sexuality along three axes of scientific discourse: pedagogical discourse with its focus on "the specific sexuality of children"; medical discourse, which raised the question of the "sexual physiology peculiar to women"; demographical discourse with its concern for birth regulation (cf. 116; cf. also Miles 1993, 21ff.). Fictional Gothic universes are located within this heightened scrutiny or rather problematization of sexuality—"the sexuality of children, mad men and women, and criminals; the sensuality of those who did not like the opposite sex; reveries, obsessions, petty manias, or great transports of rage" (Foucault 38f.; cf. also Miles 1993, 21).

Equally important changes were also taking place in the popular consciousness of death. The late eighteenth century was characterized by a growing and "unprecedented antipathy toward death in all its aspects" (Castle 130), which had its roots in "[c]hanging affectional patterns, the breakdown of communal social life, and the increasingly individualistic and secular nature of modern experience" (ibid.). Despite the efforts of science and philosophy to banish the fear of death through rational analysis (e.g., the increase in anatomical research), the widespread fear of premature burial, the first wave of which was during the 1740s and the second wave from approximately 1770 until 1780, testified to a growing anxiety regarding death (cf. Ariès 515ff.).[1] In the eighteenth century, the "previous cultural familiarity with death, its integration into life, turns into a retreat from death in a double gesture of denial and mystification" (Bronfen 86)—denial and mystification of death thereby correlating with the workings of a taboo (cf. Meier 175). These changes in the popular consciousness of sexuality and death during the first hey-day of Gothic fiction constitute an important foil for the following analyses of works written by Matthew Lewis and Ann Radcliffe. The analysis begins with Lewis's *The Monk* as a typical example of male Gothic, which incorporates "masculine plots of transgression of social taboos by an excessive male will, and explorations of the imag-ination's battle against religion, law, limitation and contingency" (Milbank 54), before moving on to Radcliffe's *The Italian*.

The main plot of Lewis's *The Monk* features the hypocritical Capuchin superior Ambrosio, who is idolized throughout Madrid for his apparent asceticism and virtue as well as his moving or rather sublime sermons. Ambrosio's satanic downfall sets in after his asso-ciate in the monastery, the novice Rosario, reveals himself to be a woman, namely Matilda, and seduces Ambrosio. The pent-up pas-sions of Ambrosio are thus released and, after tiring of Matilda, he finds a new object of desire in the fifteen-year-old Antonia, who is a paragon of virtue and innocence. The acts of depravity perpetrated by Ambrosio accumulate in a fast-rising rate, as he lets himself be drawn into sorcery and commits murder and incest. His first victim is Antonia's mother, Elvira, whom he kills to prevent her from pub-licly revealing his plans to seduce or rape Antonia. With demonic help, Ambrosio induces a state akin to death in Antonia, and carries her off to a crypt, where he brutally rapes and kills her on her awak-ening. Arrested for his crimes and faced with torture by the inqui-sition, Ambrosio, after initial reluctance, sells his soul to the devil in order to escape. The devil, however, cheats Ambrosio, and, after revealing that Matilda was a demon and that Ambrosio committed matricide and incest when he killed Elvira and raped Antonia, dashes Ambrosio from great height to the ground, where he suffers a tortur-ous and prolonged death. This main plot is thematically linked to a second plot about two lovers, Raymond and Agnes, who, after many painful struggles and obstacles, are reunited at the end of the novel. The two plots converge in a final climax, during which the rescuers of Agnes, who is imprisoned in a convent, also find Ambrosio in the crypt with the murdered Antonia.

This brief summary in itself already testifies to the fact that the central plot of the novel, which is focused on the monk Ambrosio, is

The Organic Uncanny ❧❧ 139

"structured around uncontrollable sexual desire and 'perverse' sexual transgression" (Haggerty 2004–5 [n. pag.])—the spectrum ranging from homosexuality to rape, incest and necrophilia. As Haggerty notes, the illicit desire of homosexuality is blatantly invoked in the relationship between Ambrosio and Rosario / Matilda. Due to the wide-spread assumption throughout the eighteenth century in England that sodomy was brought over to the homeland from Italy (and France) and that the monastery or convent were quite often breeding places for this 'contagion', Lewis is able to introduce homosexual overtones in his story by the mere combination of Catholicism / Italy, a monastery and the bonding between a monk and a blushing novice (cf. ibid.). The invocation of illicit homoeroticism becomes more pronounced due to moments of intimacy between Ambrosio and Rosario (cf. ibid.), for example when Ambrosio presses Rosario's hand "with tenderness" (*TM* 53) and tells him that when he first beheld him, he "perceived sensations…till then unknown" (*TM* 54) to him. Rosario's confession that he is in fact a woman ultimately does not neutralize the suspicion of same-sex desire, for the 'unveiling' of Rosario as female turns out to be, at least if the devil is to be believed, a re-veiling of the demon (whose gender is unclear) in a female costume (cf. Fincher [n. pag.]). Furthermore, one may argue that Rosario / Matilda's potentially ambiguous gender is aggravated by her performative "gender bending" (ibid.): She is capable both of manipulatively acting according to female gender stereotypes or rather behaving like the 'effeminate' Rosario (cf. *TM* 221: "she had resumed the character of the gentle interesting Rosario") and of assuming "a sort of courage and *manliness* in her manners and discourse" (*TM* 200; emphasis added).

In *The Monk*, the invoked "homoerotic desire is buried under a tableau of heterosexual libidinal excess" (Tuite [n. pag.]). The very excessiveness of the heterosexual libidinal economy (for example Ambrosio's lustful nights with Matilda, his erotic fantasies about Antonia and his raping her) reads as a symptom of an underlying anxiety about gender identity. In the Gothic world of Lewis's *The Monk*, the body is a text which is open to misinterpretation. The reader's expectations and the character's beliefs about the identity of bodies are constantly reversed (cf. Fincher [n. pag.]) as every 'unveiling' only constitutes a 'reveiling' in a different form (cf. ibid.; Tuite [n. pag.]). The uncanny quality of such 'inauthentic' bodies is expressed by Rosario / Matilda's status as one of Lucifer's "crafty spirit[s]" (*TM* 375) by the end of the story. Ultimately, the staged violation of

140 ▩ *Stella Butter and Matthias Eitelmann*

the taboo of homosexuality can be read as voicing "fears about the invisibility of queer bodies and desires" (Fincher [n. pag.]) in a time characterized by an increased monitoring of the body and sexuality (cf. ibid.).

The 'perverse' sexual transgression staged in *The Monk* also encompasses incest and necrophilia—two stock themes of Gothic literature of the time. Indeed, some critics have even gone as far as to speak of "Incest as the [!] Meaning of the Gothic novel" (Perry 261), claiming that the "Gothic novel's cultural work was to invest the incest motif with a new kind of foreboding" (ibid.). Gothic's 'cultural work' regarding incest may be better understood against the socio-cultural backdrop of the ongoing conflict between (what Foucault has termed) the 'deployment of alliance' and the 'deployment of sexuality'. While the relations of sex used to be regulated exclusively by the former paradigm, that is the "feudal systems of marriage, kinship, and inheritance" (Pollak 14), the eighteenth century witnessed, as noted above, the rise of a new apparatus of social discipline, namely the deployment of sexuality, which is concerned with an intensification of bodily sensations and which grants new importance to the conjugal family unit (cf. Foucault 106; Miles 1993, 22). The paradigm of (modern) sexuality conceives the family as "the most active site of sexuality" (Foucault 109) and "incest as both the model and the limit of desire" (Pollak 15).[2] While incest is strictly prohibited by the laws of alliance because it implies the "violation of genealogical principles and hence the short-circuiting of true succession" (Perry 269), it is something 'solicited (and refused)' by the deployment of sexuality in order for the family to be "a hotbed of constant sexual incitement" (Foucault 109; see also Perry 269). Given the fact that the deployment of sexuality did not eradicate the laws of alliance, but instead was superimposed on and often in conflict with these, incest constitutes a "peculiarly dense transfer point between two overlapping but distinct forms of cultural power" (Pollak 17). Gothic universes tap into these 'dense transfer points' of conflicting paradigms and explore contemporary fears and pleasures regarding the dispersion of sexuality across the family body (cf. Perry 275).[3]

Necrophilia, as another prevalent 'perverse' sexual transgression common in Gothic novels, takes on various shapes and forms in *The Monk*. One of the most prominent examples is the episode of the "Bleeding Nun." This episode is integrated into the second plot revolving around the 'star-crossed lovers' Don Raymond and Donna Agnes. The union of Agnes and Raymond—two nobles who have

The Organic Uncanny ✦ 141

fallen in love with each other—is ill-fated because Agnes's parents are (due to superstitious reasons) set on her taking the veil. In order to flee from the castle where she is being held by her family and elope with Raymond, the rationally-minded Agnes decides to disguise herself as the legendary Bleeding Nun, a ghost whom the inhabitants of the castle are in fear of. Raymond, however, suddenly finds himself in a (typical Gothic) nightmare when he discovers that the woman whom he spirited away from the castle and whom he pledged his body and soul to is not Agnes, but the Bleeding Nun or rather "an animated corpse" (*TM* 140). As it turns out, the Bleeding Nun is the ghost of Raymond's great-aunt, Beatrice de las Cisternas, who had during her life-time broken free of her enforced life in a convent to live as the concubine of Baron Lindenbergh; his brother Otto, whom she fell in love with, instigated her to murder his brother and afterward killed her. Since that time, she has been condemned to haunt the Castle of Lindenbergh as the Bleeding Nun—dressed in a blood-stained nun's habit, with a lamp and a large knife. The combination of the nun's veil and the blood stains points to the binary opposition in terms of gender stereotypes which Beatrice represents: While the veil is associated with female chastity, the symbol of blood implies defloration as well as menstruation and thus female sexuality (cf. Morse 52f.). One may argue that Beatrice literally becomes uncanny because she represents the return of the repressed, or rather those organic drives which are excluded in the ideal of de-sexualized womanhood dominant at the time.[4] In the case of Beatrice, the organic uncanny takes the shape of aggressive female sexuality.

The necrophilic fusion of sexuality and death in the figure of the Bleeding Nun, "a symbol of explosive female sexuality" (Kilgour 158), is striking.[5] The nightly haunting of Raymond by this 'animated corpse' is definitively sexual in nature, as she 'presses her cold lips to his' (cf. *TM* 141) and 'touches him with her rotting fingers' (cf. *TM* 142). Whereas the necrophilic nature of Raymond's sexually (and incestuously) charged encounters with his great-aunt Beatrice / the Bleeding Nun serve to heighten the horrors of an aggressive female sexuality, the necrophilic overtones in Ambrosio's rape of Antonia amidst the rotting bodies in a vault emphasize female passivity and objectification (cf. *TM* 324ff.).

The fact that necrophilia is part and parcel of most Gothic novels of the time raises the question as to what the reasons are for this marked affinity during the (mid-)eighteenth century between sexuality and death. One possible explanation is offered by the cultural construction of an "analogy between the aggressivity of death and the violence of love" (Bronfen 86) throughout this period. In a time of Enlightenment belief in rational control over inner and outer nature, sexuality and death were perceived as disruptive forces which could disturb "the autonomy and rationality of the self and...provok[e] a transgression of morality" (ibid.). An effective figure for this fear is necrophilia as it combines these two threatening realms of 'savage nature'. This observation, however, requires considerable socio-historical specification. In his study on sexuality and death in British Gothic novels, Franz Meier (175) emphasizes that the aristocracy, which constituted the dominant social class during the eighteenth century, and the middle classes displayed markedly different 'taboo concentrations' regarding sexuality and death. For the aristocracy, whose sexual permissiveness during the 'Regency' period in particular is notorious (albeit with the obligatory 'double standard' of sexual behavior), it is primarily death and less sexuality which poses a taboo. Meier relates this taboo concentration to the fact that the power and wealth of the aristocracy has a genealogical basis: while death contains the potential threat of a loss of power due to an extinction of the bloodline, sexuality is a means of continuing the very same. In contrast, the middle classes make use of a distinct sexual morality (or rather sexual taboos) to distance themselves from the aristocracy (cf. ibid.). In a time of social and economic conflict between the aristocracy and the middle classes, both make use of a distinct taboo structure as one way of marking their position. Despite these processes of social demarcation by means of differing taboo structures, the very fact that both sexuality and death share the role of the taboo provides a link between them, which becomes further pronounced due to the close interaction between the aristocracy and the middle classes in the wake of their social conflict (cf. ibid.).

Gothic novels play on cultural anxieties regarding death and sexuality by drastically undermining the cultural myths and taboos set up as a means of taming and regulating these areas of experience. The popular notion of sentimental reunion in the afterlife, which can be read as a form of 'mystification' of death, is explicitly evoked by Antonia when she tells Ambrosio, "we shall one day meet in heaven: there shall our friendship be renewed" (*TM* 293). Antonia's 'resurrection' in the family vault to a necrophilic universe of brutal rape and murder not only caters to the prevalent hysterical fear of premature burial, but sets the stark reality of rotting flesh, of the

The Organic Uncanny ❈❈❈ 143

organic uncanny, against the vision of blissful disembodied spirits in the afterworld. In a similar vein, Ambrosio's seven-day death torment at the end of the novel—Satan's gruesome parody of Genesis (cf. Kilgour 162)—does not leave the reader with a sense of satisfactory closure in the sense that in the death of the villain a metaphysical justice prevails. Instead, the "theatrical excess of his broken, insect-eaten 'corpse' calls into question the divine justice that has inflicted such gruesome torments upon it. . . . [The] closure [is] destabilised by its very excess (it appears less divine, than pagan, brutal and arbitrary)" (Miles 2000, 54). Scenes such as the description of Ambrosio's death with its lurid details of myriads of insects feasting upon his sores, eagles tearing his flesh and scratching out his eyeballs, serve to emphasize "the condition of being flesh and blood" (Clive Barker, qtd. in Booe 8). It is the defiled and degraded body which is granted center stage and as such it seems fitting that the novel closes with "the river [carrying away] the corpse of the despairing monk" (*TM* 377).

The School of Terror: Ann Radcliffe's 'Polite Gothic'

Whereas the abject body is described with "libidinous minuteness" (Miles 2000, 41) in Lewis's *The Monk*, one finds very different strategies of transgression in the Gothic works of Ann Radcliffe, who "stood as the unrivalled head of her own school of [Gothic] fiction" (ibid. 2004, vii). Radcliffe's distinction between 'terror and horror', which she introduced in her posthumously published essay "On the Supernatural in Poetry" (1826), constitutes a helpful point of departure for identifying and contextualizing the different literary practices of Lewis and Radcliffe in their negotiation of tabooed areas. In her famous and much quoted essay, Radcliffe argues that only terror is a source of the sublime and is therefore to be preferred to horror: "Terror and horror are so far opposite, that the first expands the soul, and awakens the faculties to a high degree of life; the other contracts, freezes, and nearly annihilates them" (Radcliffe 1826, 150). The difference between terror and horror is directly linked with materiality (cf. Miles 2000, 41). Whereas terror depends on "uncertainty and obscurity" (Radcliffe 1826, 150) and is thus very much a matter of the mind or imagination, horror is a result of the threat made manifest in concrete shape, that is, the real presence of a ghost or actual physical injury carried out. Radcliffe's interest in the landscapes of the mind, rather than the supernatural as such, offers one reason why she consistently explains the (seemingly) supernatural as the result of natural causes in her Gothic works (cf. Miles 2000, 50). The differences between Radcliffe and Lewis may be succinctly summed up in a series of oppositions: female versus male Gothic, explained versus unexplained supernatural events, and terror versus horror (cf. 45). With regard to the treatment of taboo, Radcliffe's focus on sublime terror means that she avoids the direct description of shocking events, actions or objects (cf. Shapira 455).

While Lewis's *The Monk* follows "'Sadean' sensationalism" (Miles 2000, 41) and revels in descriptions of the abject body, Radcliffe's Gothic and its treatment of corporeality is indebted to the novel of sensibility and follows the code of delicacy (cf. ibid.). Radcliffe's emphasis on a "decorous management of the body" (ibid.), especially the female body, in her Gothic worlds, is linked to the precarious status of female authors in the eighteenth century. The cultural ideal of chaste and delicate womanhood, with its concomitant decorous erasure of the female body, "severely limits women's ability to represent the body at all in language, a matter of obvious consequence for the woman writer" (455).

Lewis's shocking treatment of the body in *The Monk* posed a profound challenge for Radcliffe's 'polite Gothic', which was based on an idealist notion of sensibility (cf. Miles 1995, 170f.). According to this notion of Enlightenment thinking, humans possess an innate moral instinct, which leads them to find scenes of vice abhorrent while approving of scenes of benevolence. The staging of virtue in distress in literature was therefore seen as a means of improving sensibility and thus true virtue by addressing the benevolent side of mankind. Such notions of sensibility are scandalously satirized in *The Monk*, which stages 'virtue in distress' as having a titillating effect (cf. ibid.). Moreover, Lewis also radically questions the notion of sensibility "as *heightened consciousness*, as the capacity to *penetrate beyond physical surfaces*" (Conger 114)—to the soul veiled by the human face or God veiled by the face of nature (cf. ibid. 133). A stark contrast to such a notion is formed by the mask-like faces in *The Monk*, which even characters with heightened sensibility (e.g., Antonia, Elvira) are not capable of reading (cf. ibid.), to name just one example. In the place of an idealist notion of sensibility, Lewis asserts a materialist one where sensibility is primarily associated with the sensual (cf. ibid. 119ff.).

Radcliffe rose to the challenge *The Monk* presented for her own aesthetics by answering with a fictional revision of Lewis's novel—*The*

The Organic Uncanny ❦ 145

Italian. Radcliffe's last novel published during her lifetime presents an especially interesting example of her literary negotiation of taboo and transgression, for *The Italian* entails a "re-working and re-assessment of her art" (Miles 1995, 156) in the light of the ideological emphases of the times[6] and the profound challenge posed by the sensationalism of *The Monk*.

The Italian to some extent marks a departure from the typical Radcliffean plot (cf. ibid. 150), for it is not the heroine, Ellena, who is persecuted by the marital plans of her family and is in flight from an abhorrent patriarch; instead, it is the male suitor, Vivaldi, who meets with the strong opposition of his aristocratic parents, especially his mother, the Marchesa, when he informs them of his wish to marry the genteel, but poverty-stricken orphan Ellena. The Marchesa conspires with her confessor Schedoni to thwart Vivaldi's marital plans. Ellena is kidnapped and whisked away to the dreadful convent San Stefano, but rescued sometime later by Vivaldi. The lovers' clandestine marriage is prevented by Schedoni, who arranges for the Inquisition to apprehend Vivaldi while Ellena is taken to a sinister shelter to be murdered. When Schedoni's villainous accomplice Spalatro refuses to stab Ellena to death, Schedoni decides to carry out the crime himself, but changes his mind when he discovers that Ellena seems to be his long-lost daughter. Realizing that the marriage of his daughter with the heir of the Vivaldi family is the perfect means to gratify his ambition to power, money, and influence, Schedoni is now set on making the match between Ellena and Vivaldi possible. Meanwhile, in the dungeon of the Inquisition, Vivaldi has several mysterious encounters with an ecclesiastic, who later turns out to be Nicola di Zampari (a former associate of Schedoni's). Nicola, who is set on harming Schedoni, brings information about his former life and crimes to light: Schedoni murdered his brother, the Count di Bruno (Ellena's real father), and raped his brother's wife. As a result of these revelations, Schedoni is arrested by the Inquisition, but evades their punishment by poisoning himself and Nicola. In the end, Ellena discovers that her mother is still alive and is in fact the nun Olivia, whom she had formed an attachment to during her time in the convent San Stefano. Vivaldi and Ellena, whose spotless aristocratic genealogy and respectable heritage is established, marry with the consent of the parents.

The markedly different styles Radcliffe and Lewis employ in their treatment of tabooed areas are especially apparent when taking a closer look at the scene in which Schedoni is about to murder Ellena. Whereas in *The Monk* the proliferation of transgressions is rendered explicitly and with relish, incestuous rape is first only hinted at in this scene in *The Italian*, and second not actually committed. Overtones of rape are brought to the reader's mind both on account of "the iconography of the scene (Schedoni first removes the 'lawn' from Ellena's breast [before he plans to stab / penetrate her with a phallic knife]) and the allusions to Lewis" (Miles 1993, 171), that is, the scene is modeled on Ambrosio's nightly penetration of Antonia's chamber to rape her (cf. ibid.). Moreover, the quotation from Walpole's *The Mysterious Mother* (1768)—a play concerned with incest—that serves as epigraph of the very first chapter of *The Italian*, in combination with Schedoni's discovery that Ellena apparently is his daughter also implies the incest taboo (cf. ibid.). The transgressive sexuality of incest is invoked at the beginning of Radcliffe's novel, but the act is forestalled (figuratively) when Schedoni discovers, along with the identity of Ellena, a surprisingly tender "fullness of his heart" (*TI* 274; cf. ibid.). By contrast, in the parallel scene in *The Monk*, Elvira's frustration of Ambrosio's attempted incestuous rape of Antonia leads him to commit a different act of barbarity (matricide) before following his plans of rape through at a later time. Rewritings of central scenes such as these in *The Italian* have caused critics to describe Radcliffe's "revisionary efforts" (Conger 129) as 'sensibility restored' (ibid.).

Whereas Lewis's *The Monk* is littered with abject bodies (cf. Shapira 466), Radcliffe "de-emphasizes the body's material presence and implicitly contains its scrutiny within a polite discourse of sensibility" (464). A case in point is the distancing of death as abject corporeality: Instead of the sensual descriptions of corpses (e.g., their look and smell) offered in Lewis's Gothic worlds, one encounters only metonymic displacements (e.g., "bloody garments," *TI* 458; cf. Shapira 465) or a displacement of the body "from the primary diegetic surface…[to its embedding in] visions, anxious fantasies, tales of dubious truth-value" (Shapira 465). Lewis's *The Monk* gleefully draws attention to what the discourses of delicacy and sensibility underpinning Radcliffe's Gothic novels leave out: the materiality and abject quality of the defiled and corrupted organic body. The organic uncanny or rather "[t]he body that Radcliffe laboured to conceal returned, with a vengeance, and took its place at the forefront of the Gothic" (466).

The Organic Uncanny ❦ 147

By presenting a decorous version of Lewis's text, Radcliffe both signaled her own propriety (473) and engaged in a re-negotiation of her idealist notion of sensibility—a re-negotiation that bears deep traces of ambivalence. On the one hand, Radcliffe presents sensibility in *The Italian* as the faculty which renders humans humane and may prevent them from nefarious taboo violations such as murder (cf. also Miles 1995, 164). Thus, it is only in a (brief) moment of awakening sensibility that the Marchesa feels any stirrings of compassion for Ellena, whom she is plotting to have murdered by Schedoni. Moreover, the portrayal of the order of Our Lady of Piety posits the convent as a (utopian) female realm, where "sensibility is [realigned] with private, feminine virtues, to present it as an alternative mode of self-fulfillment" (Conger 139). However, the ambivalence about an idealist notion of sensibility running through *The Italian* becomes clear in view of Schedoni's voicing "the language of philosophical libertinage in accents reminiscent of De Sade's blasphemous free-thinkers" (Miles 1995, 162). Schedoni articulates a world of moral relativism by arguing that custom and law are merely "vulgar prejudice" (*TI*, 202) and that morality is to be drawn from an inner sense of justice (cf. *TI* 203: "Why should we hesitate to do what we judge to be right [i.e., Ellena's murder]!"; cf. Miles 1995, 164). The supposedly innate sense of justice (and by extension morality) Vivaldi and Ellena constantly appeal to is thus seriously thrown into question (cf. ibid.). The "'sub-textual' doubt" (172) woven into the fabric of Radcliffe's earlier Gothic novels regarding the "validity of sensibility as both the instrument and the character of a dawning [enlightened] new age" (ibid.) becomes markedly more pronounced in *The Italian* (cf. ibid.).[7]

All in all, the analyses of Lewis's *The Monk* and Radcliffe's *The Italian* have shown that despite the formulaic structure of Gothic novels with its stock theme of transgressions of all sorts, the treatment of the tabooed areas of sexuality and death are fundamentally different in these two styles of Gothic writing. The vivid portrayal of the organic uncanny and the parodying of a Radcliffean sensibility in *The Monk* testify to a "materialist ethic" (Conger 143) that gives rise to a world of brutal violence and self-destruction "in which fellow-feeling can effect little more than graceful death" (ibid.). In contrast, the appeal to an idealistic ethical system with its insistence on going beyond "the level of material sensation" (144) and the tribute paid to the discourse of delicacy make for a decidedly different negotiation of taboo and transgression in Radcliffe's *The Italian*.

New Gothic: Angela Carter's *The Magic Toyshop* (1967)

Themes characteristic for Gothic texts of the eighteenth century— that is, "the legacies of the past and its burdens on the present; the radically provisional or divided nature of the self; the construction of peoples or individuals as monstrous or 'other'..." (Spooner 8)— continue to be prominent in Gothic texts of the nineteenth and twentieth centuries as well as in contemporary Gothic literature. New Gothic, as the return of Gothic motifs and stereotypes in contemporary fiction is generally referred to, has boomed since the late 1960s, with the Gothic "compositional vocabulary (scenic and linguistic)" (Sage and Smith 1) surfacing in all kinds of genres (cf. Sage 89). Various textual strategies are made use of in order to evoke the Gothic literary tradition, often in an act of innovative genre renewal, for example by means of genre hybridization or meta-fictional foregroundings (cf. Butter and Eitelmann). What is striking about contemporary Gothic, is the increasing popularity of 'comic Gothic' with its focus on evoking ambivalent laughter in the recipient (as opposed to 'serious Gothic', which is aimed at generating fear and terror).[8] The comic mode has far-reaching implications for this genre's handling of taboo and transgression.

While the (organic) uncanny continues to be featured in a wealth of comic Gothic novels—the New Gothic novels of Patrick McGrath (e.g., *The Grotesque* [1989], *Spider* [1990]) or Iain Banks (e.g., *The Wasp Factory* [1984]) may be taken as a case in point—, it is the exuberance of the carnivalesque (*sensu* Mikhail Bakhtin) which gives (New) Comic Gothic its distinct flavor and which in turn shapes the negotiation of tabooed areas in these literary works. Both the organic uncanny and the carnivalesque are concerned with the "degradational return to 'the material bodily principle'" (Morgan 25), they differ, however, in their emotive qualities (cf. ibid.): Whereas the 'material bodily principle' in the carnivalesque has a regenerating and liberating aspect— terror is "turned into something gay and comic" (Bakhtin 39)—, the biological plenum of the organic uncanny is devoid of "the elements of built-in upswing, of rejuvenation" (Morgan 25). In many cases, however, elements of the uncanny and the carnivalesque interplay so that a clear-cut distinction is not always possible.[9]

Angela Carter's *The Magic Toyshop* (1967) offers an especially interesting example of how the pronounced carnivalesque in comic Gothic bears consequences for the handling of the stock theme of tabooed

The Organic Uncanny ❦ 149

sexuality. The use of conventional Gothic motifs—which, from the beginning, have been suffused with rigid male-female dichotomies and patriarchal hierarchies—enables Carter to emplot a profound critique of the subject's enmeshment in gender stereotypes and to expose the destructive and violent implications thereof. At the same time, however, the transgressional aspects are given a new twist uncommon for traditional Gothic: in this case, incest as utopia.

The plot of *The Magic Toyshop* focuses on fifteen-year-old Melanie, whose parents died in a plane crash. She and her younger siblings, her brother Jonathan and her mentally challenged sister Victoria, then move into the house of her mother's brother: her Uncle Philip Flower, who is the owner of the toyshop which the title of the novel refers to. Similar to the villains in Gothic fiction, Uncle Philip terrorizes his wife Margaret (who has tellingly fallen silent since their wedding night) and her Irish brothers Finn and Francie. His patriarchal reign of terror is most obvious in the cellar of his toyshop where Philip has set up a puppet theater on which he stages his perverse visions of ideal gender relationships. Moreover, he abuses Melanie as a submissive marionette by making her play the role of Leda in his production that adapts the Greek myth of Leda and Jove. In his interpretation, the encounter is depicted as a brutal rape scene, concentrating on the question of how "Almighty Jove in the form of a swan wreaks his will" (*TMT* 166). For Finn, who is sexually attracted to Melanie and who is forced to witness Melanie's traumatization, this performance eventually functions as a catalyst: He breaks out of his uncle's oppression and destroys the grotesque swan. In the following, the destruction of the swan is celebrated by the other members of the family in a boisterous and orgiastic manner. In the course of the carnivalesque celebration, Melanie realizes that her aunt Margaret and Francie have an incestuous relationship—which Philip also finds out when he surprisingly returns right at the climax of the celebration. As a consequence of his discovery, the palpable violence escalates as Philip sets his house on fire. The novel closes with the idyllic prospect of a future love relationship between Melanie and Finn, in phrases reminiscent of the biblical narrative of the Garden of Eden: "At night, in the garden, they faced each other in a wild surmise" (*TMT* 200). Yet, the idyll sketched at the end is highly questionable as "the young lovers' Eden is hardly paradise, and the death of the tyrant-god condemns them, in a truly Sartrean sense, to be free" (Smith 358).

The preceding short summary illustrates the extent to which *The Magic Toyshop* follows the generic foil of the Gothic novel and the key function which the transgression of the incest taboo has at the climax of the novel. The plot is, as is typical of the Gothic genre, structured around the theme / motif of the 'damsel in distress', which, albeit latent at first, culminates in Melanie's symbolic rape through Uncle Philip's grotesque swan at the end of the performance. A Gothic framework is invoked through explicit intertextual references (e.g., to Edgar Allan Poe and the Hammer horror films[10], cf. *TMT* 93, 122) as well as through the Gothic description of the toyshop itself—"a dark cavern of the shop" (*TMT* 39), which reminds Melanie of "Bluebeard's castle...[with] chopped up corpses neatly piled in all the wardrobes" (*TMT* 83).

It is significant that the fairytale of Bluebeard, which functions as a reference foil of Melanie's experiential reality in her uncle's household, is essentially an archetypal tale of taboo-violation in which the prohibited entrance into the secret room signifies the initiation into sexual secrets (cf. Bettelheim 299–303). The evoked fairytale of Bluebeard draws attention to the fact that Melanie's gender identity is modeled to a great extent on patriarchal concepts of femininity, for European fairytales thrive on gender clichés and constitute a means of perpetuating gender dichotomies of ideal masculinity and femininity in oral or literal traditions (cf. Wagener 122f.). The ubiquity of these gender stereotypes in the Western (literary) imagination is highlighted by the sheer density of intertextual allusions in *The Magic Toyshop*, ranging from diverse fairytales such as the above-mentioned Bluebeard or Sleeping Beauty, to biblical texts as well as to Yeats's "Leda and the Swan." Carter, though, challenges such patriarchal concepts of femininity by exposing their discursive nature as well as their inherent physical and psychological violence. The 'violence of gendering' (cf. Wyatt) is especially foregrounded by focalizing the experiences in Bluebeard's castle through a female perspective, namely Melanie's.

The patriarchal ideal of reducing woman to an object status is realized aesthetically and most pointedly in Philip's puppet theater the moment Melanie takes at his command the part of Leda. By making the atmospheric violence (of gendering) explicit in a scene in which Melanie is "subjected to rape by simulacrum" (Smith 349), Carter breaks the taboo of sexual violence. As soon as the puppet swan attacks Melanie during the performance, she acts as her uncle's

The Organic Uncanny ❦ 151

script demands, turning into a marionette and thereby completely submitting to him. The oversized and thus grotesque proportions of the wooden swan, though, debunk the patriarchal notion of natural superiority. The staging of Leda's rape, which is also Melanie's in a metaphorical sense, is pervaded by a moment of dark ridicule: "The gilded beak dug deeply into the soft flesh. She screamed, hardly realising she was screaming. She was covered completely by the swan but for her kicking feet and her screaming face. The obscene swan had mounted her" (*TMT* 167). The tension between elements of terror and comic absurdity in this scene may provoke 'ambivalent laughter' (cf. Fuß 100) as a reader response, which is typical for the comic strain of New Gothic novels.

Uncle Philip's script for Melanie in his play, modeled on patriarchal notions of femininity, eventually implies the obliteration of the self, which becomes manifest when Melanie 'learns' in the course of her traumatic experience to see herself as an object and not as an active agent (cf. *TMT* 166). Melanie's 'lesson in femininity' highlights how gender identity is in effect a cultural construct rather than a natural ontological reality: the clearly allocated gender roles in Philip's play literally follow a patriarchal script, thus exposing gender identity as mere spectacle and performance.[11]

What challenges the Gothic patriarchal bulwark in *The Magic Toyshop* and shakes it to its very foundations, however, is the breaking of the incest taboo at the climax of the novel. Ultimately, a double breaking of the incest taboo is staged: first, by depicting a culturally tabooed incestuous relationship; and second, by de-tabooing the incest taboo and recoding it as a utopian concept challenging patriarchal notions. The disruption of patriarchal values through means of the depicted incest becomes manifest in the literal destruction of the Gothic fortress, that is the magic toyshop, on Philip's discovery of the incestuous love between his wife and her brother (cf. Monson-Rosen 234). It is precisely at this point that Philip loses his omnipotent status within his extended family. The significance incest is granted in *The Magic Toyshop* implies a specific functionalization and resemanticization of incest which differs drastically from the way the incest taboo was approached in Lewis' *The Monk* or Radcliffe's *The Italian*. In Carter's *The Magic Toyshop*, incest is envisioned as a utopian counter-concept which demolishes any culturally constructed gender boundaries. In this way, the traditionally heterosexual romance plot is contrasted with an alternative eroticized brother-sister-relationship consummated in a transgressional celebration of sexuality, or rather in a carni-valesque orgy:

> The incest model then serves to inscribe a heterosexual love that is outside the realm of the interwoven structures of societal patriarchy, heterosexual hegemony, and conventional romance. Carter offers a model for a relationship conceived outside of naturalizing patriarchal law, and, in violating that most primal of laws, she shakes the myth of patriarchy at its very core. (236)

The utopian notion of incest is even more strengthened by the fact that an incestuous relationship is not limited to Margaret and Francie but also refers to Melanie and Finn for they, too, develop a symbolic brother-sister-relationship as is emphasized several times in the novel (234ff.). The "post-patriarchal heterosexuality" (235) that gradually evolves between Melanie and Finn is visualized succinctly in Finn's destruction of Uncle Philip's grotesque swan—which, in effect, implies Philip Flower's symbolic castration. A proper debunking of the phallic body takes place when Finn reports how he hid the swan under his coat and imagines how passers-by must have perceived him at this exact moment: "It must have looked, to a passer-by, as if I was indecently exposing myself, when the swan's neck stuck out" (*TMT* 173). The phallus, swelled up to huge propor-tions and visible to everybody due to its unreal over-size, is thus exposed as a mere construct of patriarchal myth-making—a real-ization that corresponds to the parodistic functional potential of Gothic fiction: "The Gothic mode is essentially a form of parody, a way of assailing clichés by exaggerating them to the limits of gro-tesqueness" (Fiedler 452).

As this brief discussion of Carter's *The Magic Toyshop* as an exam-ple of the comic strain of New Gothic shows, Gothic's negotiation of taboo and transgression cannot be reduced to stock formulaic struc-tures, but instead encompasses a wealth of ever changing forms and functions. In contemporary culture, Gothic has "consolidated its position as the material of mainstream entertainment" (Spooner 25), with Gothic films and TV series (e.g., *American Gothic* [1995–96]; *Buffy the Vampire Slayer* [1997–2003]) enjoying huge commercial suc-cess. While Gothic works are not in all cases necessarily subversive, but may instead be deeply conservative, even racist, xenophobic, and sexist, Gothic does provide "a language and a set of discourses with which we can talk about fear and anxiety" (30)—especially fears

The Organic Uncanny ❦ 153

related to taboos surrounding the organic uncanny. This may help to explain the popularity and relevance of Gothic in present times.

Notes

1. Throughout the sixteenth, seventeenth, and eighteenth centuries death was perceived as a liminal state. Death only became real or rather absolute at the moment of bodily decomposition—that is why the embalmment of the body was seen to prolong the moment until absolute death (cf. Ariès 514). The eighteenth century, however, marked a shift in mentality insofar as the liminal state between life and death was no longer conceptualized as life infringing on death (e.g., the corpses display signs of life, such as sweating, the growth of nails and hair), but rather that death encroaches on life: The signs of death are lodged in the midst of life—as in the case of apparent death (cf. ibid.). The literary tradition of the erotic macabre which flourished throughout the sixteenth, seventeenth, and eighteenth centuries thus has its roots in decidedly different perceptions of death. For detailed information on changing attitudes toward death in Western society see Philippe Ariès' seminal study *The Hour of Our Death* (1981); for a concise summary of cultural constructions of death in English society during the eighteenth and nineteenth centuries, see Meier and Bronfen.

2. Cf. Pollak 14 with reference to Foucault 109: "[I]ncest...is constantly being solicited and refused; it is an object of obsession and attraction, a dreadful secret and an indispensable pivot. It is manifested as a thing that is strictly forbidden in the family insofar as the latter functions as a deployment of alliance; but it is also a thing that is continuously demanded in order for the family to be a hotbed of constant sexual incitement." Modern sexuality and kinship relations are deeply enmeshed: The conjugal family unit became the privileged point for the development of the deployment of sexuality *and* at the same time "reciprocally dependent for its survival on the production of incestuous desire."

3. As Miles 1993, 25f., drawing on Foucault and Stone, emphasizes in his study on *Gothic Writing*, the "head-on clash between two systems of values" (Stone 157), one of which "demanded total conformity in deeds and words and even in secret thoughts to the collective [patriarchal] will as expressed by the state and the official Church" (ibid.), while the other "insisted on the right of the individual to a certain freedom of action and inner belief" (ibid.), or in Foucault's terminology, the tension between the deployments of alliance and sexuality, goes a long way in explaining the (at first glance) puzzling phenomenon that Gothic novels dwell extensively on the power of patriarchy despite its

marked weakness in the late eighteenth century. For a depiction of the loosening of patriarchal structures during the eighteenth century (cf. ibid.).

4. While the eighteenth century witnessed sexual permissiveness, the 'double standard' of sexual behavior was still upheld among the upper classes: "According to this convention, the husband enjoyed full monopoly rights over the sexual services of his wife, who was expected to be a virgin on her wedding night.... On the other hand, the man was expected to have gained some sexual experience before marriage, and any infidelities after marriage were treated as venial sins which the sensible wife was advised to overlook. Thus, both fornication and adultery were exclusively male prerogatives at this social level..." (ibid. 315). While a "man's honour depended on the reliability of his spoken word; a women's honour [depended] on her reputation for chastity" (316).

5. For a discussion of significant parallels between the figure of the Bleeding Nun and Agnes cf. Kilgour 157ff.

6. For a concise depiction of the change in attitudes and value judgements regarding sensibility, especially in the wake of the French Revolution, cf. Miles 1995, 149–73.

7. For an in-depth analysis of Radcliffe's ambivalent treatment of sensibility in *The Italian*, cf. ibid., 145–73.

8. In their seminal study on comic Gothic, Avril Horner, and Sue Zlosnik point out that even traditional Gothic has a close affinity to the comic mode, which often results from the sheer excessiveness with which the protagonists' feelings are depicted: "[T]he stylized theatricality of the Gothic device...is always teetering on the edge of self-parody" (12).

9. Cf. also Spooner 68f.: "In what I am calling the 'Gothic-Carnivalesque', the sinister is continually shading into the comic and vice versa."

10. The Hammer films of the 1950s to early 1970s are heavily indebted to the Gothic tradition with their famed adaptations of *Dracula* and *Frankenstein*.

11. The foregrounding of the constructivist character of gender identity is a recurrent theme from the very beginning of *The Magic Toyshop*, culminating in Philip's performance. Even before Melanie moves into her uncle's house, her bodily self-exploration is paralleled with the expeditions of various male conquerors ("Cortez, da Gama or Mungo Park"; *TMT* 1); the poses she imitates in front of her mirror resemble the paintings of male artists, and her awakening sexuality conspicuously goes along with her reading D.H. Lawrence's *Lady Chatterley's Lover* (cf. *TMT* 1f.). The dominance of male authorities in the context of her adolescence undermines the notion of an autonomous development and emphasizes the discursive character and the cultural specificity of gender identity (cf. Wyatt 69).

The Organic Uncanny ❖ 155

Works Cited

Ariès, Philippe. *Geschichte des Todes*. 1982. Munich: dtv, 1993.

Bakhtin, Mikhail. *Rabelais and His World*. Bloomington: Indiana UP, 1984.

Bataille, Georges. *Die Erotik*. Ed. Gerd Bergfleth. Munich: Matthes and Seitz, 1994.

Bettelheim, Bruno. *The Uses of Enchantment. The Meaning and Importance of Fairy Tales*. Harmondsworth: Penguin, 1978.

Booe, Martin. Interview with Clive Barker. "Deliciously Terrifying." *U.S.A. Weekend*. January 26–28, 1990. 8.

Bronfen, Elisabeth. *Over Her Dead Body. Death, Femininity and the Aesthetic*. Manchester: Manchester UP, 1992.

Butter, Stella, and Matthias Eitelmann. "*New Gothic*: Angela Carter." *Der zeitgenössische englische Roman. Genres—Entwicklungen—Modellinterpretationen*. Ed. Vera Nünning. Trier: WVT, 2007. 163–79.

Carter, Angela. *The Magic Toyshop*. London: Virago Press, 1994.

Castle, Terry. *The Female Thermometer. 18th-Century Culture and the Invention of the Uncanny*. Oxford: Oxford UP, 1995.

Conger, Syndy M. "Sensibility Restored: Radcliffe's Answer to Lewis's *The Monk*." *Gothic Fictions. Prohibition/Transgression*. Ed. Kenneth W. Graham. New York: Ams Press, 1989. 113–49.

Fiedler, Leslie. *Love and Death in the American Novel*. New York: Stein and Day, 1960.

Fincher, Max. "The Gothic as Camp: Queer Aesthetics in *The Monk*." *Romanticism on the Net* 44 (2006). *érudit*. February 17, 2009 <http://www.erudit.org/>.

Foucault, Michel. *The History of Sexuality*. Vol. 1. London: Penguin, 1990.

Freud, Sigmund. "Totem und Tabu." *Studienausgabe. Fragen der Gesellschaft. Ursprünge der Religion*. Ed. Alexander Mitscherlich, Angela Richards, and James Strachey. Vol. IX. Frankfurt: Fischer, 2000. 287–444.

Fuß, Peter. *Das Groteske: Ein Medium des kulturellen Wandels*. Köln: Böhlau, 2001.

Haggerty, George E. "The Horrors of Catholicism: Religion and Sexuality in Gothic Fiction." *Romanticism on the Net* 36–37 (2004–5). *érudit*. February 17, 2009 <http://www.erudit.org/>.

Horner, Avril, and Sue Zlosnik. *Gothic and the Comic Turn*. Basingstoke: Palgrave Macmillan, 2005.

Kilgour, Maggie. *The Rise of the Gothic Novel*. London: Routledge, 1995.

Lewis, Matthew. *The Monk. A Romance*. London: Penguin, 1998.

MacLachlan, Christopher. "Introduction." *The Monk. A Romance*. By Matthew Lewis. London: Penguin, 1998. vii–xxv.

Meier, Franz. *Sexualität und Tod. Eine Themenverknüpfung in der englischen Schauer- und Sensationsliteratur und ihrem soziokulturellen Kontext (1764–1897)*. Tübingen: Niemeyer, 2002.

156 &&& *Stella Butter and Matthias Eitelmann*

Milbank, Alison. "Female Gothic." *The Handbook to Gothic Literature.* Ed. Marie Mulvey-Roberts. London: Macmillan, 1998. 53–57.

Miles, Robert. *Gothic Writing 1750–1820. A Genealogy.* London: Routledge, 1993.

———. *Ann Radcliffe. The Great Enchantress.* Manchester: Manchester UP, 1995.

———. "Ann Radcliffe and Matthew Lewis." *A Companion to the Gothic.* Ed. David Punter. Oxford: Blackwell, 2000. 41–57.

———. "Introduction." *The Italian or the Confessional of the Black Penitents. A Romance.* By Ann Radcliffe. Introd. and Notes Robert Miles. London: Penguin, 2004. vii–xxix.

Monson-Rosen, Madeleine. "'The Most Primeval of Passions'. Incest in the Service of Women in Angela Carter's *The Magic Toyshop.*" *Straight Writ Queer: Non-Narrative Expressions of Heterosexuality in Literature.* Ed. Richard Fantina. Jefferson, NC: McFarland, 2006. 232–43.

Morgan, Jack. *The Biology of Horror. Gothic Literature and Film.* Carbondale: Southern Illinois UP, 2002.

Morse, David. *Romanticism: A Structural Analysis.* London: Macmillan, 1982.

Perry, Ruth. "Incest as the Meaning of the Gothic Novel." *The Eighteenth Century* 39.3 (1998): 261–78.

Pollak, Ellen. *Incest and the English Novel, 1684–1814.* Baltimore: Johns Hopkins UP, 2003.

Punter, David. "The Modern Gothic." *The Literature of Terror. A History of Gothic Fictions from 1765 to the Present Day.* Vol. 2. London: Longman, 1996.

Radcliffe, Ann. "On the Supernatural in Poetry." *New Monthly Magazine and Literary Journal* 16 (1826): 145–52.

———. *The Italian or the Confessional of the Black Penitents. A Romance.* 1976; 2000. Introd. and Notes Robert Miles. London: Penguin, 2004.

Royle, Nicholas. *The Uncanny.* Manchester: Manchester UP, 2003.

Sage, Victor. "Gothic Novel." *The Handbook to Gothic Literature.* Ed. Marie Mulvey-Roberts. London: Macmillan, 1998. 81–89.

Sage, Victor, and Allen Lloyd Smith. "Introduction." *Modern Gothic: A Reader.* Eds. Victor Sage and Allan Lloyd Smith. Manchester: Manchester UP, 1996. 1–5.

Shapira, Yael. "Where the Bodies Are Hidden: Ann Radcliffe's 'Delicate' Gothic." *Eighteenth-Century Fiction* 18.4 (2006): 453–76.

Smith, Patricia Juliana. "The Queen of the Waste Land: The Endgames of Modernism in Angela Carter's *Magic Toyshop.*" *Modern Language Quarterly* 67.3 (2006): 333–61.

Spooner, Catherine. *Contemporary Gothic.* London: Reaktion Books, 2006.

Stone, Lawrence. *The Family, Sex and Marriage in England 1500–1800.* Abr. ed. Harmondsworth: Penguin, 1979.

Tuite, Clara. "Cloistered Closets: Enlightenment Pornography, The Confessional State, Homosexual Persecution and *The Monk*." *Romanticism on the Net* 8 (1997). *érudit*. February 4, 2009 <http://www.erudit.org/>.

Wagener, Christel. "*Story in a Story*: Märchen und Mythen bei Angela Carter." *Recent British Short Story Writing*. Vol. 50 of *Anglistik & Englischunterricht*. Eds. Hans-Jürgen Diller, Stephan Kohl, Joachim Kornelius, Erwin Otto, and Gerd Stratmann. Heidelberg: Winter, 1993. 115–30.

Wyatt, Jean. "The Violence of Gendering: Castration Images in Angela Carter's *The Magic Toyshop*, *The Passion of New Eve*, and 'Peter and the Wolf'." *Angela Carter. Contemporary Critical Essays*. Ed. Alison Easton. New York: St. Martin's Press, 2000. 58–83.

CHAPTER VIII

THE AGE OF TRANSITION AS AN AGE OF TRANSGRESSION? VICTORIAN POETRY AND THE TABOO OF SEXUALITY, LOVE, AND THE BODY

Sarah Heinz

The Victorian era has been described as an age of transition and change in which the traditional system of belief was not only questioned but also transgressed. At the same time, it is often considered to be emblematic of conservatism, prudery and a stability which borders on stagnation. The Victorians are seen as people with an almost pathological dread of everything connected to the body, even, as Fryer notes, hiding the legs of the table and the piano-forte under frilled pantalets (cf. 35). But they are also, as Altick argues, seen as belonging to a society which welcomed reform or experiment, and committed itself to the idea of progress (cf. 107). In this context, the poetry of the Victorian era is much more than a mere mirror of these contradictory impulses. Both groups of English poets of the time, whether radicals like Browning or conservatives such as Tennyson, use literature to confront deep-seated anxieties in a time of crisis.

Taboos and their transgression are a central issue in the assessment of this inherently contradictory era and its poetry. My main thesis is based on Tzvetan Todorov's view in *Genres in Discourse* that transgression does not destroy a norm but on the contrary makes this norm visible. This view is complemented by Stephen Greenblatt's view of culture as a system of mobility and constraint (cf. 225–32). In this sense, Victorian poetry will be analyzed as a transgression that makes nineteenth-century laws and taboos visible while at the same time asking questions about their legitimacy. While the poetry of the era questions the ineffability and sanctity of taboos, these taboos are also reestablished as points of reference in a period that thinks of itself as an age of transition. The focus of attention will be on the depiction of sexuality, love, and the body since Victorian society puts these issues under a strong social and moral taboo. Nevertheless, their status as taboo is intensely scrutinized in Victorian poetry. This paradox will be interpreted within the main framework with a view to two countervailing, even contradictory movements: the backward impulse of poets of regeneration such as Tennyson and the forward impulse of radical poets such as Browning.

Theoretical Background: Violating and Reestablishing Taboo by Transgression

In their study of language and taboo, Keith Allan and Kate Burridge write that "[n]othing is taboo for all people, under all circumstances, for all time" (9). Taboos arise out of social constraints on an individual's behavior because a breach of taboo will cause discomfort, harm or injury. In that sense, taboos are not objects with a demonic power as nineteenth-century anthropologists described them but rather conventionalized rules. But if taboos are neither absolute nor timeless and if they are really products of a specific time and society, then they can tell us something about that selfsame society in which they were created. According to such a view, taboos are social conventions that, as Sigmund Freud observed, "have no grounds and are of unknown origin" although "to those who are dominated by them they are taken as a matter of course" (18).[1] In spite of their arbitrariness, taboos therefore have a strong, unifying effect.

Tzvetan Todorov interprets transgression as a means for making visible the borders as well as limitations of a law or system, not a destruction of it: "…in order to exist as such, the transgression requires a law—precisely the one that is violated. We might even go further and observe that the norm becomes visible—comes into existence—owing only to its transgressions" (14). With respect to literary works and their transgression of the laws of genre, Todorov states later: "One has to think that every time, in these exceptional works where a limit is reached, the exception alone is what reveals to us that 'law' of which it also constitutes the unexpected and necessary deviation" (ibid.). Although Todorov uses his concept for genre criticism, it can be applied to the broader notion of culture as a complex system which necessarily includes constraints and mobility as

Stephen Greenblatt has described it. For Greenblatt, cultures can be defined in terms of a specific ratio of mobility and constraint. Even the most rigid regime requires some minimal measure of movement to reproduce itself over time, while even the most liberal and open societies have to accept some limits to remain functional. Greenblatt's conclusion therefore closely resembles Todorov's notion of the necessity of transgression for the establishment as well as for the questioning of laws and rules:

> Indeed the limits (of culture) are virtually meaningless without movement; it is only through improvisation, experiment, and exchange that cultural boundaries can be established.... What is set up, under wildly varying circumstances and with radically divergent consequences, is a structure of improvisation, a set of patterns that have enough elasticity, enough scope for variation, to accommodate most of the participants in a given culture. A life that fails to conform at all, that violates absolutely all the available patterns, will have to be dealt with as an emergency—hence exiled, or killed, or declared a god. But most individuals are content to improvise, and, in the West at least, a great many works of art are centrally concerned with these improvisations. (Greenblatt 228f.)

Literature is therefore more than an indicator of social change or part of the historical background of a society. For both Greenblatt and Todorov, literary texts are instruments for changing a specific culture's ratio of mobility and constraint. Literature can transgress rules and laws in the space of an 'as if', which has a decisive impact upon the members of a culture, a fact which can explain the intended function of censorship: "Restrictions on language and weapons have the same motivation" (Allan and Burridge 17). In that sense, Victorian poets do not merely write about but rather fight for and against rules and laws in a society where the ratio of mobility and constraint has become increasingly flexible.

Victorian Poetry: Mobility and Constraint

In often contradictory terms, a belief in progress and change and a longing for the (imagined) stability of the past set the tone for Victorian self-images and representations. In Queen Victoria herself the basic contradictions of her age become apparent. Victoria is seen as an example of the exclusion of the body from public discourse. At the same time, Queen Victoria's happy marriage, her nine children,

162   Sarah Heinz

and her lifelong mourning after the death of Prince Albert point to the importance of the erotic, the body, and sexuality in the Victorian era. This has led to an almost pejorative use of the adjective Victorian as well as to a negative view of the whole age as a "gross historical monster," whose essence "was known to be an insensate devotion to respectability, with all that this suggests of compromise and conformity, of concealment and dissembling" (Trilling and Bloom 3).[2]

The Victorians themselves constructed a very different image of their society and time, heavily stressing progress and improvement (cf. Altick 107). This contradictory relation between exclusion and inclusion, stability and change, between reform and reactionary impulses can be detected in nearly every part of Victorian life (cf. Armstrong). Poets, painters and philosophers were often similarly alarmed and excited by the transformations Britain was undergoing and hence Victorian poetry "on the one hand glances back wistfully at fading beauty and romance, and on the other hand confronts the new industry and the new and exciting conditions of life with a measure of alertness and enthusiasm" (Richards 1). Voices like William Johnson Fox, the editor of the *Monthly Repository*, a radical Utilitarian and Unitarian journal, and Browning's "literary godfather" (Armstrong 28), demanded fundamental change and a transgression of all borders erected by old institutions:

> One fact, however, is sufficiently evident, that we are in a state of transition: that old things are passing away and giving place to new....The Church cannot remain as it is....The Law cannot remain as it is....Education cannot remain as it is....The means for disseminating information cannot remain as they are....Above all, the relative condition of the working class cannot remain the same. (Fox qtd. in Armstrong 25f.)

This questioning of the status quo and the demand for a new order was met by the demand for a regeneration of society, not a revolution, which was led by a group of intellectuals called "the Apostles," to which Victorian poets like Tennyson and Arthur Hallam belonged. In this context, Isobel Armstrong speaks of two systems of concentric circles, one dissenting and radical, the other subversive and conservative (cf. 27). Still, both groups wanted British society to change and they "explored a theology which transgressed orthodoxy and both saw literature and politics as inseparable from one another" (28). Questions of race, class, and gender, of culture and politics were tackled in journals and public debate, but especially in the poetry of the time. To an extent that was formerly unknown, Victorian poetry thus encompasses a vast and complex body of productions "by authors of both sexes in every social class from all districts in the British Isles (and indeed the colonies)" (Cronin, Chapman and Harrison viii).[3]

"My Life Is Bitter with Thy Love": Sexuality, Love, and the Body

In the first volume of his projected history of sexuality, Michel Foucault states that thinking about sexuality and the body has been dominated by what he terms the repressive hypothesis: Sexuality has been analyzed as something that culture and society try to repress and control through laws, moral codes and exclusion, in other words by making sexuality a taboo. Foucault contested this view by claiming that all discourses that seem to limit and control sexuality in this way help to create and proliferate the selfsame discourse they seemingly want to eliminate: "A censorship of sex? There was installed rather an apparatus for producing an ever greater quantity of discourse about sex, capable of functioning and taking effect in its very economy" (Foucault 23).[4] The machinery that set out to prevent people from talking about sex and the body therefore helped to establish a discourse in which sexuality could be expressed in the first place.

The fact that Victorian poetry is far more concerned with sex and the body than one might expect is a first hint at this proliferation of the discourse of sex (cf. Marcus). Nevertheless, the repressive hypothesis cannot completely be cancelled out, as John Maynard has explained: "If we see an ever broadening production of sexuality throughout both the nineteenth and twentieth centuries..., we can also see some major arcs in the battle of control and release: a new concern with respectability developing with the Victorian era and perhaps cresting in the 1880s and 1890s..." (544).[5] Victorian poets explore sexuality and the body through depictions of those contested and tabooed areas which both validate and transgress moral codes but which primarily make these taboos visible and expressible for the reader. Sexuality becomes something one could talk about, albeit only in discourses about preventing sexuality.

In the following, I want to examine six poems which shed light on the role of sexuality, love and the body in Victorian poetry as a structure of mobility and constraint. Thereby, the conservative as well as the radical position will be taken into consideration. Swinburne's "Anactoria" (1866) and Browning's "Meeting at Night" (1845) will be discussed as radical questionings of Victorian moral codes, while Tennyson's *Idylls of the King* (1859–1885) serve as a warning of the dangers of female sexuality. George Meredith's *Modern Love* (1862) will then be analyzed as a questioning of love in the depiction of a marriage in which both husband and wife commit adultery. In a last step, William Ernest Henley's *In Hospital* (1873–1875) is compared with Coventry Patmore's ode "To the Body" (1877). While Henley presents the body in pain and thereby contests concepts of propriety as well as beauty and health, Patmore's ode stresses the wholeness and sanctity of the human body.

Algernon Charles Swinburne is very often seen as a Victorian poet who merely wrote to provoke his contemporaries and was as notorious for his offensive themes as for his wild lifestyle. Indeed, topics such as lesbianism, sadomasochism, necrophilia, or paganism are directed at a Victorian sense of propriety, openly speaking about the unspeakable: "Part of the strategy of...(his) writing was to question by shock" (Armstrong 387). Nevertheless, a poem like "Anactoria" helps one to understand how a radical depiction of female desire also establishes boundaries which are not to be crossed.

In "Anactoria," it is interesting to observe that Swinburne chooses a Hellenic background to present lesbian love. The erotic poem is "the first important poetic representation in English of Sappho—hitherto edited into heterosexuality—as a lesbian" (O'Gorman 480). In the depiction of the sadomasochistic desires of a woman toward a woman—in exuberant, sometimes even excessive language—several taboos are openly transgressed. Nevertheless, the Hellenic background also distances the dangerous topic from contemporary Victorian society. Furthermore, the genre of the dramatic monologue with its emphasis on immediacy, specificity in space and time and the speaker's, not the poet's, internalized and isolated subjectivity makes it possible to speak about Sappho's desire and sexuality without openly making claims upon sexuality and desire in general and in the present. That way, the dramatic monologue, the "flagship genre of Victorian poetry" (Slinn 80), becomes a "poetry of experience" (cf. Langbaum) for poet, speaker and reader that provides Victorian poets with a medium for multiple forms of cultural critique. In this sense it also becomes "psychological poetry" (Faas 30).

The speaker of the poem is the Greek lyric poet Sappho, who is in love with and extremely jealous of Anactoria. Swinburne here uses original quotations in translation from Sappho's own "Ode to Anactoria" ("To a Beloved Woman") and is strongly influenced

Age of Transition: Age of Transgression? ❧ 165

by de Sade's *La Nouvelle Justine*, which Swinburne read in 1862 (cf. O'Gorman 480). Right at the beginning of the poem, Sappho openly acknowledges her desire for Anactoria's body as well as the destructiveness and pain of this desire:

> I feel thy blood against my blood: my pain
> Pains thee, and lips bruise lips, and vein stings vein.
> Let fruit be crushed on fruit, let flower on flower,
> Breast kindle breast, and either burn one hour. (ll. 11–14)

In the intense eroticism of these lines Sappho closely connects her love with death and pain and rather wants to see Anactoria dead than in the hands of a man: "I would my love could kill thee; I am satiated / With seeing thee live, and fain would have thee dead" (ll. 23–24).

While Anactoria is described with 'feminine' adjectives such as "sweet," "soft," "fair" and "delicate," Sappho's reaction is marked by aggression and a love that is so intense that it seems like hate. At the same time, Sappho's hate-love is naturalized by addressing Aphrodite, who is presented as creator of earth and love: "have we not lips to love with, eyes for tears, / And summer and flower of women and of years?" (ll. 95–96) Here, taboos are not only transgressed but their validity is radically questioned. A woman desiring another woman is presented as something that is as natural as "fields that wear / Lilies" (ll. 99–100) and equal to heterosexual desire: "Are there not other gods for other loves?" (l. 102) As this love is part of natural cycles, it cannot and need not be repressed and the speaker of the dramatic monologue colorfully proliferates and variegates the language of sexuality and the body in the poem. The poem therefore self-consciously provokes and plays with the taboos of Victorian moral codes, but it also marks these taboos as contingent by positioning the poem "between provocation in literature and sexuality as an aspect of life" (Maynard 558).

Nevertheless, Sappho's desire to kill, devour, and consume Anactoria is a transgression that is not only marked by love but also by jealousy and violence. Her desire is not only bound to the love object itself, but to its destruction and death: "Would I not plague thee dying overmuch? / Would I not hurt thee perfectly? not touch / Thy pores of sense with torture, and make bright / Thine eyes with bloodlike tears and grievous light?" (ll. 133–36) The repetitiveness of the syntax, the increase in question marks and the more and more pounding rhythm of the stanzas illustrate that Sappho's love is not

166　❦　*Sarah Heinz*

merely the natural love of Aphrodite. Here, Swinburne's presentation of a love that is close to madness resembles Robert Browning's "Madhouse Cells" (1842), two dramatic monologues which focus on "the diseased…logic of a disturbed mind" (O'Gorman 171), as in "Porphyria's Lover," where the reader enters into the mind of a speaker who killed his beloved to preserve the 'good minute' of their relationship. Here, a love and sexual desire that turns toward destruction is a transgression that does not question a taboo that must be overcome (cf. Johnson 103). It rather foregrounds a taboo that becomes visible in Sappho's aggressive and destructive desire. This becomes apparent when Sappho compares herself to Zeus:

> Me hath love made more bitter toward thee
> Than death toward man; but were I made as he
> Who hath made all things to break them one by one,
> If my feet trod upon the stars and sun
> And souls of men as his have always trod,
> God knows I might be crueller than God. (ll. 147–52)

Sappho's love for Anactoria has turned into something beyond natural cycles like life and death and beyond the natural law of the gods. Swinburne thereby connects the provocative depiction of female desire and the questioning of moral taboos concerning sexuality with an attack on religion and a reflection of the role of poetry, all the while stressing that there are boundaries whose transgression is perilous to speaker as well as auditor. "Anactoria" becomes a complex whole that imagines a shift in the ratio of constraint and mobility experienced in Victorian society.

Robert Browning's short poem "Meeting at Night" also confronts the taboo of speaking about desire and sexuality, but in contrast to "Anactoria" it features a male speaker. He approaches the house of his lover in a boat at night and enters the farmhouse through the window. The two stanzas of this poem focus entirely on the description of male desire through its externalization onto the feminized landscape. The cove of the grey sea overshadowed by a low half-moon is "gained" with "pushing prow" and the speaker "quench(es) its speed i' the slushy sand" (ll. 5–6). While the male speaker actively penetrates both land and sea to "quench" his speed, his female counterpart waits "thro' its joys and fears" for the "two hearts beating each to each" (ll. 11–12). Browning's use of sexual metaphors like cove, moon, slushy sand or warm-scented beach for the woman enhances the activity of

Age of Transition: Age of Transgression? 167

the man's desire, which culminates not with the two hearts beating in unison at the end of the poem but rather with the "blue spurt of a lighted match" (l. 10). Although he thereby transgresses Victorian moral codes through obvious sexual innuendo, Browning keeps the traditional gender hierarchy firmly in place (cf. Maynard 561). In this sense, the radical poet Browning, who often wrote against patriarchal control, seems to be less transgressive although no less provocative than Swinburne.

It is particularly interesting to note that Tennyson, who is often seen as Browning's antagonist or at least the proponent of the second, conservative circle of Victorian poets, partly inverts this gender hierarchy of active male and passive female in his *Idylls of the King*, his Arthurian cycle of poems. In this poem about "heroism, nationhood and sexual responsibility" (O'Gorman 62), the destruction of Arthur's kingdom is explained through the illicit desire and adultery of Lancelot and Guinevere as well as the ruinous influence of "saucy" Vivien. In both Guinevere and Vivien female desire and sexuality is emphasized while Merlin, Arthur, and even Lancelot remain passive. When Vivien tries to charm Merlin after he has left Arthur's court in "Merlin and Vivien," "he lay as dead / And lost to life and use and name and fame" (1601, ll. 211–12). When she tries to seduce Arthur, he "(h)ad gazed upon her blankly and gone by" (1600, l. 159) and Merlin mocks "(t)hat Vivien should attempt the blameless King" (ibid., l. 162). Browning's mythical heroic males, with the emphasis on activity and prowess, are transformed in Tennyson into peerless but also sexless men, confronted with and irritated by dangerous female desire. This becomes especially apparent in the differences and similarities between the presentation of Vivien and Guinevere. The Queen is "Heaven's own white / Earth-angel, stainless bride of stainless King" (1598, ll. 79–80) and wears green and gold, "glittering like May sunshine on May leaves" (ibid., l. 86). Vivien wears

> A twist of gold...round her hair; a robe
> Of samite without price, that more exprest
> Than hid her, clung about her lissome limbs,
> In colour like the satin-shining palm
> On sallows in the windy gleams of March. (1602, ll. 219–23)

While Guinevere clearly takes the position of the pure wife and angel, Vivien is the lascivious pagan whore and serpent, a fact which is again stressed by her savage hymn to Eros and the body's lust in "Balin and Balan": "Old priest, who mumbled worship in your quire—/ Old monk and nun, ye scorn the world's desire, / Yet in your frosty cells ye feel the fire!" (1588, ll. 438–40) In that sense, Vivien can be interpreted as a character that closely resembles Sappho in her wild and aggressive desire for love as well as for power and destruction. Nevertheless, both women share the same colors, gold and green, and both are associated with spring and thereby with awakening sexuality. Not only Vivien but also Guinevere is ruled by desire and love and it is her adultery that breaks the round table apart. In "Guinevere," she acknowledges this guilt while simultaneously absolving Lancelot of his part in the crime, again making him the faultless but also passive recipient of female desire: "Mine is the shame, for I was wife, and thou / Unwedded: yet rise now, and let us fly, / For I will draw me into sanctuary, / And bide my doom" (1728, ll. 118–21).

This blurring of the clear boundary between Vivien and Guinevere creates central problems in Tennyson's poem as he transgresses the split between wife and whore and collapses them. Tennyson can only evade the dangerous potential of this image of women's desire by turning Guinevere and Lancelot into helpless victims of fate: "They are both noble lovers who must yield to desire that they themselves consider unworthy and that so manifestly destroys the realm, as it was felt to destroy the domestic world in Victorian society" (Maynard 552). Vivien on the other hand must remain the evil, lewd pagan who simply wants to destroy everything that is good and pure. In spite of their activity and the lacking strength of the men, these gender roles eventually restrict the scope of female power and desire. By transgressing the clear-cut line between angel and whore, Tennyson therefore does not destroy gender roles but rather emphasizes them.

Nevertheless, the poem can also be read as a critical assessment of Victorian role models for both men and women: "Tennyson's Arthurian *Idylls of the King*...represents a society encumbered with custom and habit, struggling with a damaging mind / body split which determines its culture and forms of thought" (Armstrong 382). The split between body and mind is portrayed in both women, who represent the two sides of womanhood that cannot be kept separate throughout the poem. Tennyson is therefore less provocative with regard to sexual metaphors and less radical in form and content than Swinburne or Browning, but he also transgresses Victorian taboos

Age of Transition: Age of Transgression? ❧ 169

on adultery and female desire by showing that men and women are caught up in stereotypical positions that must be overcome.

George Meredith's sonnet sequence *Modern Love* challenges Tennyson's view of Arthur as the helpless victim of Guinevere's adultery: "While Tennyson's *Idylls of the King* lays the blame on Guinevere and tries not to criticize the peerless but sexless Arthur, some kind of adultery is present on both sides in Meredith's poem" (Maynard 553). In its sonnet form and its content, Meredith critically assesses the tradition of courtly love and the language as well as poetic form with which love is usually expressed: "In presenting instead of a lover's declaration to his beloved the anatomy of a failing marriage, it denies the familiar terrain of the poetic form it so narrowly avoids" (O'Gorman 328). In the 'modern' marriage that is depicted in glimpses of single moments and events, both husband and wife are ruined by role expectations, social conventions, and their failure to conform to them. Immediately at the beginning of the first sonnet, the misery of this 'modern love' is presented: "Like sculptured effigies they might be seen / Upon their marriage-tomb, the sword between; / Each wishing for the sword that severs all" (ll. 14–16). Mutual love, passion and desire have ended for this "ever-diverse pair" (l. 786), but their marriage does not end until the wife kills herself with poison in sonnet forty-nine. In Meredith's sonnets, marriage is not the eternal bond of two people destined for each other but rather a fancy for a season, as sonnet thirteen emphasizes: "'I play for Seasons; not Eternities!' / Says Nature, laughing on her way. 'So must / All those whose stakes is nothing more than dust!'" (ll. 193–201)

As in "Anactoria," the story of adultery in this commonplace, middle-class marriage is not explained through fate as in Tennyson's *Idylls of the King*, but through the nature of love and sexuality itself. What Victorians at the time of the publication of *Modern Love* found so shocking is the presentation of love's most holy institution, marriage, as fleeting, superficial, and based on as well as destroyed by the sexual needs of both husband and wife. Propriety and the ideal of the eternal bond are not only transgressed but their status as ideal is itself fundamentally questioned (cf. Edmond 209f.). This transgression amounts to much more than a challenge to the institution of marriage: "It [marriage] took on the function of a trope of harmony in which the settling of domestic conflicts between the sexes could represent a national capacity for liberal compromise claimed to be a special trait of Englishness" (Saville 526). The hypocritical role play of the couple in the company of others makes clear that even

170 ❧ *Sarah Heinz*

seemingly happy marriages and therefore the whole nation may suffer from the same deficiencies:

> At dinner, she is hostess, I am host.
> Went the feast ever cheerfuller? She keeps
> The Topic over intellectual deeps
> In buoyancy afloat. They see no ghost.
> With sparkling surface-eyes we play the ball:
> It is in truth a most contagious game:
> *Hiding the Skeleton* shall be its name.
> Such play as this the devils might appal!...
> Fast, sweet, and golden, shows the marriage-knot.
> Dear guests, you now have seen Love's corpse-light shine. (ll. 257–72)

Meredith therefore not only lays claim to an assessment of one individual marriage but of the whole of Victorian society that hides its skeletons from public eyes. He presents the modern experience of sexual relations and love as marked by pain, messiness and ordinariness; and even the adulterous affairs of husband and wife could not be more different from the high-minded and courtly rituals of Lancelot and Guinevere in Tennyson's *Idylls*. Although it is mostly narrated by the husband and therefore strongly shaped by his misogynistic stance, which can be interpreted as shaping his "unreliable narration" (Fletcher 87), *Modern Love* transgresses male and female gender roles by showing that it is not fate that binds these people to each other but a constricting vision of marriage and love. Victorian society is here seen as an age that clings to a conservative and outdated world view that must be transgressed.

In a short look at two final poems I want to substantiate my point with respect to the depiction of the human body itself. With the rise of medicine, anatomy and the natural sciences, the body and the individual's relation to it not only attracted the attention of Victorian poets. For the whole nation it became "a focal point for a number of discourses and contemporary anxieties such as individual and social health, political control, insanity, sexuality, and gender" (Stedman 59). While on the one hand the body is increasingly dissected and transformed into matter, it is on the other hand celebrated as the beautiful and healthy vessel of the eternal soul. Coventry Patmore's ode "To the Body" from his collection of poems *The Unknown Eros* presents the human body as "creation's and creator's crowning good" (l. 1) and as "Little, sequestered pleasure-house / For God and for His Spouse" (ll. 11–12). The body

Age of Transition: Age of Transgression? 171

resembles its creator in its beauty and grace. The human experience of the world through the medium of the body foreshadows heaven. Patmore, best-known for his idealization of the Victorian wife into the 'angel in the house,' praises the body for its beauty and the pleasure it brings. Nevertheless, this pleasure is not the violent passion of Swinburne's Sappho, Browning's quenching of desire or the fulfillment of sexual needs as in the adulterous affairs in *Modern Love*. Instead of transgressing the taboo of depicting bodily functions and base sexual needs, Patmore cleanses the body of all that openly connects it to sexuality, pain and disfigurement. The last seven lines of the poem, whose rhythm strongly resembles the Lord's Prayer, therefore reverberate with religious metaphors and adjectives:

> Or, if the pleasure I have known in thee
> But my poor faith's poor first-fruits be,
> What quintessential, keen, ethereal bliss
> Then shall be his
> Who has thy birth-time's consecrating dew
> For death's sweet chrism retained,
> Quick, tender, virginal, and unprofaned! (ll. 47–53)

Although acknowledging its role in sexuality and its connection to earthly desires and profanities, Patmore reduces the body to an outward extension of the eternal soul: "In *The Unknown Eros* Coventry Patmore finds earthly love a premonition of sexual ecstasy in heaven, here at least a truly religious experience: love with God superseding even heavenly married love itself" (Maynard 555). There could be no starker contrast to this vision of clean, heavenly bodies than William Earnest Henley's *In Hospital*, which is an account of Henley's own period in hospital in 1873 during which he had a foot amputated. In twenty-eight poems recollecting the setting, the people in hospital, the surgery as well as the pain and suffering, Henley presents the human body as alone, vulnerable and damaged:

> You are carried in a basket,
> Like a carcase from the shambles,
> To the theatre, a cockpit
> Where they stretch you on a table. (ll. 57–60)

The speaker of the poem has become a patient—"Case Number One" (l. 220)—who is directly and bodily involved in, though

172 ❧ *Sarah Heinz*

as a narrator somehow removed from what is done to him and what he speaks about. This immediacy of the events is mirrored in Henley's plain language and the titles of the single poems, for example, "Before," "Operation," and "After," or "Staff-Nurse: Old Style" and "Staff-Nurse: New Style." The body has turned into a carcase, an expression that is usually connected to dead animals which are cut up into meat. The description of pain and the body after surgery openly transgresses taboos of propriety that normally limit what can be said about corporeality and health, not only when Henley describes his own pain after the operation but also later when he describes the patients singing and dancing in the poem "Interlude":

> Stumps are shaking, crutch-supported;
> Splintered fingers tap the rhythm;
> And a head all helmed with plasters
> Wags a measured approbation. (ll. 324–27)

While for Patmore the body is a little pleasure-house whose connection to earth and human suffering is turned into a vision of beauty and eternal life, for Henley the focus is on the fragile and sick body in this life, which has nothing religious or ethereal. The hospital is a huge and dirty worldly institution full of nurses, scrubbers, doctors and leaking cisterns, and the patient's hope for recovery remains uncertain: "It's the spring. / A sprightliness feeble and squalid / Wakes in the ward, and I sicken, / Impotent, winter at heart" (ll. 432–35). The fertility and hope of spring cannot touch the poet in hospital until he is finally discharged in the last poem. But even then he does not address god or his good fate, and the wonderful world that he perceives does not consist of the beauty and holiness that Patmore described. On the contrary, the poet's senses are stimulated by "the spell of the streets" (l. 529), "the flat roar and rattle of wheels" (l. 531) and the "smell of the mud in my nostrils" (l. 535). The world he returns to is an ordinary, dirty, and industrialized cityscape, but it still makes the patient feel "dizzy, hysterical, faint" with his freedom: "These are the streets. . . . / Each is an avenue leading / Whither I will!" (ll. 546–48) In Henley's poem, the body is therefore not only presented as weak and in pain but even in its recovered state it is a fundamentally profane and human body. Thereby, *In Hospital* transgresses both the taboo on the depiction of the body and the taboo on faith and doubt, firmly establishing the body itself as the final border of humanity which cannot be transgressed toward an eternal life.

Conclusion

The transgression of taboos in Victorian poetry underlines the contradictory structure of the whole age as well as the general function of literature as a means for changing the ratio of mobility and constraint in a given culture. While Victorian poets challenge and transgress moral codes and norms in their depiction of sexuality, love, and the body, they also emphasize the basic function of taboos in their society by making them visible and by providing a language in which to talk about them. Far from simply removing or destroying laws and limitations, Victorian poetry therefore creates a literary space in which these can be tested, assessed, and eventually changed. Both the conservative and the radical poets of the time demonstrate that taboos must be questioned but that it is also impossible to completely leave them behind. Consequently, the poetry of the Age of Transition might truly be described as texts about transgression in the sense of being concerned with taboos and their role in a society whose ratio of mobility and constraint has become flexible, a characteristic that we share with the Victorians even today.

Notes

1. "Taboo prohibitions have no grounds and are of unknown origin. Though they are unintelligible to us, to those who are dominated by them they are taken as a matter of course." ("Die Tabuverbote entbehren jeder Begründung; sie sind unbekannter Herkunft; für uns unverständlich, erscheinen sie jenen selbstverständlich, die unter ihrer Herrschaft stehen." [Freud]).

2. In this context Trilling and Bloom quote Lytton Strachey's *Eminent Victorians*, published in 1918, "which undertook to 'shoot a sudden revealing searchlight into obscure recesses, hitherto undivined,' the implication being that the Victorian Age was a vast hypocrisy, from whose face the mask was now at last to be torn" (3). This appropriation of the Victorians by the twentieth century—in literature, social politics, film, or visual culture—has recently been re-examined by Simon Joyce.

3. The body of texts used in the following includes only male Victorian poets. Although the Victorian era saw a rise in women's poetry, it was

174 ❦ *Sarah Heinz*

the male poets who were best-known, most widely read and it is no coincidence that it was the male conservative Tennyson who became Poet Laureate in 1850. The considerable influence of women poets of the era has been established in more recent studies, cf. Armstrong 318–77; Leighton, and the essays in Chapman.

4. "Censure sur le sexe? On a plutôt mis en place un appareillage à produire sur le sexe des discours, toujours davantage de discours, susceptible de fonctionner et de prendre effet dans son économie même" (Foucault).

5. This concern with propriety cresting in the 1880s and 1890s can be observed in the scandal and public interest surrounding the Wilde Trial of 1895, where Oscar Wilde was tried under the Criminal Law Amendment Act of 1885. In this context it is interesting that this law did not include women and homosexual acts, pointing to a completely different perception of female sexuality and desire. Summarising the Act, Richard Ellmann writes: "When it was pointed out to Queen Victoria that women were not mentioned, she is reported to have said, 'No woman would do that'" (386).

Works Cited

Allan, Keith, and Kate Burridge. *Forbidden Words: Taboo and the Censoring of Language*. Cambridge: Cambridge UP, 2006.

Altick, Richard. *Victorian People and Ideas*. London: J.M. Dent and Sons, 1974.

Armstrong, Isobel. *Victorian Poetry: Poetry, Poetics and Politics*. London: Routledge, 1993.

Browning, Robert. "Meeting at Night." *The New Oxford Book of Victorian Verse*. Ed. Christopher Ricks. Oxford: Oxford UP, 2002. 125.

——. "Porphyria's Lover." *Victorian Poetry: An Annotated Anthology*. Ed. Francis O'Gorman. Oxford: Blackwell, 2004. 172–73.

Chapman, Alison, ed. *Victorian Women Poets*. Woodbridge: D.S. Brewer, 2003.

Cronin, Richard, Alison Chapman, and Antony H. Harrison. "Editor's Preface." *A Companion to Victorian Poetry*. Eds. Richard Cronin, Alison Chapman, and Antony H. Harrison. Oxford: Blackwell, 2002. viii–ix.

Edmond, Rod. *Affairs of the Hearth: Victorian Poetry and Domestic Narrative*. London: Routledge, 1988.

Ellmann, Richard. *Oscar Wilde*. Harmondsworth: Penguin, 1988.

Faas, Ekbert. *Retreat into the Mind: Victorian Poetry and the Rise of Psychiatry*. Princeton: Princeton UP, 1988.

Fletcher, Pauline. "'Trifles light as air' in Meredith's *Modern Love*." *Victorian Poetry* 34.1 (1996): 87–99.

Foucault, Michel. *The Will to Knowledge. History of Sexuality 1*. Trans. Robert Hurley. London: Penguin, 1998.

Fox, William Johnson. *Monthly Repository* N.S. VI (January 1832): 1–4.

Freud, Sigmund. *Totem and Taboo.* Trans. James Strachey. London: Routledge and Kegan Paul, 1950.

Fryer, Peter. *Mrs Grundy: Studies in English Prudery.* London: Dennis Dobson, 1963.

Greenblatt, Stephen. "Culture." *Critical Terms for Literary Studies.* Eds. Frank Lentricchia and Thomas McLaughlin. 2nd ed. Chicago: U of Chicago P, 1995. 225–32.

Henley, William Earnest. *In Hospital. Victorian Poetry: An Annotated Anthology.* Ed. Francis O'Gorman. Oxford: Blackwell, 2004. 571–86.

Johnson, E.D.H. *The Alien Vision of Victorian Poetry.* Hamden: Archon Books, 1963.

Joyce, Simon. *The Victorians in the Rearview Mirror.* Athens: Ohio UP, 2007.

Langbaum, Robert. *The Poetry of Experience: The Dramatic Monologue in Modern Literary Tradition.* New York: Norton, 1957.

Leighton, Angela. *Victorian Women Poets: Writing Against the Heart.* Charlottesville: UP of Virginia, 1992.

Marcus, Steven. *The Other Victorians: A Study of Sexuality and Pornography in Mid-Nineteenth Century England.* London: Weidenfels and Nicolson, 1966.

Maynard, John. "Sexuality and Love." *A Companion to Victorian Poetry.* Eds. Richard Cronin, Alison Chapman, and Antony H. Harrison. Oxford: Blackwell, 2002. 543–66.

Meredith, George. "Modern Love." *Victorian Poetry: An Annotated Anthology.* Ed. Francis O'Gorman. Oxford: Blackwell, 2004. 328–49.

O'Gorman, Francis, ed. *Victorian Poetry: An Annotated Anthology.* Oxford: Blackwell, 2004.

Patmore, Coventry. "To the Body." *Victorian Prose and Poetry.* Eds. Lionel Trilling and Harold Bloom. New York: Oxford UP, 1973. 678–79.

Richards, Bernard. *English Poetry of the Victorian Period 1830–1890.* 2nd ed. London: Longman, 2001.

Saville, Julia F. "Marriage and Gender." *A Companion to Victorian Poetry.* Eds. Richard Cronin, Alison Chapman, and Antony H. Harrison. Oxford: Blackwell, 2002. 526–42.

Slinn, E. Warwick. "Dramatic Monologue." *A Companion to Victorian Poetry.* Eds. Richard Cronin, Alison Chapman, and Antony H. Harrison. Oxford: Blackwell, 2002. 80–98.

Stedman, Gesa. *Stemming the Torrent: Expression and Control in the Victorian Discourses on Emotions, 1830–1872.* Aldershot: Ashgate, 2002.

Strachey, Lytton. *Eminent Victorians.* London: Chatto and Windus, 1974.

Swinburne, Algernon Charles. "Anactoria." *Victorian Poetry: An Annotated Anthology.* Ed. Francis O'Gorman. Oxford: Blackwell, 2004. 480–86.

Tennyson, Alfred Lord. "Idylls of the King." *The Poems of Tennyson.* Ed. Christopher Ricks. London: Longman, 1969. 1460–756.

176 ✸ *Sarah Heinz*

Todorov, Tzvetan. *Genres in Discourse.* Trans. Catherine Porter. Cambridge: Cambridge UP, 1990.

Trilling, Lionel, and Harold Bloom. "Victorian Prose." *Victorian Prose and Poetry.* Eds. Lionel Trilling and Harold Bloom. New York: Oxford UP, 1973. 3–13.

CHAPTER IX

METRICAL TABOOS, RHYTHMIC TRANSGRESSIONS: HISTORICO-CULTURAL MANIPULATIONS OF THE VOICE IN NINETEENTH- AND TWENTIETH-CENTURY POETRY

Clive Scott

This chapter examines the meanings of meter as an historico-cultural regime designed to suppress or sublimate certain impulses connected with poetry's maximization of the materiality of language, and to identify as off limits certain kinds of perception derivable from the reading of verse. The nineteenth and early twentieth centuries constitute the chapter's field of enquiry, but this period is investigated neither systematically nor exhaustively. Instead, the chapter selectively treats poets or works that peculiarly dramatize the issues and developments relating to metro-rhythmic taboos and transgressions. These issues and developments are broadly outlined in the chapter's opening section. Reference is made, from time to time, to Barthes's *Le Plaisir du texte* (1973); readerly taboo is, after all, the site of Barthesian *jouissance* / bliss: "Bliss is unspeakable, inter-dicted" (21), rhythm a pleasure of the voice that cannot be spoken.

Preliminaries: Voice, Meter, Rhythm

The large paradox which underlies the pages following is a simple one: what metricality casts as taboo is precisely that organ which it seems designed to promote: the voice. The textualization of the voice is the first step to its removal from activity, since the writing of voice is both a translation of voice and a reporting of voice; a translation in the sense that the multiplicity of voice-types and pronunciations is reduced to one (the pronunciatory system [IPA]) of the standard alphabet, an "abstraction" of the voice (unless expressly transcribed as dialect, etc.); and a reporting in the sense (a) that the written language purportedly "reports" actual speech, and (b) that speech written can be reappropriated by any speaker. The metricalization of voice not only orders and "transcendentalizes" voice, takes voice out of itself, but it also tends to dictate the way in which we listen to, or hear, voice. Voice becomes the vehicle of meter, rather than vice versa, and, in this sense, serves a principle "higher" than itself. Meter is one of the ways in which a text establishes its linguisticity, and in so doing pushes paralinguisticity to the margins, as a textual auxiliary. And it is by virtue of this constitutive linguisticity that the text becomes greater than any single event which might seek to actualize it in a form other than its written-ness. In this sense, one of the taboos enforced by meter is any thorough-going appropriation of text, any singularization of text, by the performative act.

I have elsewhere suggested that the importunities of voice, the messiness of its variables, the inability of linguistics to come to meaningful terms with voice-quality (cf. Laver), have been side-stepped by the device of constituting verbal music as the true study of linguistic acousticity:

> For many, music may seem little more than a convenient way of ousting the voice, of justifying the elocutory disappearance of the poet, by implying that words have a music of their own and that the instrument that best plays that music is not a particular voice but the perfectly tuned International Phonetic Alphabet. (370)

There are two aspects of this particular tendency that I wish to highlight: first, I want to underline the obvious, namely the discrepancy that exists between what our eyes can teach themselves to hear and what the ear hears. As I look through a text I notice the predominance in a particular passage of a particular phoneme. In this process I am making three assumptions: (i) that sounds are isolatable from the phonetic stream; (ii) that the importance of a sound is indicated by its frequency / repetition; (iii) that sound is semanticizable, because this is poetry and every element clamors to speak in many tongues. When the poem is performed, read aloud, all these assumptions become questionable. But it is the assumption contained in (iii) that I wish to stop over as my second point. The semanticizing of sound is a process in which the identification of a sound, and the ability to describe it, are more important than the sounding of that sound in any particular mouth. But what if a poem communicates a voice rather than vice versa? What if a poem discovers its meaning *only* by its embodiment in a particular voice? What if the reading aloud of poetry is considered as an event in life-writing, the life-writing of the reader, or more especially, of the reader's voice? This is the direction in which Barthes's notion of "writing aloud" takes us:

> *Writing aloud* is not expressive; it leaves expression to the pheno-text, to the regular code of communication; it belongs to the geno-text, to *signifiance*.... Due allowance being made for the sounds of the language, *writing aloud* is not phonological but phonetic; its aim is not the clarity of messages, the theatre of emotions; what it searches for (in a perspective of bliss) are the pulsional incidents, the language lined with flesh, a text where we can hear the grain of the throat, the patina of consonants, the voluptuousness of vowels, a whole carnal stereophony. (cf. 66)

If this kind of writing is more concerned with the grain of the voice than with the voice's expressive coherence, more concerned with the accidents of pronunciation than with communication, then we must certainly radically adapt our notion of what the proper scansional / descriptive tools are. What Barthes strains to hear through language-sounds is not a signified but the articulated body of the speaker, as if listening to speech in close-up.

As an historico-cultural force, as an ideology, meter is a distancing and disciplining of voice, which guarantees *a certain range* of poetic licenses, establishes a channel of intersubjective communication, insinuates attitudinal or generical associations, safeguards, archi-textual, and intertextual continuities; and this affiliation of metrical patterns with verse-genre (elegy, ode, etc.) entails the imposition of an appropriate voice. Meter's authority derives not only from its being the imprint of the nation, the patriarchy, tradition, a whole range of text-transcendent vested interests, but also from its positing no locus of enunciation, from its ritualizing the voice. We might also claim that metrical patterning encourages, if not compels, the through-reading of the line, since it is only by through-reading that

180 ⬧ *Clive Scott*

we can comfortably perceive the regularity of the meter. This then entails a regime of reading which reinforces the teleological linearity of text and censors interruption, fragmentation, rubato, anything which speaks of the free-rhythmic.

In generative terms, meter stands to rhythm as competence to performance, as deep structure to surface structure, determining what is possible within the rules of rhythmic transformation. But an opposite, Bergsonian, view is equally attractive: namely, that the writing and reading of poetic texts proceeds from an inner durational state, from the deep self, to a surface which comprehends the communal. In other words, meter is not the deep structure out of which rhythmic variation is generated as a surface structure; rather, the inner duration or dynamic of personal experience, the rhythm of the *moi profond*, is the deep structure, out of which the *moi superficiel*, the critically and socially interactive self, the metrical self, develops, in order to communicate and share. Meter simplifies rhythm so that we can all reach some basis of agreement with our reading neighbors, so that a contract of conventionality can be established. This is to imply that rhythm and meter are not complementary, are not concrete and abstract versions of the same thing, but rather are oppositional principles, rhythm pulling in the direction of the paralinguistic, the unconscious, the unpredictable, the heterogeneous, the qualitative, the continuous, and meter, correspondingly, supporting the claims of the linguistic, the conscious, the predetermined, the homogeneous, the quantitative and the discontinuous.

Episodes from the Nineteenth Century: Wordsworth, Hopkins, Henley

To gain a broad view of the functions of meter at the beginning of the nineteenth century, one can do much worse than consult the "Preface" (1802) to the *Lyrical Ballads*, in which Wordsworth, according to W.J.B. Owen, "probes, more deeply than any considerable earlier critic, into the psychological bases of the effect of ordinary metrical patterns" (qtd. by Mason 80). For Wordsworth, meter is, first and foremost, that which assures communicative effectiveness; meter serves a model of poetry in which the poet imparts something to the reader, and thus has a phatic function, keeping clear and unencumbered the channel of communication. But meter is also the central key to a contract with the reader, a contract "that certain classes of ideas and expressions will be found in [the Author's] book, but that others will be carefully excluded" (58). This latter clause tells us of the

Metrical Taboos, Rhythmic Transgressions ❧ 181

decorums that it is meter's business to guarantee and safeguard. One might also suspect that meter is a guarantor of reflectiveness, is the mechanism which ensures that "influxes of feeling are modified and directed by our thoughts, which are indeed the representatives of all our past feelings" (62). Wordsworth looks to his own poetry to act as a countervailing force to "this degrading thirst after outrageous stimulation" (65) by which the populace has been latterly impelled. But it is true that meter, too often, is called upon to justify the excesses of the poetical: personifications, figures of speech, poetic diction. What is important for Wordsworth is that we should know how to value meter for its intrinsic merits, not as a pretext for auxiliary licenses. Meter is the guarantee of a commonness of ground between poet and reader, constituting fixed laws ("regular and uniform") to which both are subject and, while not interfering with expression, heightening and improving the associated pleasure (cf. 79). But perhaps the most important passage in the "Preface" for our purposes is this one:

> But, if the words by which this excitement is produced are in themselves powerful, or the images and feelings have an undue proportion of pain connected with them, there is some danger that the excitement may be carried beyond its proper bounds. Now the co-presence of something regular, something to which the mind has been accustomed in various moods and in a less excited state, cannot but have great efficacy in tempering and restraining the passion by an intertexture of ordinary feeling, and of feeling not strictly and necessarily connected with the passion. This is unquestionably true, and hence, though the opinion will at first appear paradoxical, from the tendency of metre to divest language in a certain degree of its reality, and thus to throw a sort of half consciousness of unsubstantial existence over the whole composition, there can be little doubt but that more pathetic situations and sentiments, that is, those which have a greater proportion of pain connected with them, may be endured in metrical composition, especially in rhyme, than in prose. (81)

In these lines, Wordsworth develops two ideas: 1) that meter can act as a second, simultaneous voice, or channel of communication, serving to counteract the highly charged with a restraining discourse of the reassuringly familiar, a moderating "intertexture"; 2) that meter is a force for abstraction, which de-substantiates the materiality of language and of that of which language is the vehicle. Wordsworth then goes on to affirm the converse of the first proposition, namely, that meter can help to invest words with passion when they are not

182   Clive Scott

of themselves wrought up to the proper intensity. This is to endow meter with a tutelary role, to ascribe to it an independence of effect which the poet, apparently, is happy to concede to it, in view of its powers of compensation and supplementation.

Wordsworth's words incline us to view metrical stress as something which leavens and directs sense. And it is the very regularity of stress-occurrence that allows for this transformation of expressive sense-stress into metrical stress. In Hopkins's sprung rhythm, two things of significance happen to stress: (a) we may distinguish between pho-nological accents (stresses of sense) and metrical stresses (stresses of the verse) and these may not entirely correspond to each other. When the distribution of metrical stress becomes irregular, when the foot ceases to be a determining unit, then stress is more naturally driven by sense, acquires greater autonomy. In other words, stress is perceived less as implanted by metrical need, a stress of compliance, and more as something discovered and affirmed by the voice, a stress more para-linguistically motivated; (b) the stress of sprung rhythm, the stress we must search for and create, is both "more *of* a stress" than that of common rhythm "in which less is made of stress" (Pick 98, letter to R.W. Dixon, 22 Dec. 1880) and, consequently, "the making of a thing more, or making it markedly, what it already is; it is the bringing out of its nature" (116, letter to Patmore, 7 Nov. 1883). Stress, for Hopkins, is "instress," the energy which actualizes an object's "inscape," its quiddity, and embodies the force which inscape exerts on the mind. Inasmuch as stress, and the rhythms it creates, express the subjective idiosyncrasies of the perceiver of inscape, and the time-bound relativ-ity of the perception, then stress is not metrical. Inasmuch as stress witnesses to the inescapable and timeless imprint in inscape of God's hand, then it has the tendency to metrify itself. But, all in all, if stress, for which Hopkins provides intensifying devices (clusters, alliteration, slurring of unstressed syllables, outrides, hovering accent), is the site of epiphany, then it must resist codification, since codification would de-individualize and vulgarize the epiphanic experience. Hopkins's stress is thus also the site of Barthesian bliss rather than Barthesian pleasure, asocial, unsettling cultural and psychological assumptions. Ironically, this kind of experience of God's work breaks a taboo, is transgressive, allows into the ordered consistency of ritual and litany, the eruptions, unsuppressible, tumultuous, of personal revelation.

W.E. Henley's shift toward free verse, in his collection *In Hospital* (written 1873–75; publ. 1888) is impelled by the wish to find a medium that will allow a dynamic and unmediated response, not to epiphany, but to real events. He presents his hospital experience not as emotion recollected in tranquillity, but as the anxious, vulnerable, spontaneous reactions to ongoing events. These are what Henley calls his "impressions": he refers to his poems as "those unrhyming rhythms in which I had tried to quintessentialize, as (I believe) one scarce can do in rhyme, my impressions of the Old Edinburgh Infirmary" (vii). In his article "The Decadent Movement in Poetry" (1893), Arthur Symons commended *In Hospital* as an artistic experiment and suggested that Verlaine's "theory of poetical writing—'sincerity, and the impression of the moment followed to the letter'—might well be adapted as a definition of Mr Henley's theory or practice" (867).

Free verse in Henley, then, mediates between the pressures of an external world, to whose every shift it is able to adapt itself, and the inward life of the poet, which is itself unlike any other life, with a rhythm all of its own, just as the Impressionist painter's brush both records every subtle nuance and change in atmospheric conditions, and, in the very rhythm of its strokes, expresses a perceiving subjectivity.[1] And this mediatory activity of the medium takes place in real time, in the midst of event. If we through-read lines from *In Hospital*—for example, Lord Lister doing his rounds of the ward:

> So shows the ring
> Seen from behind round a conjurer
> Doing his pitch in the street.
> High shoulders, low shoulders, broad shoulders, narrow ones,
> Round, square, and angular, serry and shove;
> While from within a voice,
> Gravely and weightily fluent,
> Sounds; and then ceases; and suddenly
> (Look at the stress of the shoulders!)
> Out of a quiver of silence,
> Over the hiss of the spray,
> Comes a low cry, and the sound
> Of breath quick intaken through teeth
> Clenched in resolve. And the Master
> Breaks from the crowd, and goes,
> Wiping his hands,
> To the next bed, with his pupils
> Flocking and whispering behind him ("Clinical," ll. 23–40)

—we may find ourselves drawn to the lulling chant of dactyls (/ x x). But if we read like this, we would miss the voice hidden in the dactyls,

184 &&& *Clive Scott*

we would miss the realization that a sequence of dactyls has, within its metrical rectitude, if not a chaos, at least a broad range of conflicting configurations of experience: choriamb (/ x x /) ("So shows the ring"; "Seen from behind"; "serry and shove"; "Comes a low cry"; "Wiping his hands"); adonic (/ x x / x) ("Out of a quiver"; "Flocking and whispering" [?]); ionic (x x / /) ("To the next bed"); second paeon (x / x x) ("and angular"; "and suddenly"); third paeon (x x / x) ("and then ceases"; "of the shoulders"; "quick intaken"; "And the Master"; "with his pupils"); anapaest (x x /) ("in the street"; "of the spray"; "and the sound"); amphibrach (x / x) ("of silence"; "behind him"); iamb (x /) ("Of breath"; "through teeth"; "and goes"). There are dactyls, too. This phrasalization of meter restores not only the expressive power of punctuation as respiratory accompaniment, but releases the diverse array of existential and psychic charges, the pulsional energies, which metrical continuity conceals by endowing them, precisely, with a purely metrical *raison d'être*; furthermore, it reminds us that free verse is heterometric or heterorhythmic, not just by virtue of changes of pattern from line to line, but also by rhythmic pluralism, or pluralism of rhythmic interpretation, within the single line.

Directions in the Twentieth Century: Pound, Lawrence, Eliot

Although the Imagists had hard words to say about verbal impressionism,[2] Imagism is unthinkable without the Impressionist example, and I want to turn to that cliché of Imagist transformation of the hazy into the crystalline, Pound's "In a Station of the Metro," but for its metrico-rhythmic instructiveness.

What this trip to the Underworld of the metro entails is a return, not just with an indistinct gallery of faces crystallized into an image, but with a transformation of our apprehension of the poetic line. When Pound first published this poem in *Poetry* (Apr. 1913), he presented each line as three units, with spaces separating the units, and with the first line's line-terminal punctuation as a colon rather than a semi-colon:

```
x x   / x x   x / x
In a Station of the Metro

 x] x   x/ x      x   x  / x     x   x /   (x)
The] apparition   of these faces   in the crowd:
```

```
/ x      x  x  /    x        /
Petals   on a wet, black   bough.
```

In a letter to Harriet Monroe of March 30 1913, Pound insisted on this disposition: "In the 'Metro' hokku, I was careful, I think, to indicate spaces between the rhythmic units, and I want them observed" (1951, 53). What this disposition reveals is a poem whose opening, particularly if one includes the title, is sustained by a third paeon (x x / x). In order to regularize this pattern over the first line, I am treating the line-initial definite article as an extrametrical upbeat (anacrusis) or as an elision ("Th'apparition"). And I am assigning a silent or unrealized off-beat to "crowd." It is possible to imagine the spectral survival of the third paeon in the second line, in the phrase "on a wet black," if one imagines an off-beat on "black." But I might leave "black" with its stress and produce a line without any echoes of its partner-line: a trochee (/ x) ("Petals"), an ionic (x x / /) ("on a wet, black") and finally a stressed monosyllable ("bough").

Alternatively, if one retains the stress on "black," then one might feel the need of a sequence of unrealized off-beats after each of the stressed monosyllables, not only to ensure that each item of the phrase "wet, black bough" has a reverberative wake, but also so that each of these items is like an acoustic after-image of the initial trochee "Petals":

```
/ x      x  x  / (x) / (x)     /  (x)
Petals   on a wet, black     bough
```

My final scansion proposes another spectral survival of the third paeon. I simply read the second line as if the third paeon should be made up with unrealized off-beats and by the demotion of the stress on "black" to an off-beat, thus:

```
(x) (x)   / x      x  x  /    x    (x) (x)  /  (x)
          Petals   on a wet, black      bough
```

This second line begins then to have wrapped into it the silent acoustics of inwardness; only fragments of the third paeon are now audible, expression becomes more abstract, non-vocal, opens speech on to spaces unexplored.

This shift, from one line to the next, to a rhythmic perception without *point de repère* is perhaps signaled by the shift from

186 ⚬⚬⚬ *Clive Scott*

a notational first line, involving definite articles and a demonstrative adjective, to a second-line composite image made up of zero and indefinite articles. In his account of the originating incident which took place as he was emerging from the metro in the place de la Concorde in 1911, an account which appeared in the *Fortnightly Review* of September 1 1914—a shorter version of which had appeared in *T.P.'s Weekly* on June 6 1913—, Pound says of the poem: "I dare say it is meaningless unless one has drifted into a certain vein of thought" and adds "In a poem of this sort one is trying to record the precise instant when a thing outward and objective transforms itself, or darts into a thing inward and subjective" (qtd. in Ruthven 153). As we turn the corner of the first line, it is precisely this "darting into" that occurs, and we have to find our place in a certain vein of rhythmic thought; we cross the threshold into a new state of rhythmic consciousness, which the original line-terminal colon captures, but which the semi-colon of the final printed version does no justice to. This darting is connected with a drifting, in which, perhaps, if we align it with Barthes's drifting, we "[pivot] on the *intractable* bliss that binds [us] to the text (to the world). Drifting occurs whenever social language, the sociolect, *fails me*..." (18f.).

The "failure" of the sociolect, of any voice promoting cultural values, is an inevitable concomitant of Barthesian *jouissance*, and its aggressive presentness:

> *criticism always deals with the texts of pleasure, never the texts of bliss*:... thus criticism speaks the futile bliss of the tutor text, its *past or future* bliss: *you are about to read, I have read*: criticism is always historical or prospective: the constatory present, the *presentation* of bliss, is forbidden it; its preferred material is thus culture, which is everything in us except our present. (21f.)

This is a proposition with which Lawrence might have concurred. In Lawrence's view, a poetry written in the perspective of past and future, the poetry that is imprinted with the forms of memory and memorability, is a poetry already over, distanced from perception by its own glittering finality. It is a poetry which also embodies a loss of nerve, a flight from the existential precariousness of the present, the risk of unprocessed encounter with the quick of Time. For Lawrence, free verse, far from being fragmented regular verse, is an indissociable blend of form and medium, the medium of ongoing experience itself, in which nothing repeats itself, in which there are no anchorages of recurrence:

> It is never finished. There is no rhythm which returns upon itself, no serpent of eternity with its tail in its own mouth. There is no static perfection, none of that finality which we find so satisfying because we are so frightened. (87)

The present, the taboo time, is a particular existential experience of presentness, the instant(aneous) present, the immediate present, the sheer present, which coincides with, is dependent upon, the intense presentness to itself of the self, the epitome of self in its wholeness, risen to the surface, as it were, in all its sensory vulnerability, but also, assertiveness.

Lawrence's "Humming-Bird" (1st publ. 1921) owes much to Crèvecœur's portrait of the humming-bird ("the most irascible of the feathered tribe" [184]) in *Letters from an American Farmer* (1782):

I can imagine, in some otherworld	/ x x / x x x / x x
Primeval-dumb, far back	/ x x / / /
In that most awful stillness, that	
only gasped and hummed,	x x x / x / x x / x / x /
Humming-birds raced down the avenues.	/ x x / x x / x x
Before anything had a soul,	x x / x x / x /
While life was a heave of Matter, half inanimate,	x / x x / x / x / x / x x
This little bit chipped off in brilliance	x / x / / x x / x
And went whizzing through the slow,	
vast, succulent stems.	x x / x / x / / / x x /

I believe there were no flowers then,
In the world where the humming bird flashed ahead of creation.
I believe he pierced the slow vegetable veins with his long beak.

Probably he was big
As mosses, and little lizards, they say, were once big.
Probably he was a jabbing, terrifying monster.

We look at him through the wrong end of
    the long telescope of Time,
Luckily for us.

The humming bird itself is the present, the present of selfhood, come impatiently to accelerate and awaken to itself all that is slow in the pre-conscious world. The rhythm here conforms to no preexisting shape, nor offers itself as the potential mould for future utterances.

188   Clive Scott

A curious paradox of Lawrence's verse is that it must be prosaic in order to be poetic: it must slacken any drive that rhythm has toward metricity, however fragmentary, in order to promote, valorize, its authenticity as the dynamic of experience itself. Line four might be described as dactylic, but that would be to suggest an intention it has not got, to imply a *principle* of repetition in something which merely finds itself repeated. To speak dactyls is to yield to metrical scansion's need to quantify and measure; verse withstands meter, so that time cannot be transformed into space, or proximity and coincidence (of voice and rhythm) transformed into distance and separation, or the mobile and planar into the static and perspectival. Metrical analysis immobilizes verse and thus, perversely, eradicates, makes a taboo of, sound's actuality.

Eliot's "Reflections on *Vers Libre*" (1917), on the other hand, reveals a poet made uneasy by free verse, looking for a model of supervised (by meter) or responsible (exercised for special purposes) freedom—"the ghost of some simple metre should lurk behind the arras in even the 'freest' verse;…freedom is only true freedom when it appears against the background of an artificial limitation" (187). *The Waste Land* (1922) frequently traffics with iambic pentameter, but one may feel that these passages are vouchsafed on sufferance, that their significance is more intertextual than operative, a remembered integrative discourse, a cherished socio-symbolic filter, having the completeness of the ideologically intact. In *The Waste Land*: fragmentation and only incipient reconstruction; metrical principles glimpsed; rhythmic improvisations enforced. How, in this world, do we read rhythm into sense, sense into rhythm?

In the opening lines of "What the Thunder Said"—

After the torchlight red on sweaty faces	/ x x / x / x / x / x
After the frosty silence in the gardens	/ x x / x / x x x / x
After the agony in stony places	/ x x / x x x / x / x
The shouting and the crying	x / x x x / x
Prison and palace and reverberation	/ x x / x x x / x / x
Of thunder of spring over distant mountains	x / x x / x x / x / x
He who was living is now dead	/ x x / x x / /
We who were living are now dying	/ x x / x x / / x
With a little patience	x x / x / x

(ll. 322–30)

—I detect two rhythmic traces: in the first "hemistichs" of the lines, the predominance of the adonic (/ x x / x—with added syllable or foot), and in the second, a third paeon (x x / x—with added "trochee" in ll. 326–27). Inasmuch as line 330 is a line of resolution or synthesis, we might say that it is the "spirit" of the third paeon that ultimately presides. But what is that "spirit"? It is the vehicle of an entropic movement, it seems, to do with the dispersal of energy, the loss of power, fruitless resistance, sterile effort. Things die away into multiplicity or distance. The adonic and its variants, on the other hand, and not surprisingly given that they occupy the first hemistich, have a certain impulsiveness in them, a certain expectancy, a certain tension, as one moves to a threshold at which one wishes to conjure new hope.

I want to pick up this rhythmic play a few lines further on, at the last element of line 345:

If there were water   / x x / x

The familiar adonic returns with the note of expectancy transformed into optative hypothesis ("if [only]"). The opposing principle expresses itself spondaically:

And no rock   x / / (bacchic)

This immobilization, congealment, petrification in spondee we have already encountered, in the equally bacchic "is now dead," and in the antispast "are now dying" (x / / x), but the rocky looks for release in the adonic reduced by a syllable to choriamb, and then liquefied by a following iambic dimeter (+ feminine syllable):

If there were rock   / x x /
And also water   x / x / x
        (ll. 347–48)

The emergent iambic then plays itself out:

And water   x / x
A spring   x /
A pool among the rock   x / x / x /
        (ll. 349–51)

culminating in another fusion with the choriamb (cf. ll. 347–48), made more liquid by an extra medial weak syllable:

If there were the sound of water only   / x x x / x / x / x

190 &&& *Clive Scott*

But the three weak syllables are countered by three strong ones, prefaced by an adonic:

> Not the cicada   / x x / x
> And dry grass singing   x / / / x (bacchic + trochee)
>   (ll. 353–54)

As this line-group comes to an end, we must clearly read the onomatopoeic sequence as iambic, the silencing of whose offbeats produces a concatenation of stresses at its end—

> Drip drop drip drop drop drop drop   x / x / (x) / (x) / (x) /

—with, at line 358, a resurgence of the third paeon followed by a trochee, which we first heard at ll. 326–27:

> But there is no water   x x / x / x

But what are the meanings of this excursion into "What the Thunder Said"? We cannot talk about the metricity of these lines, since no obligations or expectations play any part. We inhabit an acoustic landscape in which our ears are alerted to the murmurings within the words, infra-structural phrasings, sub-textual promptings. If meter is a kind of surveillance system or method of control, the guardian of standards, discipline, shape, then what we have before us is a voyage of self-discovery, reading our own hearing, hearing our own "interpretation," where interpretation is not about comprehension, but about modality, modalization, correspondences between rhythms and affective colorings, which are nonce creations without authority. And because they are without authority, because they are the autobiography of a reading, these identifications of rhythmic impulses take analysis into areas it does not willingly occupy, where there will be no interpretive community, no attempted consensus, and where meaning will have to yield to psychic association.

It may be that, for Eliot, the very writing of "What the Thunder Said" was a way of entering a world that was out of bounds, itself the waste land, where certain bearings are lost, where we are thrown back on more primitive resources and more intuitive responses. But if "What the Thunder Said" is, by virtue of its very transgression a dark journey of the soul into rhythmically forbidden territory, it is also, by the same token, a journey into Barthesian *jouissance*, where we may pleasurably live out our neuroses, where the voice, the body vocalized, can freely pursue its own ideas, as an anachronic subject, drifting in the non-acculturated.

Notes

1. Symons is of the view that: "The poetry of Impressionism can go no further, in one direction, than that series of rhymes and rhythms named *In Hospital*" (867).
2. In this connection, one thinks particularly of Pound's remark about the hapless Symons—"But is a slave to impressionism, whether the impression be precious or no" (1960, 365)—and his more general observation: "These 'impressionists' who write in imitation of Monet's softness instead of writing in imitation of Flaubert's definiteness, are a bore, a grimy, or perhaps I should say, a rosy, floribunda bore" (1960, 400).

Works Cited

Barthes, Roland. *The Pleasure of the Text*. London: Jonathan Cape, 1976.

Crèvecœur, J. Hector St. John de. *Letters from an American Farmer and Sketches of Eighteenth-Century America*. Ed. Albert E. Stone. Harmondsworth: Penguin, 1981.

Eliot, T.S. "Reflections on *Vers Libre*." *To Criticize the Critic and Other Writings*. London: Faber and Faber, 1978. 183–89.

Henley, W.E. *Poems*. London: David Nutt, 1904.

Laver, John. *The Phonetic Description of Voice Quality*. Cambridge: Cambridge UP, 1980.

Lawrence, D.H. "Introduction to 'New Poems'." *Selected Literary Criticism*. Ed. Anthony Beal. London: Heinemann, 1967. 84–89.

Pick, John, ed. *A Hopkins Reader*. New York: Oxford UP, 1953.

Pound, Ezra. *The Letters of Ezra Pound 1907–1941*. Ed. D.D. Paige. London: Faber and Faber, 1951.

———. *Literary Essays of Ezra Pound*. Ed. T.S. Eliot. London: Faber and Faber, 1960.

Ruthven, K.K. *A Guide to Ezra Pound's "Personæ" (1926)*. Berkeley: U of California P, 1969.

Scott, Clive. "*État présent*: French Verse Analysis." *French Studies* 60 (2006): 369–76.

Symons, Arthur. "The Decadent Movement in Literature." *Harper's New Monthly Magazine* 87 (1893): 858–67.

Wordsworth, William. *Lyrical Ballads*. Ed. Michael Mason. London: Longman, 1992.

CHAPTER X

'LOGICIZED' TABOO: ABJECTION IN GEORGE ELIOT'S *DANIEL DERONDA*

Anna-Margaretha Horatschek

> "I" is heterogeneous....Thus braided, woven, ambivalent, a heterogeneous flux marks out a territory that I can call my own because the Other, having dwelt in me as alter ego, points it out to me through loathing
>
> —*Kristeva 1982, 10*

Sigmund Freud, Herbert Mead, Michel Foucault, and Judith Butler—despite their fundamental differences—agree that the individual has to internalize the rules of the dominant culture in order to be acknowledged as a subject. In his seminal essay *Totem and Taboo* which has shaped our present-day discourse about taboo and transgression, Freud puts forth the thesis that societies instrumentalize taboos in order to enforce these rules by implementing differentiations between good and bad, normal and abnormal, natural and unnatural. Mead follows this lead with his contention that the development of "a complete self" (155) depends on its conformity with the "generalized other" (154). This generalized other does not only contribute to the formation of self, but prohibits any fundamental deviation from its rules. Foucault's analyses address historically specific discursive mechanisms, including taboos, which are employed to regulate sexuality (cf. Foucault). Butler radicalizes the relationship between personal identity and social norms and asks:

> To what extent do regulatory practices of gender formation and division constitute identity, the internal coherence of the subject, indeed,

194   Anna-Margaretha Horatschek

the self-identical status of the person? To what extent is identity a normative ideal rather than a descriptive feature of experience? (16)

Julia Kristeva's essay *Powers of Horror* ties in with these basic premises, yet introduces a significant shift of perspective with relation to Freud's explications. As she states: "Relying on numerous readings in ethnology and the history of religions…, Freud notes that the morality of man starts with 'the two taboos of totemism'—*murder* and *incest*" (57). Significantly for Kristeva, however, in the course of the essay

> [Freud] leaves off speculating on incest ("we do not know the origin of incest dread and do not even know how to guess at it" [162]) in order to center his conclusion in the second taboo, the one against murder, which he reveals to be the murder of the father. (ibid.)[1]

Kristeva takes her starting point from this disruption in Freud's arguments and specifically addresses the taboo "that Freud points to when he brings up dread, incest and the mother; one that, even though it is presented as the second taboo founding religion, nevertheless disappears during the final elucidation of the problem" (ibid.). She provocatively suggests that the disappearance of the mother in Freud's writing dramatizes the second taboo, lying ontologically and epistemologically prior to the murder of the father—namely the murder of the mother. In Kristeva's reading, Freud himself falls prey to the cultural taboo concerning the unconscious memory of the symbolic murder of the mother as the primary condition for any form of identity bound to the Symbolic Order as the realm of the father.

Further, for Kristeva, literature is a privileged site for interrogating that boundary between subjectivity and the pre-subjective realm which is characterized by

> the instability of the symbolic function in its most significant aspect—the prohibition placed on the maternal body (as a defence against autoeroticism and incest taboo). Here, drives hold sway and constitute a strange space that I shall name, after Plato (*Timeius*, 48–53), a *chora*, a receptacle. (14)

Literary texts explore the limits of language and playfully engage with the border to forbidden territories beyond the empire of the Symbolic Order:

> In a world in which the Other has collapsed, the aesthetic task—a descent into the foundations of the symbolic construct—amounts to

retracing the fragile limits of the speaking being, closest to its dawn, to the bottomless 'primacy' constituted by primal repression.... Great modern literature unfolds over that terrain: Dostoyevsky, Lautréamont, Proust, Artaud, Kafka, Céline. (18)

Yet, as this essay will argue, not only modern literature, but Victorian novels as well are immersed in psychological patterns:

In the largest sense, the importance of psychology to a study of the novel lies in... their mutual implication: their shared formal concerns (ways of writing, or narrating, the self), their shared imaginative powers (ways of picturing the mind), and their shared goals (a satisfyingly complete image of the mind's processes).... thus it was... that George Eliot, along with her partner G.H. Lewes, studied comparative anatomy in order to understand the workings of the nerves and brain. The novel, in brief, was part of the story of psychology, just as surely as psychology is part of the history of the novel form. (Dames 93f.)

Following these premises, I shall outline the function of taboo and abjection in George Eliot's novel *Daniel Deronda* (1988 [1876]). With Kristeva's "EXILE WHO ASKS, 'WHERE?'," I shall not ask "...as to his 'being', [but rather] concerning his place. 'Where *am I?*' instead of 'Who *am I?*'" (Kristeva 1982, 8). I shall read the novel as an exponent of a normative model of self-formation that is dramatized by transgressive behavior, and in so doing, I will focus on the female characters of Gwendolen Harleth and 'the Alcharisi', the mother of the Jewish title hero. My thesis is that both these characters' fates illustrate and finally enforce the cultural norms of a masculine self which is demarcated by taboos. These taboos are lodged in primal and secondary repression according to the rules of a masculine order of the symbolic. This order is represented by the eponymous hero Daniel Deronda and his line of biological and social Jewish forefathers. However, before I turn to the novel, I shall address a few preliminary questions and outline Kristeva's model of individuation.

Most literary texts dealing with taboos only make a topic of violating taboos—they are not violating taboos themselves. In the process of narrativization, as Schaffers (25) argues, the event is processed for the cultural archives. As this transformation assimilates taboos to the discourse of the Symbolic Order and thereby domesticates them, the question arises: How do we recognize taboos, especially if they are unconscious to a large degree? For Kristeva, feelings of horror, fear or dread, disgust, revulsion, and nausea or physical reactions like vomiting, fainting, or trembling signal that the individual is

196 &&& *Anna-Margaretha Horatschek*

confronted with the tabooed limits of those aspects of reality which his or her culture has circumscribed as 'normal', 'real', or 'true', and which are included in the semantic field of a cultural reality. In a similar vein, Jürgen Habermas reads such symptoms of physical distress as paleo-symbolic signs which stem from pre-linguistic phases of individuation and should not be mistaken as empty signs, as they are based on experiences and carry meaning.[2] In Kristeva's psychological model of subject formation, these paleo-symbolic signs announce the proximity of the abject, a theoretical space which the pre-oedipal child has to leave in order to become a subject. In this process,

> a space becomes demarcated, separating the abject from what will be a subject and its objects,... prior to the springing forth of the ego, of its objects and representations. The latter, in turn, as they depend on another repression, the 'secondary' one, arrive only *a posteriori* on an enigmatic foundation that has already been marked off.... (Kristeva 1982, 11)

This act of separation is what Kristeva calls primal repression, "which fashions the human being.... 'I' am not but do *separate, reject, ab-ject*" (ibid. 13). Only after this abjection does the secondary repression lead to "being *like*" through an act of identification: "The *mimesis*, by means of which he becomes homologous to another in order to become himself, is in short logically and chronologically secondary" (ibid). Thus, the 'abject' indicates the *chora*, a psychological state which exists prior to the separation of subject and object, of consciousness and the unconscious, and prior to the ego and to the entrance into the Symbolic Order:

> On such limits and at the limit one could say that there is no unconscious, which is elaborated when representations and affects (whether or not tied to representations) shape a logic. Here, on the contrary, consciousness has not assumed its rights and transformed into signifiers those fluid demarcations of yet unstable territories where an 'I' that is taking shape is ceaselessly straying. We are no longer within the sphere of the unconscious but at the limit of primal repression that, nevertheless, has discovered an intrinsically corporeal and already signifying brand, symptom, and sign: repugnance, disgust, abjection. (11)

According to Kristeva, these symptoms arise whenever the subject is confronted with phenomena that undermine his or her grip on reality and self. These phenomena initiate a regression to this very first stage of the self-formation of "the future subject," which has to "leave the natural mansion" (13) and destroy the child's pre-oedipal sense of unity with the mother in order to establish the primary difference of self and other. As Young argues:

> Thus the border of separation can be established only by expelling or rejecting the mother, who until then is not distinguished from the infant, so that the expulsion that creates the border between inside and outside is an expulsion of itself, its continuity.... The abject is other than the subject but only as just the other side of the border. So the abject is not opposed to and facing the subject, but next to it, too close for comfort.... The abject provokes fear and loathing because it exposes the border between self and other as constituted and fragile and because it threatens to dissolve the subject by dissolving the border. (201f.)

Consequently, the abject challenges not only the ego but the truth-and-reality-claims of cultural codifications which are internalized as superego. Any approach to the world of human self abjection "notifies us of the limits of the human universe" (Kristeva 1982, 11).

For the following interpretation I shall read all those signs that disrupt the order of socially controlled behavior, such as tears, sobs, faints and cries as

> the metaphors of non-speech, a 'semiotics' that linguistic communication does not account for...evoking sorrowful humanity [as] representatives of a 'return of the repressed' in monotheism. They re-establish what is non-verbal and show up as the receptacle of a signifying disposition that is closer to so-called primary processes. (Kristeva 1986, 174)

In my reading they signify a moment of transgression into tabooed territories of the *chora*.

Gwendolen Harleth—the young, beautiful, and naively narcissistic protagonist of George Eliot's novel *Daniel Deronda* (1876)—is confronted twice with abjection in the very moments she reaches out imaginatively to secure an identity in perfect compliance with the social norms of her society. Inspecting the house where she has to move with her family because of financial difficulties, the young woman contemplates her beauty in a mirror, when "a hinged panel of the wainscot at the other end of the room" opens and discloses

198 **Anna-Margaretha Horatschek**

"the picture of an upturned dead face, from which an obscure figure seemed to be fleeing with outstretched arms" (20). We are left in the dark as to the origin of this picture during the entire novel. Thus the narrative places the image of its first appearance right next to Gwendolen's mirror image, which epitomizes the gender norms of her social surroundings. Seen in light of Kristeva's model, this scene dramatizes the hypothesis: "To each ego its object, to each superego its abject" (Kristeva 1982, 2). Gwendolen's mimetic identity *"like"* (13) the cultural norms, which is the product of secondary repression, is superseded by the disruptive incursion of primal repression, when the amorphous non-identical existence of the child has been rejected, abjected, and separated into an 'I' and the Other:

> The corpse, seen without God and outside of science, is the utmost of abjection. It is death infecting life. Abject. It is something rejected from which one does not part, from which one does not protect oneself as from an object. Imaginary uncanniness and real threat, it beckons to us and ends up engulfing us. (4)

In the scene mentioned above, and for the rest of the novel, Gwendolen will be similarly haunted by the image of "a white dead face from which she was ever trying to flee and for ever held back.... And it came—it came" (*DD* 577 and 592).

The picture imposes its presence for a second time at a moment that was intended as a triumphant public presentation of Gwendolen's mimetic self. The occasion arises when Gwendolen represents Hermione in a *tableau vivant* of the last scene of Shakespeare's *The Winter's Tale*. Hermione has unjustly been suspected of adultery and according to the order of her husband, King Leontes, should have been killed. However, in the final scene of the drama Hermione is presented on stage as a statue, that mysteriously comes to life at the sound of music. In Shakespeare's drama, the miracle is revealed as a ruse which has been played on the king as well as on the audience, since Hermione has been hidden for sixteen years and has not been killed. Thus the supposed corpse has been alive all this time and now can re-enter life through the art of sculpting and music. Yet when in Gwendolen's "imitation of acting" (*DD* 48)—just like in Shakespeare's play—the order is given "Music, awake her, strike!", and the genial pianist Herr Klesmer "struck a thunderous chord..., the movable panel... flew open on the right opposite the stage and disclosed the picture of the dead face and the fleeing figure brought out in pale definiteness by the position of the wax-lights" (*DD* 49).[3] Whereas Shakespeare's drama shows the triumph of life over death, the novel's scene reveals the unsettling presence of death in life. Gwendolen's reaction to this disclosure displays all the characteristics of abjection, since, accompanied by

> a piercing cry...Gwendolen...stood...with a change of expression that was terrifying in its terror. She looked like a statue into which a soul of Fear had entered: her pallid lips were parted; her eyes...were dilated and fixed....Gwendolen fell on her knees and put her hands before her face. She was still trembling, but mute, and it seemed that she had self-consciousness enough to aim at controlling her signs of terror, for she presently allowed herself to be raised from her kneeling posture and led away.... (ibid.)

In Kristeva's words:

> That elsewhere that I imagine beyond the present, or that I hallucinate so that I might, in a present time, speak to you, conceive of you—it is now here, jetted, abjected, into 'my' world. Deprived of world, therefore, I *fall in a faint*. In that compelling, raw, insolent thing in the morgue's full sunlight, in that thing that no longer matches and therefore no longer signifies anything, I behold the breaking down of a world that has erased its borders: fainting away. (1982, 4)

At this moment Gwendolen experiences that "[t]he more or less beautiful image in which I behold or recognize myself rests upon an abjection that sunders it as soon as repression, the constant watchman, is relaxed" (*DD* 13).

Whereas Gwendolen's 'mimetic' self, in compliance with the visual norms of what a woman has to look like, signifies the product of secondary repression, namely "*mimesis*, by means of which [she] becomes homologous to another in order to become [her]self" (ibid.), the dead face incorporates the abject: "[T]he corpse, the most sickening of wastes, is a border that has encroached upon everything....The border has become an object" (3f.). For Gwendolen, the face of the corpse represents all those "things which were meant to be shut up" (*DD* 20), namely a psychic reality the young woman has unconsciously known and tried to repress for years: To be a princess means to be a "princess in exile" (*DD* 32), whose identity is hinged on an 'I'. The narrating voice describes Gwendolen's split between her awareness of the "the vastness in which she seemed

200 ✦ *Anna-Margaretha Horatschek*

an exile" (*DD* 52), and the conscious will for a socially assimilated, mimetic 'I' as

> the iridescence of her character—the play of various, nay, contrary tendencies. For Macbeth's rhetoric about the impossibility of being many opposite things in the same moment, referred to the clumsy necessities of action and not to the subtler possibilities of feeling.... but a moment is room wide enough for the loyal and mean desire, for the outlash of a murderous thought and the sharp backward stroke of repentance. (*DD* 33)

The reference to Macbeth leaves no doubt that Gwendolen's mimesis of the Victorian gender stereotype hides murderous thoughts. But before these thoughts will become manifest against her husband Grandcourt, Gwendolen commits a symbolic murder against the mother of his illegitimate children. During his entire courtship the prospective husband has not mentioned Lydia Glasher, who nine years earlier left her husband Colonel Glasher and a child, and has since had two daughters and two sons with her lover. Grandcourt expects her to concur with his plans to marry another woman, but his long-term mistress forces herself on Gwendolen and makes her promise not to accept Grandcourt: "My husband is dead now, and Mr Grandcourt ought to marry me. He ought to make that boy his heir." Gwendolen is fully aware that "I am a woman's life" (*DD* 128), but she takes this life and breaks her promise by accepting Grandcourt's proposal. With this decision, she excludes the mother of her husband's children from a proper place in the social world in order to gain an admired identity herself through the wealth and rank of her husband. However, the young wife learns that the marriage reduces her to the status of a beautiful ornament and robs her of any possibilities for a place of her own. In addition, her awareness of her treason undermines the stability of her identity. What she does not know is that Grandcourt has found out about his mistress' meeting with his future wife and thus is fully informed about Gwendolen's moral failing. Consequently, the couple's relationship is poisoned by their mutual secrecy about tabooed knowledge: Whereas Grandcourt exploits his power over Gwendolen's psyche with sadistic lust, the young woman mourns the loss of her personal integrity. Broken by her husband's tyrannical imposition of his will, Gwendolen's hate culminates in her hesitation to throw a rope when he falls overboard their sailing ship. When her ensuing attempts to

'Logicized' Taboo   201

save him prove fruitless, she has become "a murderess" (*DD* 591) in her own eyes.

Gwendolen's dread as well as her hysterical sobs after his death are markers of her regression to the border between the conscious 'I' and an ontologically primary basis of her psyche which she fears. In her confession to Daniel Deronda she admits: "I told you from the beginning—as soon as I could—I told you I was afraid of myself" (ibid.). Her tortured narration makes clear that the act formed the manifestation of psychological processes which have accompanied her entire life:

> All sorts of contrivances in my mind—but all so difficult. And I fought against them—I was terrified at them—I saw his dead face...ever so long ago I saw it; and I wished him to be dead. And yet it terrified me. I was like two creatures. I could not speak—I wanted to kill—it was as strong as thirst—and then directly—I felt beforehand I had done something dreadful, unalterable—that would make me like an evil spirit. And it came—it came. (*DD* 592)

The overriding significance with which the narration imbues the wished for murder of Gwendolen's father-husband in comparison to her active social annihilation of the mother Lydia Gasher forms a structural analogy to Freud's superimposition of the murder of the father over the ontologically prior and more fundamental murder of the mother in his writings.

While Gwendolen herself has no explanation for "her susceptibility to terror," the narrator explicitly relates her "fits of spiritual dread" to "the religion taught her" (*DD* 51f.):

> Solitude in any wide scene impressed her with an undefined feeling of immeasurable existence aloof from her, in the midst of which she was helplessly incapable of asserting herself. The little astronomy taught her at school used sometimes to set her imagination at work in a way that made her tremble; but always when some one joined her she recovered her indifference to the vastness in which she seemed an exile; she found again her usual world in which her will was of some avail, and the religious nomenclature belonging to this world was no more identified for her with those uneasy impressions of awe than her uncle's surplices seen out of use at the rectory. (*DD* 52)

According to Kristeva, a secularized attitude toward religion leads more readily to those primal repressions at "the limits of the human

202 &&& *Anna-Margaretha Horatschek*

universe" (1982, 11), as Christian morality can function as a kind of culturally inserted bulwark against the psychological proximity of the abject:

> In the contemporary practice of the West and owing to the crisis in Christianity, abjection elicits more archaic resonances that are culturally prior to sin; through them it again assumes its biblical status, and beyond it that of defilement in primitive societies. (17f.)

In this context, Gwendolen's "tremor on suddenly feeling herself alone, when, for example, she was walking without companionship and there came some rapid change in the light" (*DD* 52), indicates her susceptibility for intimations of a radical loneliness. In Kristeva's diction, this is

> the culminating form of that experience of the subject to which it is revealed that all its objects are based merely on the inaugural *loss* that laid the foundations of its own being. There is nothing like the abjection of self to show that all abjection is in fact recognition of the *want* on which any being, meaning, language, or desire is founded....if one imagines...the experience of *want* itself as logically preliminary to being and object—to the being of the object—then one understands that abjection, and even more so abjection of self, is its only signified. (1982, 5)

Gwendolen can counter this regression "when someone joined her" (*DD* 52) and—in psychoanalytical terminology—supplies the Lacanian mirror (cf. Horatschek 2004, 614) to assure her of the—imaginary—presence of a self. Yet the novel as a whole is not satisfied with this individual counterstrategy against regression, but propagates an entire system of secularized morality as a substitute for Christian morals. According to Kristeva,

> [a]n unshakable adherence to Prohibition and Law is necessary if that perverse interspace of abjection is to be hemmed in and thrust aside. Religion, Morality, Law. Obviously always arbitrary, more or less; unfailingly oppressive, rather more than less; laboriously prevailing, more and more so. (1982, 16)

It is Daniel Deronda's task to fend off the abject and represent and install a prohibitive system of rules, perfectly in tune with the cultural necessity to constrain the proximity of the archaic realm harboring

'Logicized' Taboo   203

the primordial lack of the psyche. Toward the end of this very long novel, the eponymous hero and mentor of Gwendolen Harleth reads her "dread" as the language of a moral self which has been covered up by the superficial values of upper class Victorian England: "Turn your fear into a safeguard. Keep your dread fixed on the idea of increasing your remorse ... [*sic*] Take your fear as a safeguard. It is like quickness of hearing. It may make consequences passionately present to you" (*DD* 577).

Deronda's admonishments repeat George Eliot's opinion that an authentic morality has to replace religious doctrines in an utterly secularized world. In dire need of a transcendental signified that might provide anchorage for moral demands, the 'Victorian Sage' resorted to the general practice of the Victorian age and transferred models of natural science as explicatory systems onto social, gender and ethical problems (cf. Richardson), envisioning the realm of ethics as ruled by a 'moral law' which functions in analogy to natural law. Accordingly, the structure of the secularized 'ethical law' is defined by the classical episteme and the "Natural History of social bodies" which are incarnate in the cultural practice of the present.[4]

The novel places this counter-world of moral authenticity, historical responsibility, duty and sympathy in Jewish thinking and music, embodied in the title hero. Daniel's admonishments replace the worn out Christian doctrines as bulwarks against the abject, and the structures of the moral law superimpose the horizon of cultural restrictions over the anarchic realm of the abject. Paleo-symbolic manifestations of the abject, enmeshed in physicality, have to 'pass through' the realms of the incarnate law and hence arrive at the doors of consciousness as signs of moral rules inscribed in the body. Daniel Deronda has transformed the abject into an embodied morality that obeys the logic of the natural sciences.

With logicized morals substituting religion, the tide of anarchic impulses is supposed to be stemmed: According to this model of self-formation, Gwendolen has to overcome her narcissistic hermeticism and face her innate morality to find "her fuller self" (ibid.). She must insert herself into the general laws of morality, which are not those held by the majority in her social surroundings, but those dramatized by the novel's title hero. For him, her sobs do not tell about her inaugural loss and existential loneliness, but are symptoms of her naturally existent moral self. Deronda employs these signs as warnings not to transgress the order of things pre-established in the moral law, but to adhere to the rules

204   *Anna-Margaretha Horatschek*

of this quasi-natural Symbolic Order and to keep inside the confines of its regime. Outside of this realm there is horror: "[T]hink that a severe angel, seeing you along the road of error, grasped you by the wrist, and showed you the horror of the life you must avoid" (*DD* 658). With a view to Julia Kristeva's model of individuation, *Daniel Deronda* thus pushes Gwendolen symbolically from the point of primal repression toward the point of secondary repression, where individuality is achieved by the rules of mimesis. He presents the moral law as "an other with whom I identify" (Kristeva 1982, 10) in order to realize one's true self.

Significantly, Deronda's mother Leonora Princess Halm-Eberstein—who conforms neither to the conventions of English society, nor to the rules of the Jewish community, nor to the moral law represented by Daniel Deronda—is eaten up by a disease that might be cancer. Read as symptom and paleo-symbolic sign, the body of the princess speaks its own language, "a language that gives up, a structure within the body, a non-assimilable alien, a monster, a tumor, a cancer that the listening devices of the unconscious do not hear, for its strayed subject is huddled outside the paths of desire" (11).

This may seem surprising, as she seems to have followed nothing but her desire to become an artist. In order to achieve this goal, she deliberately married a weak man—for she must marry according to the law of her Jewish father—, then gave away her baby son who interfered with her career without any qualms, and when finally she sees him as a grown up man and reveals her relationship to him, she does not admit any motherly feelings:

> No princess in this tame life that I live in now. I was a great singer, and I acted as well as I sang. All the rest were poor beside me. Men followed me from one country to another. I was living a myriad lives in one. I did not want a child.... I did not want to marry. I was forced into marrying your father—forced, I mean, by my father's wishes and commands; and besides, it was my best way of getting some freedom. I could rule my husband, but not my father. I had a right to be free. I had a right to seek my freedom from a bondage that I hated. (*DD* 537)

During this interview, her son is "clutching his coat-collar as if he were keeping himself above water by it, and feeling his blood in the sort of commotion that might have been excited if he had seen her going through some strange rite of a religion which gave a sacredness to crime" (ibid.).

His fear of drowning is not astonishing as he perceives his mother as the watery nymph Melusina, derived from French legends. "She was a remarkable-looking being.... Her worn beauty had a strangeness in it as if it were not quite a human mother, but a Melusina, who had ties with some world which is independent of ours" (*DD* 536). This mythical creature insisted on the preservation of a realm of her self hidden from the male gaze of knowledge, and was betrayed by her human lover, because he could not bear to leave her strangeness intact. Deronda's mother is well aware of her being stigmatized as a monster: "Every woman is supposed to have the same set of motives, or else to be a monster. I am not a monster, but I have not felt exactly what other women feel—or say they feel, for fear of being thought unlike others" (*DD* 539).

The text cannot bear this outrageous feminine reality. Measured with the rod of the moral law represented by Daniel Deronda, she is abjected and associated with "[t]he traitor, the liar, the criminal with a good conscience..." because they "disturb...identity, system. Order. What does not respect borders, positions, rules. The in-between, the ambiguous, the composite...any crime, because it draws attention to the fragility of the law, is abject..." (Kristeva 1982, 4). Yet although Princess Halm-Eberstein evaded the lot of what her father called "'the Jewish woman',", who had to "adore the wisdom of [laws], however silly they might seem to me" (*DD* 540), she always "had an awe of my father" (*DD* 542). This awe wins out in the end, as "a fatal illness" (*DD* 539) and "evil enchantments" (*DD* 540) force her "to obey my dead father...and deliver to you what he commanded me to deliver" (*DD* 541), although she still feels "'the same Leonora'—she pointed with her forefinger to her breast—'here within me is the same desire, the same will, the same choice...'" (*DD* 540).

The novel does not answer the question of whether her illness voices the law and punishment of the father, or whether it articulates Leonora's flaunted desires and her heart being "pressed small, like Chinese feet" (541). According to Kristeva's model, the abjected body of the rebellious mother manifests itself in defiance of the law of the father; interpreted in analogy to Deronda's reading of Gwendolen's dread, the moral law demands justice and retribution for having been flaunted a lifetime.

206 ᙓᙔ *Anna-Margaretha Horatschek*

The implementation of this moral law opens up a deep-structural alternative to the values of English society as well as to the petrified law of Leonora's Jewish father in the novel. It enables a moral critique of the superficiality and inauthenticity of a society either too lax or too restrictive, and yet claims to be in agreement with human nature. In this concept of the psyche, there is no abject. Instead the novel—like the bible—succeeds in *"logicizing* of what departs from the symbolic, and for that very reason it prevents it from being actualized as demonic evil. Such a logicizing inscribes the demonic in a more abstract an [*sic*] also more moral register as a potential for guilt and sin" (Kristeva 1982, 91).

For Kristeva it is the twelfth-century Jewish philosopher, astronomer, doctor and lawyer Moses Maimonides who explicates this *"logic of distribution* and behaviour on which the symbolic community is founded: a Law, a reason" (91f.). Tellingly, the most important authority for Gwendolen's mentor Deronda is the Jewish visionary Mordecai, who repeatedly refers to Maimonides as his authority. According to Kristeva, the entire tradition following Maimonides works at the expulsion of the abject, "the archaic relation to the mother," as her very presence threatens that

> *strategy of identity,* which is, in all strictness, that of monotheism.... In other words, the place *and* law of the One do not exist without a *series of separations* that are oral, corporeal, or even more generally material, and in the last analysis relating to fusion with the mother. [Judaism] carries into the private lives of everyone the brunt of the struggle each subject must wage during the entire length of his personal history in order to become separate, that is to say, to become a speaking subject and/or subject to Law. (106)

In phylogenetic as well as in individual 'strategies of identity', biblical taboos "are responses of symbolic Law, in the sphere of subjective economy and the genesis of speaking identity"; any "breach of the order regulated by taboo" (94) must be re-established by a sacrifice so as "to have access or not to a place—the holy place of the Temple" (93). Further:

> [T]his sets up at once the problem of the relations between *taboo* and *sacrifice.* It would seem as though God had penalized by means of the flood a breach of the order regulated by taboo. The burnt offering set up by Noah must then re-establish the order disturbed by the breaking of taboo. (94)

The holy place of the Temple is the place of the Law of God, the Father. For the individual genesis read in view of psychoanalytical structures, this realm of the father is represented by the Symbolic Order, and it takes the sacrifice of the mother in order to gain—or insure—access to this 'Temple'. Leonora's outrageous rejection of her motherhood discloses this tabooed prerequisite of the individual's admittance to the Symbolic Order, which is covered up by the hypostazation of motherhood. To admit and justify this act destroys the working conditions of any taboo which relies on the opacity of its meaning. Because of the uncanny disclosure and the shameless affirmation of the 'murder' of her motherhood, the Alcharisi is stigmatized as a monster and banished from the order of society; from the world of the novel she is expulsed by her death.

In contrast, Klesmer, a Jewish musician and her male counterpart, represents the cultural ideal of enclosing art—which for Kristeva "is rooted in the abject it utters and by the same token purifies, . . . the essential component of religiosity" (17)—in the confines of moral laws. Trying to cure Gwendolen of her delusions about becoming a famous actress, he tells her:

> . . . you wish to try the life of the artist; you wish to try a life of arduous, unceasing work. . . . You must know what you have to strive for, and then you must subdue your mind and body to unbroken discipline. . . . Genius at first is little more than a great capacity for receiving discipline. . . . Your muscles—your whole frame—must go like a watch, true, true, true, to a hair. (*DD* 216–19)

It is Klesmer and Daniel Deronda who survive as normative characters. Both have effectively silenced the voices of the abject manifested in Gwendolen and Leonora, which were directed against the law of authoritarian forefathers such as the hero's grandfather Daniel Charisi. At the end of the novel, his doctrine is handed on to Deronda—and the reader—by Kalonymos as the accumulated wisdom of tradition which shows the way into the avid grandson's future:

> He said, 'Let us bind ourselves with duty, as if we were sons of the same mother.' That was his bent from first to last—as he said, to fortify his soul with bonds. It was a saying of his, 'Let us bind love with duty; for duty is the love of law; and law is the nature of the Eternal.' So we bound ourselves. (*DD* 617)

208 ❧ *Anna-Margaretha Horatschek*

Once again the order of male bonding overlays the role of the mother and replaces primal immersion with consciously gendered structures.

Gwendolen is not granted any prominent place in this patriarchal order. "[F]or the first time being dislodged from her supremacy in her own world, and getting a sense that her horizon was but a dipping onward of an existence with which her own was revolving" (*DD* 689), she has to bear Daniel's farewell visit, during which he finally tells her of his plans to marry Mirah and to go to Israel. She must content herself with her beloved mentor's image as the ultimate norm of morality, which will lure and command her into the laws of a patriarchal world. But the abject will not be repressed without a struggle. After Deronda has left, "[t]hrough the day and half the night she fell continually into fits of shrieking, but cried in the midst of them to her mother, 'Don't be afraid. I shall live. I mean to live. . . . I shall be better' " (692).

Notes

1. Kristeva refers to Freud, *Totem and Taboo*, 1913, in vol. 13 of *Complete Works*. Freud develops his myth of the murder of the archaic father in his essay *Moses and Monotheism*.

2. For an explication of this concept cf. Horatschek 1998a: Paleosymbols are primal symbolic forms generating meaning which are precursors of the ontogenetic and phylogenetic organization of symbols. "The earlier organization of symbols which does not allow the transposition of its contents into grammatically regulated communication can only be investigated through data about the pathology of speech and on the basis of an analysis of the content of dreams. We are here concerned with symbols which direct behaviour and not just with signs since symbols possess an authentic meaning-function; they represent experiences gained in interaction" (Horatschek quoting Habermas 197).

3. For the function of music in G. Eliot and Shakespeare cf. Horatschek 2004.

4. Cf. Eliot 2005, 131. Seminal studies that analyze this interrelation are by Shuttleworth, Carroll, and Ermarth. For an account of Eliot's uneasy alliance of classical thought paradigms with organicism cf. Horatschek 1998b.

Works Cited

Butler, Judith. *Gender Trouble. Feminism and the Subversion of Identity.* London: Routledge, 1990.

'Logicized' Taboo &&& 209

Carroll, David. *George Eliot and the Conflict of Interpretations: A Reading of the Novels*. Cambridge: Cambridge UP, 1992.

Dames, Nicholas. "'The Withering of the Individual': Psychology in the Victorian Novel." *A Concise Companion to the Victorian Novel*. Ed. Francis O'Gorman. Blackwell: Oxford, 2005. 91–112.

Eliot, George. *Daniel Deronda*. Ed. and introd. Graham Handley. Oxford: Oxford UP, 1988.

———. "The Natural History of German Life." *Selected Essays, Poems and Other Writings*. Eds. A.S. Byatt and Nicholas Warren. Harmondsworth: Penguin, 2005. 107–39.

Ermarth, Elizabeth Deeds. "Incarnations: George Eliot's Conception of 'Undeviating Law'." *Nineteenth Century Fiction* 23.3 (1974): 273–86.

Foucault, Michel. *Der Wille zum Wissen. Sexualität und Wahrheit 1*. Frankfurt am Main: Suhrkamp, 1983.

Freud, Sigmund. *Totem und Tabu. Einige Übereinstimmungen im Seelenleben der Wilden und der Neurotiker*. Frankfurt am Main: Fischer, 1999.

Habermas, Jürgen. "The Hermeneutic Claim to Universality." *Contemporary Hermeneutics: Method, Philosophy and Critique*. Ed. J. Bleicher. London: Routledge and Kegan Paul, 1980. 181–211.

Horatschek, Annegreth [Anna-Margaretha]. *Alterität und Stereotyp. Die Funktion des Fremden in den "International Novels" von E.M. Forster und D.H. Lawrence*. Tübingen: Narr, 1998a.

———. "The Order of Things in George Eliot's *Adam Bede*." *Anglistentag 1997 Giessen*. Eds. Raimund Borgmeier, Herbert Grabes, and Andreas H. Jucker. Trier: WVT, 1998b. 399–412.

———. "The Auditory Self: Self-Constitution by Text, Voice, and Music in English Literature." *Anglistentag 2004 Aachen*. Eds. Lilo Moessner and Christa M. Schmidt. Trier: WVT, 2004. 225–36.

———. "Spiegelstadium." *Metzler Lexikon Literatur- und Kulturtheorie*. Ed. Ansgar Nünning. Stuttgart: Metzler, 4th edition, 2008. 614–15.

Kristeva, Julia. *Powers of Horror. An Essay on Abjection*. New York: Columbia UP, 1982.

———. "Stabat Mater." *The Kristeva Reader*. Ed. Toril Moi. Oxford: Basil Blackwell, 1986. 163–83.

Mead, George Herbert. *Mind, Self and Society from the Standpoint of a Social Behaviorist*. Chicago: U of Chicago P, 1967.

Richardson, Angelique. "The Life Sciences: 'Everybody Nowadays Talks about Evolution'." *A Concise Companion to Modernism*. Ed. David Bradshaw. Malden: Blackwell, 2003. 6–33.

Schaffers, Uta. "*Geschehnisse, die für alle Zeiten der Menschheit verborgen bleiben sollten*—und wie davon erzählt wird." *Tabu und Tabubruch in Literatur und Film*. Ed. Michael Braun. Würzburg: Königshausen and Neumann, 2007. 21–44.

Shuttleworth, Sally. *George Eliot and Nineteenth-Century Science: The Make-Believe of a Beginning.* Cambridge: Cambridge UP, 1984.

Young, Iris Marion. "Abjection and Oppression: Dynamics of Unconscious Racism, Sexism and Homophobia." *Crises in Continental Philosophy.* Eds. Arleen B. Dallery and Charles E. Scott. Albany: State UP of New York, 1990. 201–13.

CHAPTER XI

REVALUATING TRANSGRESSION IN *ULYSSES*

Stefan Glomb

If one were to think of a handful of texts that have redrawn the literary map and changed the course of literary history, James Joyce's *Ulysses* would certainly be one of them, and for reasons that are closely bound up with the problem of transgression. If we take 'transgressive' to mean "denoting or relating to writing, cinema or art in which orthodox cultural, moral, or artistic boundaries are challenged by the representation of unconventional behaviour and the use of experimental forms" (*OED*; note how this definition already locates the transgressive in the realm of art rather than referring to a more general usage), *Ulysses* is transgressive on both counts listed in the last part of the definition. The novel contains many instances of unconventional or transgressive thoughts and actions, and in order to facilitate the representation of taboo areas, the boundaries of conventional modes of literary fiction needed to be transgressed. The fact that defecation, masturbation, and a variety of more or less explicit sexual fantasies are presented in the novel has contributed to its notoriety, and these features spring readily to mind when one thinks of transgression in *Ulysses*.

Contrary to this rather obvious approach, this essay will not dwell on the numerous ways in which the novel violates the dictates of propriety but will seek to develop a more fundamental understanding of transgression, which is based on the original Latin meaning 'to cross / pass' (without the pejorative coloring that the word acquired later in its history), thereby opening up a perspective that comprises much more than the breaking of taboos and conventions: "Transgression and its capacity to challenge, fracture, overthrow, spoil or question the unquestionable can no longer be contained as naughtiness

212 &&& *Stefan Glomb*

or occasional abhorration. Transgression is part of the purpose of being…" (Jenks 81). Transgression in this sense is concerned with moving beyond a state where identities and concepts (i.e., race, class, gender, religion, nationality) are stabilized, well-defined, and petrified, toward a fluidity which serves as the basis for an implicitly ethical approach fusing aesthetic, epistemological, and practical aspects: "boundaries, as Joyce describes them, are heuristic borders designed to be surpassed—not lightly, but at the appropriate time, to initiate new stages of cognitive and emotional development" (Mahaffey 168). The aim, therefore, is to show how *Ulysses* performs a revaluation of the narrow and pejorative meaning of 'transgression' toward a wider and more positive meaning without simply turning the evaluative pattern upside down: transgression as such is neither opposed nor hailed. But the ways in which the novel points out numerous instances in which the need for overstepping boundaries in one context may be just as fundamental as the need for order and stability in another give an entirely new slant on how we commonly think about transgression. One major aspect of this revaluation of transgression in *Ulysses* is the fact that that which is being transgressed is exposed as transgressive in its turn, that is the tables are turned on what has formerly been seen as the object of a violation but on close inspection turns out to be the root of the problem. Hence, this type of transgression can be seen as the "negation of a negative" (Babcock 19).

What emerges is a complex web spun out of five different facets of transgression (T) in *Ulysses*, which are part of a temporal sequence: at first, there are boundaries based on ordering structures which are felt to be transgressive since they invade and violate the subjects' personal integrity and impose limits on the scope of their development (T1: this is an unusual notion of 'transgression' since what it denotes does not originate directly in the thoughts and actions of human subjects). Second, there occurs a crossing of these boundaries and a concomitant questioning of the values connected to them (T2: this is more or less the commonly held assumption as to what 'transgression' means). T1 therefore triggers T2, and both are located within the characters' *Lebenswelt*, that is the sphere of that which occurs to them, what they think and do. T2 falls into two subcategories: T2a (violations of taboos) and T2b (a lack of compliance with ordering systems which are not, or not to the same degree, protected by taboos). Finally, T1 and T2 are constituent features of an aesthetic design which comprises yet also transcends them in that it establishes a transgressive realm in its own right (T3). Of course, everything in

Revaluating Transgression in Ulysses ❧❧❧ 213

Ulysses is part of its aesthetic make-up; yet it seems helpful to distinguish between what happens to the characters in their *Lebenswelt* and the transgressive elements employed by the novel as a whole (i.e., the techniques which are not directly linked to the characters). Again, it is necessary to distinguish between T3a (breaking of taboos) and T3b (other kinds of boundary-crossing). Transgression as a narrow and pejorative concept is therefore *aufgehoben* in the threefold Hegelian sense of the German term *Aufhebung* as negation, conservation, and the elevation to another level, and this is what is meant here by the revaluation of transgression. This conceptual framework should not be misunderstood as a hard-and-fast system comprising clearly distinguishable categories but as a broad heuristic tool charting overlapping domains since it would be highly inappropriate to analyze a novel which questions the validity and desirability of systematic rigidity by means of a rigid system. Thus, the approach proposed here does not aim at schematic reductionism but, on the contrary, sets out to demonstrate the sheer variety and interdependence of different facets of transgression in *Ulysses*.

Rather than considering Joyce's highly complex text in its entirety, this essay is based mainly on a reading of the 'Nausicaa'-chapter, a selection that can be backed up by the following three arguments, one of them obvious, the other two less so: I. (mainly concerning T2a and T3a) this chapter marks the point in the history of the reception of *Ulysses* at which, in 1920, the *Society for the Suppression of Vice in America* intervened and put an end to the novel's publication; II. (mainly concerning T2b and T3b) the chapter does not merely violate sexual and religious taboos (if that were all, there would be no need to make a lot of fuss about it these days) but, more interestingly, moves on from there to destabilize and question the conceptions in which taboos and other "thou shalt not's" (Babcock 21) are rooted; III. (concerning T3) 'Nausicaa' can be seen as a microcosm that mirrors the macrocosm of the text as a whole, that is the chapter's strategies function along the same lines as those of the entire text. T1 as that which sets off the other kinds of transgression is always involved. These three aspects provide the structure of what follows.

I

After the emotional turmoil and stylistic extravaganzas of the previous 'Cyclops'-chapter, 'Nausicaa' offers a phase of comparative calm both for Bloom and the reader. The mythological counterpart to

214   *⚹*   *Stefan Glomb*

Bloom's encounter with Gerty MacDowell on Sandymount Strand is the episode in Homer's *Odyssey* where the protagonist reveals himself to Nausicaa, daughter to the king of the Phaeacians: "He praises her beauty, likens her to a goddess, and pleads the hardship of his case. His appeal is successful; Nausicaa arranges for his safe conduct to the court, and eventually her parents arrange for his safe conduct home to Ithaca" (Gifford and Seidman 384). In Joyce's twentieth-century version, Bloom watches Gerty and her friends, and, when the two of them are left alone, masturbates to a generous display of her underwear (T2a). While this brief sketch alone would suffice to account for the outrage that the chapter caused, there are numerous additional details designed to shock the guardians of propriety as will be demonstrated shortly. What marks out the chapter in formal terms is its bipartite structure—that is the fact that its first part is presented from Gerty's point of view in what Joyce himself called a "namby-pamby jammy, marmalady drawersy" style (Budgen 161), and the second part is seen from Bloom's perspective. In this, as in some other aspects, the chapter stands in stark contrast to the 'single-eyed' view of the previous 'Cyclops'-chapter, thereby aiming at the "two-eyed reader" (Blamires 128). At the same time, this structural pattern contributes to the chapter's transgressive logic (T3b), namely the move from Gerty's maidenly thoughts to the uninhibited language of Bloom in the second half. In addition to this temporal transgressive axis, the chapter is structured by a spatial axis resulting from the fact that the meeting of Bloom and Gerty is paralleled by a men's temperance retreat in progress in the Roman Catholic Church of Mary, Star of the Sea, near Sandymount Strand. Gerty's half of the chapter presents her thoughts and her view of reality as being to a large degree filtered through and even shaped by her reading of contemporary women's magazines such as *The Princess's Novelette* or the *Lady's Pictorial*. While this creates the impression that Gerty's outlook on life is naïve, sentimental, and absurd, Joyce never takes this technique to the extreme of patronizing or ridiculing her, and this forms an additional contrast to the previous chapter where the Citizen was presented in an unambiguously ludicrous way. In the interaction with her friends Cissy Caffrey and Edy Boardman, Gerty is singled out as being much more bashful, as befits her internalized notions as to the correct shape of feminine propriety: "From everything in the least indelicate her finebred nature instinctively recoiled" (*U* 298f.).[1] The fact that Bloom is watching the three friends serves to make her even

Revaluating Transgression in Ulysses   215

more self-conscious about the way Cissy refers to one of the infants in their charge:

> —I'd like to give him something, [Edy] said, so I would, where I won't say.
> —On the beeoteetom, laughed Cissy merrily.
> Gerty McDowell bent down her head and crimsoned at the idea of Cissy saying an unladylike thing like that out loud she'd be ashamed of her life to say, flushing a deep rosy red, and Edy Boardman said she was sure the gentleman opposite heard what she said. But not a pin cared Ciss. (*U* 290)

What lends this chapter its particular appeal and poignancy is the extension of this euphemistic unwillingness to name subjects considered improper to Gerty's very thoughts, which becomes clear in her use of the word "that" as a stand-in for taboo subjects. This is mirrored by the following passage, which also shows how the Church, alongside the popular press, is instrumental in delineating and guarding the boundaries of the acceptable as well as in fixing gender stereotypes (T1):

> [Father Conroy] told her that time when she told him about *that* in confession, crimsoning up to the roots of her hair for fear he could see, not to be troubled because *that* was only the voice of nature and we were all subject to nature's laws, he said, in this life and that *that* was no sin because *that* came from the nature of woman instituted by God, he said, and that Our Blessed Lady herself said to the archangel Gabriel be it done unto me according to Thy Word. (*U* 294, emphases added)

It is all the more surprising that Gerty, notwithstanding her maidenly diffidence, is well aware of the fact that Bloom is watching her and knows perfectly well about the kind of interest that motivates him: "Her woman's instinct told her that she had raised the devil in him and at the thought a burning scarlet swept from throat to brow till the lovely colour of her face became a glorious rose" (*U* 295). The "rose" and the "rosary" mentioned earlier on the same page immediately blend into one, thereby contributing to the transgressive fusion of the sacred and the profane, the spiritual and the physical, which informs the whole chapter (T3a). Just as Bloom looks up Gerty's skirt, the priests are "looking up at the Blessed Sacrament" (ibid.), hence we "are involved in a double act of adoration" (Blamires 131).

216   Stefan Glomb

And Gerty is by no means reduced to being a passive object to the male gaze: "The eyes that were fastened upon her set her pulses tingling. She looked at him a moment, meeting his glance, and a light broke in upon her" (*U* 299). (T2b) The use of 'light' as a metaphor in the context of sexual arousal is highly unusual since that metaphor is commonly used to represent that which is taken to be opposed to (or at least clearly marked off from) sexuality and the body (in contexts as divergent as Plato's philosophy, Christian religion, and the Enlightenment), and this contributes to the aforementioned transgressive fusion (T3a). The most obvious (and offensive) means of creating this fusion, the candle, works along similar lines. Again, a more innocuous metaphorical use of 'light' is drawn into the realm of the sexual/physical (just as, conversely, this sphere is tinged with a sacred hue): the candle is both phallic in shape and liable to set fire to that which is brought near it: "Canon O'Hanlon got up again and censed the Blessed Sacrament and knelt down and he told Father Conroy that one of the candles was just going to set fire to the flowers" (*U* 296). This leads up to the chapter's (and Bloom's, i.e., the 'flower's') climax, the passage where the fireworks and the voyeur's orgasm coincide (note the "Roman" candle):

> And then a rocket sprang and bang shot blind blank and O! then the Roman candle burst and it was like a sigh of O! and everyone cried O! O! in raptures and it gushed out of it a stream of rain gold hair threads and they shed and ah! They were all greeny dewy stars falling with golden, O so lovely, O, soft, sweet, soft!
> Then all melted away dewily in the grey air: all was silent. Ah! (*U* 300)

The orgasm-cum-fireworks-cum-worship over and done with, the chapter moves on to the next stage of its "tumescence-detumescence"-pattern: "a quiet opening, a long crescendo of turgid, rhapsodic prose towards a climax, a pyrotechnic explosion, a dying fall, silence" (Gilbert 157). Even though the sexual tension has abated, Bloom's thoughts still remain firmly within the realm of the physical: he congratulates himself for not having masturbated earlier in the day ("Damned glad I didn't do it in the bath this morning over her silly I will punish you letter" [*U* 301].) as well as for his timely urination ("Good job I let off there behind the wall coming out of Dignam's. Cider that was. Otherwise I couldn't have" [*U* 303].), and, to conclude the operation, rearranges his member ("Begins to feel cold and clammy. Aftereffect not pleasant" [ibid.]. "This wet is very unpleasant. Stuck. Well the foreskin is not back. Better detach. Ow!" [*U* 306]). Simultaneously, he at some length ponders Gerty's (and other women's) menstruation ("Near her monthlies, I expect" [*U* 301].), reflects on copulation in the animal kingdom ("Dogs at each other behind. Good evening. Evening. How do you sniff? Hm. Hm. Very well, thank you" [*U* 307].), and, appropriately, allows his thoughts to revert to an earlier scene in front of the museum where he tried to verify whether stone goddesses had anuses (cf. *U* 311).

To sum up, the chapter provides numerous instances which highlight the physical side of human existence, and, in doing so, creates a blasphemous crossbreed of the sacred and the profane. What is more, it is built around a climax which, in an astoundingly efficient manner, comprises quite a number of sins: masturbation, adultery, voyeurism, exhibitionism, and pedophilia (T2a, T3a). It comes as no surprise, then, that the guardians of propriety were apoplectic (and they had not even read the "Circe"-chapter . . .).

II

So much for the obviously sordid stuff. As indicated above, what lends *Ulysses* its significance in the present context does not so much derive from the novel's forays into forbidden realms than from its move toward an altogether less restricted view of transgression. This is the concept also favored by Stallybrass and White, who adopt Barbara Babcock's coterminous designation "symbolic inversion" which "may be broadly defined as any act of expressive behaviour which inverts, contradicts, abrogates, or in some fashion presents an alternative to commonly held cultural codes, values and norms, be they linguistic, literary or artistic, religious, social and political" (Babcock 14; cf. Stallybrass and White 17). "Expressive behaviour" covers both T2 and T3 since it can be located within the sphere of the characters as well as be linked to textual strategies. Transgression in this sense comprises, but also goes beyond, the instances dealt with in the first section since it is not only the violation of taboos but also other disruptions of order which contribute to the act of rearranging the cultural codes underlying areas that are crucial to a given culture's views on what is real and what is right.

One of these areas is gender. Even though *Ulysses* is centered around two males, women (mainly, of course, Molly Bloom) are indispensable to the novel's overall makeup and thereby confirm Barbara Babcock's statement that "[w]hat is socially peripheral is

218 ◆◆◆ *Stefan Glomb*

often symbolically central" (32). In the 'Nausicaa' chapter, the case at first seems clear enough: the first half demonstrates the ways in which the mind of a young woman has been subjected to and shaped by male concepts of femininity, while the second half likewise shows her body to be the object of the male gaze. This would mean that her perspective is determined by "her instinctive compliance with cultural prescriptions for male viewing and, more particularly, [by] her narcissistic identification with mass produced images of women on display" (Sicker 97). But on closer inspection the situation proves to be less simple and straightforward, as Gerty's and Bloom's respective portrayals as well as their modes of interaction show. "But who was Gerty?" (*U* 285) Even though it is difficult to answer this question positively, it is possible to say who (or what) she is *not*. Contrary to what many critics have seen in her, she is not merely the result of male definitions since she cannot be made to fit in with a neat defining formula. The whole point is, rather, that the chapter questions the appositeness of such formulas by mixing them up and showing them to be at variance with the ways in which readers are invited to see this young woman. For all the conventionality of her thoughts, Gerty is (and perceives herself as being) never wholly in line with "the conventions of Society with a big ess" (*U* 299) (T1), and "the same theatrical Gerty who casts herself as dark temptress can simultaneously affirm, in shades of blue and white, her devotion to the Blessed Virgin and keep her 'eyebrowline' and child of Mary badge in the same toilet-table drawer" (Sicker 104). In fact, the whole range of the orthodox conceptions of femininity is brought into play in this chapter, but not a single one of them is allowed to stick since all apply equally and as a result cancel each other out. Gerty is both (and neither) saint and sinner, Mary and Eve, mother and whore, Angel in the House and New Woman, so that the "bewildering friction that results is designed to expose the gender system itself as an arbitrary and inadequate fiction, to measure its isolating mechanisms against the urgent complexity of personal desire" (Mahaffey 153). The dichotomies listed above also demonstrate the expansion of the concept of transgression implied in *Ulysses* since only the first two disruptions of order can be seen as clear violations of taboos (T2a, T3a). The last two instances, on the other hand, are more ambiguous in that the religious element is either absent (mother / whore) or shifted into metaphor (Angel in the House / New Woman), and, what is more, in the last dichotomy sexuality as the motor of taboo-defying disarrangement is no longer central (T2b, T3b).[2] The destabilization of

Revaluating Transgression in Ulysses &&& 219

gender stereotypes is also amplified by the way in which the other women are portrayed:

> Both friends fall short of the cultural ideal by displaying some trace of masculinity that might displease patriarchy. Edy wears glasses, an ungainly token of male intellectualism, while "tomboy" [*U* 294] Cis recklessly assaults gender codes by drawing "men's faces on her nails with red ink" [*U* 290] and "dress[ing] up in her father's suit and hat and the burned cork moustache and walk[ing] down Tritonville Road smoking a cigarette [ibid.]." (Sicker 122)

And finally, as an implicit criticism of the myth of feminine perfection, the text draws attention to the girls' impediments: Gerty's lameness (*U* 301), Edy's squint (*U* 295), and Cissy's "long gandery strides" (*U* 294) and "skinny shanks" (*U* 295). As Gibson argues: "'Nausicaa' insists on the reality of imperfection [and] also repudiates the concept of a hard, static body implicit in the notion of flawlessness. Bodies in 'Nausicaa' are notably in process" (135). (T3b)

A logic similar to that described above is at work in Bloom's case, even though—as is well known—men (as subjects rather than objects of definition) are traditionally less liable to be categorized as strictly as women. Nevertheless, Bloom's famous forebear Odysseus is never far from the reader's mind, and it is the tension between them which works along the same lines as the simultaneity of different gender categories in Gerty's case, for in Bloom attributes traditionally coded either male or female blend in a manner designed to transgress orthodox boundaries:

> …Joyce defines a male hero as neither brave nor vengeful, but as cautious, realistic, and slowly willing to contemplate the possibility that his relation to those he loves has inadvertently been hurtful. Joyce's most sympathetic male characters see themselves, painfully, as fallible; their heroism grows not out of boundless confidence in the rightness of physical might, but out of what might be called the moral courage to imagine freshly the perspectives of the people they have wronged. (Mahaffey 156f.)

Conversely, "[t]he only men in the novel who pride themselves on their physical prowess are an adulterer and a bigot: the exaggeratedly hot Blazes Boylan and the hypocritical Citizen" (ibid. 158). As a consequence, "the reader's expectation clashes loudly with the actual experience of reading *Ulysses*, and the cacophony that results brings

220 &&& *Stefan Glomb*

the currency of our cultural definition of gender categories comically into question" (ibid.).

Joyce combines this with another transgressive strategy: the confusion of the positions of subject and object in the interaction of the two characters. Rather than adhering to the traditional arrangement with Gerty as the passive object of the male gaze, the chapter stages a two-way traffic. It is not just Bloom who constructs Gerty as a tool for his masturbation, but also Gerty who constructs him as the object of her girlish wish fulfillment:

> Here was that of which she had so often dreamed. It was he who mattered and there was joy on her face because she wanted him because she felt instinctively that he was like no-one else. The very heart of the girlwoman went out to him, her dreamhusband, because she knew on the instant it was him. (*U* 293)

The silliness aside, Gerty clearly defies the role allocated to her within the logic of the patriarchal order. This is not a passively compliant but "a transgressive Gerty who strays beyond authorized boundaries of feminine desire and pleasure in her looks and actions" (Sicker 102). Interestingly, Bloom senses this too: "Saw something in me" (*U* 302). "She must have been thinking of someone else all the time. What harm?" (*U* 303) "Wonder how she is feeling in that region" (*U* 306). The woman gazes back: "Gerty violates the prevailing ideal of feminine innocence and unself-consciousness by taking her own voyeuristic pleasure in Bloom's masturbation until 'the distinction between watcher and watched has completely collapsed'" (Sicker 102). And again, this is combined with a mixing up of gender stereotypes: "She glanced at him as she bent forward quickly, a pathetic little glance of piteous protest, of shy reproach under which he coloured like a girl" (*U* 300). As a result, it is no longer possible to tell subject from object, so that what emerges is a reciprocal constellation (cf. Sicker 116): "She could almost see the swift answering flash of admiration in his eyes that set her tingling in every nerve. She put on her hat so that she could see from underneath the brim and swung her buckled shoe faster for her breath caught as she caught the expression of his eyes" (*U* 295). Bloom makes this explicit when he states that "it was a kind of language between us" (*U* 305).

As stated above, the logic of the transgressions staged here implies that the boundaries and orthodox concepts being transgressed (T2b, T3b) have formerly been transgressive in their turn (T1), that is they

Revaluating Transgression in Ulysses   221

are exposed as tools of domination and petrifaction, restricting the scope of life's multifarious variations to a set of handy stereotypes set to negate "the need to reinvest the clean with the filthy, the rational with the animalistic, the ceremonial with the carnivalesque in order to maintain cultural vitality" (Babcock 32).

This becomes even more obvious in the area of colonialism. The process of liberation—from the Catholic Church, from a paralyzed Ireland besotted with its own allegedly glorious past, and from English colonial rule—is the thread running through the story of Stephen Dedalus in *A Portrait of the Artist as a Young Man* and *Ulysses*, culminating in his defiant, Luciferian "non serviam" (*P* 126, 260; *U* 475). As Stephen realizes in a conversation with the English dean of studies in *A Portrait*, colonial domination has more subtle means than open violence at its disposal:

> —The language in which we are speaking is his before it is mine. How different are the words *home*, *Christ*, *ale*, *master*, on his lips and on mine! I cannot speak or write these words without unrest of spirit. His language, so familiar and so foreign, will always be for me an acquired speech. I have not made or accepted its words. My voice holds them at bay. My soul frets in the shadow of his language. (*P* 205)

As Andrew Gibson has shown in his groundbreaking study *Joyce's Revenge*, this perspective also sheds new light on 'Nausicaa'. Gerty finds herself in a similar situation, and again—as in the case of gender—this at first seems to be a model example of a young woman's mind being invaded and shaped by the colonizers' language, assumptions, and values (T1). The main instrument of this invasion is her reading matter, since the "most significant and popular women's magazines of the period were published in London" (Gibson 129). Thus the chapter is "much concerned with the relationship between Gerty and a set of discourses that produce a serviceable model of English and colonial womanhood" (133). Rather than making fun of Gerty, the narrative shows a young woman on the verge of adulthood entering a new emotional sphere which has been mapped by cultural patterns to such a degree that there seems hardly any room left for spontaneity. And yet, we can again sense the kind of counteractive undertow that characterizes her attitude toward gender. Again, T2b and T3b are closely interwoven: "To a large extent, then, Joyce makes Ireland, Irish girlhood, and 'Nausicaa' itself seem recalcitrant to a set of discursive formations imported from the dominant

222 ⚬⚬⚬ *Stefan Glomb*

culture" (135f.). While Gerty's outlook on life undoubtedly is to a considerable extent shaped by colonial discourse, it is this very discourse which also establishes room for resistance. In other words, while the dominant discourse is the only means available to her for attaining a state of literacy, what happens from then on can no longer be entirely controlled or curbed by it. As Gibson shows, the three Irish hoydens' "motherwit" allows them a creative adaptation of the dominant culture (T2b): "It warps the discourses in question, taking them in unexpected directions, entering into new, surprising, and often hilarious relationships with them. It infects them with terms, flourishes, attitudes, and kinds of experience that the discourses would in principle exclude" (146). This corresponds to the aesthetic strategy employed by the chapter as a whole (T3b), that is the way it deals with the colonial race-discourse. White skin as the norm is undermined here since the chapter "stresses the changeability and inconstancy of skin colour" (135).

All in all, then, Gerty is shown to inhabit a liminal space located at points of intersection *between* different race, class, and gender discourses, the sacred and the profane, the body and the mind, rather than *within* any of these realms. This is also underlined by the fact that she evades the structuring principles of space and time: she is a girl on the threshold of adulthood and of modernity (cf. ibid. 144), between day and night (the time of day is ca. 8:00 PM), between land and sea (Sandymount Strand). These subversions of boundaries (T3b) lead to an analysis of the ways in which the microcosm of 'Nausicaa' reflects the macrocosm of the novel as a whole.

III

Liminal spaces, points of intersection, transitions—what has been subsumed here under a wide concept of transgression is *the* aesthetic logic (both in terms of form and content) underlying *Ulysses*. This applies to the novel's multiplicity of styles, the transitions occurring between as well as within chapters, and the novel's location in relation to the concepts used in literary studies. The sheer number of styles employed in the text implies that there is no privileged way of looking at the world, no master theory, no point of rest, since every given standpoint is embedded in a number of different perspectives: "Joyce's novel refuses to recognize anything that is larger than life. Its universes are relational and relative, of reduced size and plural rather than monolithic" (Emig 20). This relational

Revaluating Transgression in Ulysses   223

character is both intertextual and intratextual: "[t]he text...dialogically exceeds its boundaries, pointing toward a multitude of other written works, and internally subverts a linear progression, as the reappearance of words sends the reader off on a tangent, back toward another context and part of the book" (Weinstock 76). Hence, readers who abandon themselves to the flow of the text experience new ways of seeing that coincide with a transgression of what has hitherto been taken to be fixed and stable. As Umberto Eco puts it:

> When a 'lump' of experience is dominated by a univocal, stable vision of the world, it can be expressed by words that are explicit judgements on what is said. But when the material of experience assails us without our possessing its interpretive framework—when we notice that the codes of interpretation can be different, more open, flexible, and full of possibilities, and yet we still don't have the key for using them— then experience must *show itself* directly in the word. (37)

Transitions between chapters (e.g., 'Ithaca' / 'Penelope', to name but one graphic example) as well as within chapters (between locations, time frames, and styles)—some of the most obvious cases being 'Wandering Rocks', 'Oxen of the Sun', and 'Circe'—are ubiquitous. That transitions in time and space are crucial to the novel can be inferred from the repeated use of two conspicuous keywords: *metempsychosis* (*U* 41, 52, **126**, 309, 334, 386, 400, 534, 562), that is "the transmigration of souls" (*U* 52), and *parallax* (*U* **126**, 338, 398, 418, 537), that is "the apparent displacement or the difference in apparent direction of an object as seen from two different points of view" (Gifford and Seidman 160; cf. McHale 51ff.). As these definitions show, the two terms denote principles of relativity, temporal (as in the move from Odysseus to Ulysses to Bloom) and spatial (as in the manifold changes of perspective), and combined they constitute the linchpin of the novel's transgressive aesthetic logic.

All of this can easily convey the impression that *Ulysses* is a prime example of postmodern free play and randomness, and this leads to the notorious discussions as to how the novel might best be placed on the map of literary categorization, for Joyce's text does not content itself with staging different kinds of transgression. As McHale contends, *Ulysses* itself (somewhat like Gerty MacDowell) is located at the intersection of categories such as 'modern' and 'postmodern': "It is at one and the same time a founding text of 'High Modernism' and

224   Stefan Glomb

a postmodernist text...; it defines and consolidates modernism yet at the same time exceeds and explodes it" (55). The same difficulty confronts those who try to classify it as either realist or symbolist (cf. Emig 24ff.). As the view put forth here implies, it might be more sensible to question the validity of these pigeonholes than to bring the novel (if it indeed is a novel) into line with them.

This leaves what is perhaps the most fundamental transgression in *Ulysses*, namely the one that moves between—that is brings together without homogenizing—ethics, epistemology, and aesthetics. The novel demonstrates the necessity of realigning the three spheres which were gradually sundered in the course of the modern age. It is important to stress that, despite its emphasis on transgression in a number of areas, *Ulysses* is by no means an "interpretive free-for-all" (ibid. 25) since it does not conduct a wholesale questioning of all conceivable boundaries. As the instances of T1 have shown, there are types of transgression which are clearly presented in a negative light (and are therefore open to negation) in that they encroach upon the freedom of individuals and force them to comply with power structures (on the collective level) and / or to give in to certain types of dominant behavior (on the individual level, cf. Boylan and the Citizen). This kind of criticism forms an integral part of the text: "as much as Joyce opposes absolutism that condemns as blasphemy any deviations from faith, he also mocks noncommittal pluralism that would evade the dilemmas and hard choices brought about by contingency" (Armstrong 150). What distinguishes the novel from moral treatises on the one hand and intellectual parlor games on the other is the fact that it serves as an exercise in transitional thought (and feeling): "one of the potential moral effects of *Ulysses* is that it can condition us... to suspend or, at any rate, postpone the moralizing tendency that consists in dispensing blame and credit, in favour of a series of constant readjustments and a fluctuating awareness of the complexity of motivation" (Senn 188). The questions it raises are: "Is there any possibility of affirmation that avoids dogmatism while nevertheless acknowledging that a commitment worth its name entails uncompromising demands?... Is there any way of avoiding the dangers of an indifferent pluralism without falling into either fanaticism or paralysed universal resistance?" (Armstrong 151) As this essay has set out to show, the 'answers' the novel 'gives' emerge from a reading process which is to a large extent shaped by the perception of the positive potential of transgression.

Notes

1. *U* refers to Joyce 1986 [1922]; *P* refers to Joyce 1992 [1916].
2. As these examples show, the categories used in this essay apply only approximately.

Works Cited

Armstrong, Paul B. *Play and the Politics of Reading. The Social Uses of Modernist Form.* Ithaca: Cornell UP, 2005.

Babcock, Barbara A. *The Reversible World. Symbolic Inversion in Art and Society.* Ithaca: Cornell UP, 1978.

Benstock, Bernard, ed. *Critical Essays on James Joyce's* Ulysses. Boston: Hall, 1989.

Blamires, Harry. *The New Bloomsday Book.* London: Routledge, 1988.

Budgen, Frank. "Nausikaa." *Critical Essays on James Joyce's* Ulysses. Ed. Bernard Benstock. Boston: Hall, 1989. 159–67.

Eco, Umberto. *The Middle Ages of James Joyce. The Aesthetics of Chaosmos.* London: Hutchinson Radius, 1989.

Emig, Rainer, ed. *Ulysses.* Houndmills: Palgrave Macmillan, 2004.

Gibson, Andrew. *Joyce's Revenge. History, Politics, and Aesthetics in Ulysses.* Oxford: Oxford UP, 2002.

Gifford, Don, and Robert J. Seidman, eds. Ulysses *Annotated. Notes for James Joyce's* Ulysses. Berkeley: U of California P, 1988.

Gilbert, Stuart. "Nausicaa." *Critical Essays on James Joyce's* Ulysses. Ed. Bernard Benstock. Boston: Hall, 1989. 149–59.

Jenks, Chris. *Transgression.* London: Routledge, 2003.

Joyce, James. *Ulysses.* Ed. Hans Walter Gabler. New York: Random House, 1986.

———. *A Portrait of the Artist as a Young Man.* Harmondsworth: Penguin, 1992.

Mahaffey, Vicki. "*Ulysses* and the End of Gender." *A Companion to James Joyce's* Ulysses. Ed. Margot Norris. Boston: Bedford, 1998. 151–68.

McHale, Brian. *Constructing Postmodernism.* London, New York: Routledge, 1992.

Senn, Fritz. "Nausicaa." *Critical Essays on James Joyce's* Ulysses. Ed. Bernard Benstock. Boston: Hall, 1989. 186–214.

Sicker, Philip. "Unveiling Desire: Pleasure, Power and Masquerade in Joyce's 'Nausicaa' Episode." *Joyce Studies Annual* 14 (2003): 92–131.

Weinstock, Jefferey A. "The Disappointed Bridge: Textual Hauntings in Joyce's *Ulysses*." *Ulysses.* Ed. Rainer Emig. Houndmills: Palgrave Macmillan, 2004. 61–80.

CHAPTER XII

TABOO, TRANSGRESSION, AND (SELF-)CENSORSHIP IN TWENTIETH-CENTURY BRITISH THEATER

Folkert Degenring

In *The Cambridge History of British Theatre*, Baz Kershaw recently described the second half of the twentieth century as probably the most consistently volatile phase in the history of the British stage (cf. 3: 291). Admitting that the story of postwar volatility is only one of many potential narratives covering that time period, Kershaw identifies four major factors that lend shape to his own account: the changing structure of the theater estate, innovations in production, the impact of technology, and changes in the role and structure of the theater audience (cf. 3: 292f.). And while, as Christopher Innes points out, the developments in British theater of the twentieth century cannot be adequately compartmentalized into distinct units—indeed, that twentieth-century British drama is defined by a "lack of clear temporal signposts" (3: 7) that would allow for such an approach—a topical reflection on taboos, their transgression and censorship in British theater can hardly avoid periodizing the twentieth century along the fault line of the Theatres Act of 1968.

Fifteen years after the coronation of Elizabeth II., the 1968 Theatres Act abolished official censorship of the stage and thus a practice that had been an aspect of the theater in Britain since the reign of Elizabeth I. While the operational system behind dramatic censorship and its intensity underwent considerable changes,[1] the regulation of the stage rested with one "centralised agency of control" (Clare 10) or another rather than local authorities following the investiture of the "full powers of dramatic censorship" (ibid.) in

228 &ss *Folkert Degenring*

the Master of Revels. It was not until the Licensing Act of 1737 and the appointment of the Lord Chamberlain as the censoring authority, however, that stage censorship became a systematic effort fully backed by an act of parliament (cf. Conolly 2). Although the powers vested in the Lord Chamberlain and the Lord Chamberlain's Office were slightly restricted by the 1788 Theatrical Representations Act and the Theatres Act of 1843, the regime established under the Licensing Act continued to define the practice of dramatic censorship until the end of the 1960s. As Leonard W. Conolly points out in *The Censorship of British Drama 1732–1824*, however, it was not just state authorities that effected the censorship of the stage. Eighteenth-century theater managers in particular modified texts and altered plays even before a manuscript was submitted for examination—in effect a form of self-censorship—but actors and even audiences also exerted a degree of influence by refusing to speak objectionable lines or vocally demanding the alteration of passages on moral, political or religious grounds (cf. 2–11).

Since the system of dramatic censorship shows a remarkable degree of continuity from the eighteenth to the twentieth century, it is perhaps not very surprising that those factors continued to exert an influence up to the abolishment of stage censorship and beyond. Guided by economic rather than political or artistic perspectives, theater managers continued their traditional roles as supporters of censorship (cf. Conolly 53f.; 107) and audiences refused to tolerate plays they found objectionable on personal principles (cf. 70). While this by no means suggests that objectionable and censurable topics and subjects remained unchanged throughout the centuries, "hallowed social taboos on open discussion of sex, religion and the establishment" (Kerensky xv) were upheld until the 1960s:

> Before that time, the actual language spoken by people in real life, especially by people without middle-class inhibitions, could not be spoken on the stage. Everyday 'four-letter' swear words were banned.... Homosexuality could not be discussed and no real sexuality of any kind could be depicted. Nudity was totally taboo. Blasphemy, including jokes about church ceremonies as well as about God, was forbidden.... Other things on the Lord Chamberlain's embargo list were representations of living people, including politicians, and jokes and criticism about the Royal Family. (xix)

The narrative of postwar theater as particularly volatile and 1968 as a metaphorical breaking point in its development should not be

Taboo, Transgression, (Self-)Censorship 229

understood, however, as suggesting that after, or indeed well before, this date taboos and their transgression were not a noteworthy factor in British theater. Nevertheless, it is indicative of the attention that both the postwar period (as an admittedly constructed whole) and 1968 as marking the end to a 'tradition' of over two centuries' worth of official censorship merit.

While censorship cannot be convincingly equated with taboo, and taboos may very well continue to exist in the absence of censorship, just what is deemed to be objectionable by censoring authorities is a good indication for the scope of political, religious, and sexual taboos. I will therefore attempt to trace some of the developments in British theater and society in the twentieth century, with a particular focus on the end of the official censorship of the stage.

If most scholars would agree that the twentieth century in British drama and theater marks a particularly vital and productive period, most would also agree that the category 'twentieth century theater' is in essence an arbitrary one (cf. Innes, Kennedy, Kosok, Maack). Indeed, the final decades of the nineteenth and the early decades of the twentieth century are marked by an element of continuity which manifests itself in the continuing dominance of the actor-manager system (cf. Kennedy 3: 11; Maack 27), the prevalence of established genres and motifs (cf. Kosok 14–18), and a relatively homogeneous target audience, namely the middle class "extending from the *petit bourgeois*... to the *haut bourgeois*" (Kennedy 3: 5).

Due to the comparatively small influence of European avant-garde movements, mainstream British theater continued to be characterized by Edwardian and even Victorian conventions as late as the end of the 1930s. Parallel to this continuation of established dramatic forms, however, British drama at the turn of the century begins to eschew formulaic, bourgeois notions of the well-made play and thus, implicitly, rejects the Victorian values represented by it (cf. 11f.). With its focus on the interrelationship of technological and social change, early Modern British drama has consequently been equated with social realism—this categorization seems overly simplistic, however. As Mark Wallis points out, "in this period of British theater there were also instances of aesthetic experiment for its own sake, of progressive belief wedded to 'conservative' forms, and of conservative ideology wedded to 'progressive' forms" (3: 167). The early period of Modern British theater is defined by at least two lines of tension: an external one, which exists between rapidly changing socio-economic conditions on the one hand and a relatively static set of norms, rules

230 ❧ *Folkert Degenring*

and values on the other, and an internal one, which exists between 'progressive' and 'conservative' themes, forms and topics. Elements of both continuity and change thus appear to be intricately bound together, in a Foucauldian sense, as "an ensemble of relations that makes them appear as juxtaposed, set off against each other, implicated in each other" (Foucault 1986, 22), thereby engendering the transgression of taboos and their subsequent censorship.

The 1843 Theatres Act required "that one copy of every new stage play, or of an alteration to an old play" (Johnston 29) intended for public performance be submitted to the Lord Chamberlain prior to the production. In essence, the act confirmed the extensive censorship powers held by the Lord Chamberlain—he could forbid any new or already licensed plays[2] without having legal cause to provide explanations or defend his decisions—even though the practical tasks of the censorship process were usually carried out by members of his staff (cf. ibid. 30; Shellard et al. 16). In 1866, Spencer Ponsonby-Farne, then comptroller of the Lord Chamberlain's Office, offered a description of the censorship process which essentially held true for the next 100 years:

> Before a play is performed it is sent to...the Examiner of Plays; he looks through that play and...if he sees anything which to his mind is objectionable he sends it to me and it is then brought to the notice of the Lord Chamberlain who gives directions on it. (qtd. in Shellard et al. 15)

Censorship of the stage in Britain can thus be described as a form of pre-censorship, since license was granted (or withheld) to a script, not to a production (cf. Johnston 30f.). The censorship process itself worked on three different levels: the institutionalized one centered on the Lord Chamberlain's Office, theater managers checking scripts before submission, and finally authors critically examining the suitability of their play's topics (cf. Shellard et al. 4).

A prominent and illuminating case in point is George Bernard Shaw's *Mrs. Warren's Profession*—not only due to its censorship history but also because "Shaw established the criteria for twentieth century British drama in its formative phase" (Innes 51). Although completed in 1894, *Mrs. Warren's Profession* was not submitted to George Redford, then Examiner of Plays, until 1898. Dealing with middle-class investment in prostitution and describing the bond of matrimony as a form of bonded labor, Shaw was anxious that the

Taboo, Transgression, (Self-)Censorship   231

play would be held to be unfit for the general public—a fear that turned out to be well-founded, when Redford not only refused to license the play but to explicate his reasons as well: Redford declined Shaw's request to that effect, stating "that the best he could do was to 'endeavour to forget that I ever read the original'" (Marshik 51; cf. Shellard et al. 16). Contrary to Richard Findlater's 1967 assessment that "censorship did not blow too hard" in terms of the number of plays that were banned—"...no great plays were overtly suppressed. Few were written, although for that sterility the Lord Chamberlain cannot take all the blame" (51)—it thus seems that theatrical censorship did indeed have far-reaching implications for the initial stages of Modern British theater. Preferring "mockery to overt confrontation" (Shellard et al. 67), Shaw's reluctance to submit *Mrs. Warren* to the scrutiny of the censors is perhaps most interesting when related to Foucault's exploration of the internalization of rules and regulations set out in *Discipline and Punish*:

> He who is subjected to a field of visibility, and who knows it, assumes responsibility for the constraints of power; he makes them play spontaneously upon himself; he inscribes in himself the power relation in which he simultaneously plays both roles; he becomes the principle of his own subjection. By this very fact, the external power may throw off its physical weight; it tends to the non-corporal; and, the more it approaches this limit, the more constant, profound and permanent are its effects: it is a perpetual victory that avoids any physical confrontation and which is always decided in advance. (202)

Since Redford refused to comment on the reasons for withholding a license for *Mrs. Warren*—he later admitted to applying "no principles that can be defined" (qtd. in Shellard et al. 63) to his judgements—it is difficult to assess precisely which aspects of the play caused particular offence. Shaw's alterations to the play in order to obtain a license for a copyright performance later in 1898[3] provides a clear indication, however: Act II, in which the eponymous Mrs. Warren defends herself, was cut and her 'profession' altered to the training of young girls as thieves (cf. Marshik 52). It must therefore be assumed that the play's transgression of taboos consisted predominantly not in the depiction of criminality and morally condemnable behavior, but rather in its portrayal of the 'New Woman' and contemporary society as both capitalist and sexist (cf. Powell 3: 78), leaving women little choice but to participate in the 'White Slave Trade', that is, prostitution, in one form or another.

232 ∞ *Folkert Degenring*

In 1909 the notorious unaccountability of the censors' decisions and public campaigning for the abolition of censorship led to a Joint Select Committee of Enquiry into stage censorship. While the enquiry's results never became legally binding, it nevertheless proposed for the first time a set of reference points for the licensing of plays. Thus, it was proposed that it should be the Lord Chamberlain's

> duty to license any play submitted to him unless he considers that it may be reasonably held—
>
> (a) To be indecent;
> (b) To contain offensive personalities;
> (c) To represent on the stage in an invidious manner a living person, or any person recently dead;
> (d) To do violence to the sentiment of religious reverence;
> (e) To be calculated to conduce crime or vice;
> (f) To be calculated to impair friendly relations with any foreign Power; or
> (g) To be calculated to cause a breach of the peace. (qtd. in Shellard et al. 63)

It is hardly surprising that a catalogue of criteria as vague as the above had little potential to drastically alter existing censorship practices. Its very vagueness, however, also demonstrates that what is considered to be taboo on the stage is subject to specific socio-historical conditions and therefore to change. Once again, *Mrs Warren's Profession* may serve as a case in point. First produced as a notionally private 'club performance', which did not fall under the Lord Chamberlain's authority, in 1902, Shaw's play was resubmitted for public performance several times over the span of over two decades. In 1917, one such submission caused the eminent poet and critic Edmund Gosse to write to Lord Sandhurst, then Lord Chamberlain, commenting that: "Censorship is in this difficulty that no-one, not even the Bishop of London, could say that it is *immoral*. It is just its preposterous morality which makes it offensive. It is like a priggish old clergyman preaching 'to men only' in a night shelter" (qtd. in Shellard et al 72). Notions of what could and could not be portrayed on the stage had clearly changed. It was not until 1924, however, that though the Lord Chamberlain's Office "accepted that the change in public attitudes might be 'regrettable', it would be 'absurd to go on refusing a License to this Play, ignoring the march of time'" (73).

Taboo, Transgression, (Self-)Censorship ❧ 233

While one factor involved in the tenacity of stage censorship in Britain is perhaps simply its long history and sheer tradition, another aspect that needs to be taken into consideration is the structure of the theater estate. Until the end of the First World War, the dominant organizational principle was that of the actor-manager, who, at the end of the nineteenth century, had successfully "breached the wall of Victorian respectability" (Kennedy 3: 7) not predominantly as excellent performer, but as successful capitalist. Thus, "the theatre was viewed—by the state, by potentially wealthy patrons, and most of all by the actor-managers—exclusively as a commercial enterprise" (16). Even though the interwar years witnessed the decline of the actor-manager system, the theater estate continued to be dominated by financial interests. The stage in London in particular "rapidly came to be dominated by financial speculators who had no stake in a venue or company…. [T]heatre became more and more a monopoly enterprise, controlled by businessmen interested chiefly in short term profit" (11).

To properly assess the impact of this factor, it must be kept in mind that it was usually theater managers, and not the playwrights, who submitted texts to the Lord Chamberlain's Office. As George Redford put it just prior to the 1909 enquiry on censorship, managers generally had

> a very shrewd idea of the proscribed limits, and are only too glad to avail themselves of an independent and recognised authority as a buffer between themselves, and the advanced school of irreconcilable Dramatists who would, if unrestrained, drive out of the theatre a very large proportion of the paying public. (qtd. in Shellard et al. 62)

While this claim should be treated with a degree of skepticism, a certain continuity with regard to this notion can be traced to the period immediately prior to the end of official stage censorship.

In 1963, for example, Henry Sherek—a successful theater manager and producer on both sides of the Atlantic—addressed the Royal Society for the Encouragement of Arts, Manufactures and Commerce on the subject of the future of the contemporary commercial theater. Replacing Peter Hall, who would later become director of the National Theatre and who admitted to finding the expression 'commercial' regarding the theater "anomalous" (442), Sherek elaborated that the main, if not sole purpose of the theater was to please the public—the success of which could be measured by whether "the play pays" (443) or not.

234 ⁑ *Folkert Degenring*

Arguing from this predominantly economic perspective, Sherek commented on the subject of so-called dirty plays. While acknowledging that "if people want dirty plays, they shall have them" (444) he stressed the potential dangers of this particular class of plays for the theater business by recounting an anecdote:

> I have cousins in Lincolnshire who have had to give up going to the theatre entirely. The children now are grown up; they do not go with them; they are married. But they said: 'We're embarrassed ourselves. We don't mind a bit of dirt' (to use a horrible expression) 'but we don't like to sit there with an awful lot of people. It's terribly embarrassing.' (444)

Not elaborating on the nature of the embarrassment caused, Sherek continued by suggesting that the censoring activities of the Lord Chamberlain's Office were clearly insufficient to prevent 'ordinary theatergoers' from accidentally attending a 'dirty' performance— and proposed a labeling system similar to the one then in use by the British Board of Film Censors. Sherek's repeated but unspecific references to 'dirty' or 'perverted' plays clearly suggest that certain topics were still considered taboo; at the same time, however, allusions to the embarrassment caused to the audience suggest that a certain amount of transgression was already taking place. In this context, he comments on failed attempts to refute the practice of stage censorship and the value of a central censoring authority:

> Speaking for myself and, in this one case only, for the Society of West-End Managers, who agree with this, I do think that it is a good thing that we have a certain measure of protection. If we go to Birmingham or some other town there is a very much smaller chance of the Watch Committee closing us down if we have the agreement of the Lord Chamberlain's Office—although it can still do so. (444)

Conforming to Redford's assessment made sixty-two years earlier, Sherek's references to the Lord Chamberlain's Office make clear that official censorship was not only accepted by some commercial theater producers and managers, but viewed as a safeguard. Furthermore, the overarching economic interest and the proposition of a labeling system suggest the demand for an additional degree of censorship applied by the theater business itself—in effect a demand for self-censorship.

Taboo, Transgression, (Self-)Censorship ❦ 235

It is perhaps particularly striking that Sherek's address dates from the year in which the state-subsidized National Theatre staged its first play—over 100 years after the first calls for its establishment (cf. Kruger 35f.). Addressing the RSA one and a half years after Sherek, Kenneth Tynan, the prominent theater critic and then Literary Manager for the National Theatre, pointed out the consequences of a purely economic perspective for the theater:

> It [the British theater] had inevitably become a short-term art, dependent on quick financial returns, concerned only to produce what the public wants now.... It was compelled to concentrate on easily digestible, uncontroversial, ego-massaging, audience-ingratiating trifles—relieved on occasion by classical revivals tailored to fit star personalities.... Subsidy offers what commercialism negates: the idea of continuity, the guarantee of permanence. (Tynan 690)

Tynan also criticized the two proposed venues for the National Theatre building, one intended for the production of classics and the other for experimental theater, pointing out that the division into a "majority theatre, performed for money, and minority theatre, performed for kicks" and "originally imposed by economic necessity" had essentially become "artificial and archaic" (693). In this context, the Lord Chamberlain's authority is seen not as an economic safeguard but as an artistic liability:

> It is not so much a question of the lines he [the Lord Chamberlain] actually cuts and the plays that he proscribes, as of the plays that don't get written because he exists...because the author knows that they will be cut—the feelings that don't even get formulated. For example, a play advocating the overthrow of the monarchy would never be allowed in this country, plays...attacking religion would seldom be allowed, plays representing living or recently deceased people are not permitted, and there are certain sexual attitudes which are equally taboo. (698)

The conflicting attitudes implicit in Sherek's and Tynan's lectures set, as it were, the stage for the repeal of censorship legislation. Two plays in particular, John Osborne's *A Patriot for Me* and Edward Bond's *Saved*, both first performed in 1965, have come to be considered as instrumental in the abolishment of dramatic censorship in the United Kingdom (cf. Shellard et al. 162f.; Johnston 225f.).

236 ❧ *Folkert Degenring*

A Patriot for Me was first submitted to the Lord Chamberlain's Office in August 1964 (cf. Shellard et al. 163) by the non-commercial English Stage Company (ESC). The play's central character, Colonel Alfred Redl, is an intelligence and general staff officer in the Austro-Hungarian army at the turn of the twentieth century. Contemporary reactions described *A Patriot for Me* as a "technically ambitious and experimental piece" (Trussler 139), with a cast of over eighty and the action spanning twenty-three years from the end of Redl's military training in 1890 to his suicide practically on the eve of the First World War. Like Osborne's earlier works *Look Back in Anger* and *Luther*, the play is a psychological exploration of an individual's condition against the background of a particular historical setting: in this case the 'condition' is Redl's homosexuality and Jewish descent—although the latter was not necessarily recognized as a concern by contemporary criticism (cf. ibid. 140; Dukore 104f.)—and the background is formed by a decadent Viennese society and the army's general staff.

Although in one instance the Lord Chamberlain's Office demanded the alteration of a supposedly blasphemous exclamation, the censor's main objection was to the play's open treatment of homosexuality—the practice of which still remained illegal and potentially punishable by imprisonment under the Offenses against the Person Act of 1861. While in 1958 the Lord Chamberlain had decided that the "subject of Homosexuality has been so widely debated, written about and talked about, that it is no longer justifiable to continue the strict exclusion of this subject from the stage," he made it equally clear that *"Licenses will continue to be refused for plays which are exploitations of the subject* rather than contributions to the problem; and similarly references to the subject which are unnecessary or have merely an exploitation value will be disallowed" (qtd. in Shellard et al. 113; emphasis in the original). *A Patriot for Me* was consequently not recommended for license on the basis that the "present text seems to be a perfect example of a piece which might corrupt, since it reveals nearly all the details of the homosexual life usually left blank even in the newspaper reports" (qtd. in Shellard et al. 164). Particular offence was caused by the drag ball in Act II, Scene I and the deletion of the entire scene demanded.

The drag ball is one of two ball scenes juxtaposed within the play. The first one—I, 6—takes place within the Hofburg, the emperor's Viennese residence, and is attended by members of the aristocracy, the diplomatic corps and high-ranking army officers. One Major remarks: "We all play parts, *are* doing so now, *will* continue to do so, and as long as we are playing at being Austrian, Viennese, or whatever we think we are, cosmopolitan and nondescript, a position palmed on us by history, by the accident of having held back the Muslim horde at the gates of Europe" (*Patriot* 115f.). After these comments on the absurdity of the roles they play (cf. Ahrens 67), the officer goes on to further question the purpose of military service: "The army, all of *us*, and the Church, sustain the Empire, which is … perspiring gaiety and pointlessness" (*Patriot* 116).

The contrasting drag ball in II, 1 serves as a mirror-image for the official ball. It is a wild and abandoned affair, and only gradually is it revealed to the audience that many of the participants are the same ones. One of the play's major topics, then, is the discrepancy between the social roles that have to be played out and the individual subject's identity or, in other words, a clash between collective and personal identities. The play's transgression therefore consists not only in the "subject of homosexuality" or even the "embraces between males and practical demonstrations of love" (Johnston qtd. in Shellard et al. 164) but in its use of the topic for the questioning of the narratives of duty, patriotism and nationality. The cuts demanded by the Lord Chamberlain would have completely undermined the play's subversive potential and were thus rejected outright by both Osborne and the English Stage Company.

Resorting to the loophole already used for the 1902 production of Shaw's *Mrs Warren's Profession*, the ESC temporarily turned the Royal Court Theatre into a club venue in order to perform the unlicensed play. While this caused a warning to be issued to the company, the Lord Chamberlain failed to take legal action—a success which encouraged the ESC to submit Edward Bond's *Saved* for licensing in 1965. Set against the backdrop of South London, *Saved* is an uncompromising and sometimes brutal exploration of the alienating effects of a capitalist and consumerist society and "the first great self-indictment of the welfare state" (Scharine 80). The play was "reluctantly recommended for license" (Shellard et al. 68) on the provision that an extensive number of cuts and alterations were made. Quantitatively, the majority of the objections refer to the characters' crude and supposedly blasphemous working-class slang. Qualitatively, the strongest objections were made to the sexual promiscuity of some of the main characters, the depiction of sexual acts and, infamously, the seemingly unmotivated stoning to death of an infant—a scathing attack on the destructiveness of capitalism's "false

238　❦　*Folkert Degenring*

culture" (*Saved* 17). As with Osborne's *Patriot*, the subversive potential of the play did not primarily lie in its 'indecency', in its 'offensive
personalities' or in its 'conduciveness to crime or vice', that is not in
the transgression of taboos themselves, but in its instrumentaliza-
tion of the transgression of taboos in order to question society's most
fundamental rules.

Bond and the ESC refused to make the required alterations and
Saved was staged as a club performance late in 1965 with the bless-
ing of the Arts Council, which awarded Bond a £1,000 writer's
grant (cf. Scharine 51). Outraged over the ESC's renewed defiance,
the Lord Chamberlain decided to press charges and in 1966 the
defendants were found guilty, put on probation for twelve months,
and fined 50 guineas [-£52.50] (cf. Shellard et al. 169). The ensuing
debate in the media and in parliament sparked by the trial countered the intended reaffirmation of censorship authority, however,
and in 1967 the Joint Select Committee on censorship of the stage
recommended "allow[ing] freedom of speech in the theater subject
to the overriding requirements of the criminal law which generally
speaking apply to other forms of art in this country. The anachronistic powers of the Lord Chamberlain will be abolished and will
not be replaced by any other form of pre-censorship, national or
local" (Johnston 233)—a recommendation implemented in the 1968
Theatres Act.

While the abolishment of censorship cannot in itself be taken to
signal an end to taboos in British theater, it is nevertheless a clear
indication of the changing attitudes of the theater estate, its audiences and an increasingly permissive society in general (cf. Kershaw 3:
293f.). If, however, the true "objective of the Theatres Act 1968
was…to replace the pre-censorship of the Lord Chamberlain with
the post-censorship of the courts" (Johnston 249), then Howard
Brenton's *The Romans in Britain* was to prove the first major testing
ground.

First performed at the National Theatre in 1980, *The Romans in
Britain* sparked a public controversy of extraordinary proportions.
Set in England in the first century BC and the sixth century AD
as well as in contemporary Ireland, the play was a violent attack on
British politics and featured "a confluence of controversial subjects
remarkable in a single work" (Beacham 36): imperialism, colonialism,
contemporary politics, British and Irish founding myths, murder,
the depiction of (attempted) homosexual rape and, for the first time
on a British stage, full male nudity (cf. Murray). Without actually

Taboo, Transgression, (Self-)Censorship ✸✸ 239

having attended a performance, Mary Whitehouse, the Secretary of the National Viewers and Listeners Association and "an indefatigable campaigner for moral reform, and something of a national institution herself" (Beacham 36), demanded an immediate prosecution under the obscenity provisions of the 1968 Theatres Act. Failing to convince the authorities to press charges on that basis, Whitehouse accused the director, Michael Bogdanov, of personally violating the Sexual Offences Act of 1956 with the production. The ensuing trial was eventually ended with a plea of no prosecution, but this outcome was not necessarily the only imaginable one.

If the attempt to post-censor *The Romans* through the courts failed and is thus indicative of the softening of taboos, the question of continued self-censorship after 1968 is more difficult to assess. One prominent case in point is Alan Bennett's *A Question of Attribution*, first performed at the National Theatre in 1988. The central character of the play is Anthony Blunt, the Soviet Spy, member of the Cambridge Five, and Surveyor of the Queen's Pictures. Exploring the topics of authenticity, forgery and deception, the play raises the question whether Elizabeth II was aware of Blunt's activities as a spy. As the first substantial portrayal of a living monarch on the British stage, the National Theatre's Board of Directors opposed the production, and Artistic Director Richard Eyre threatened to resign in order to ensure that the play was staged—an occurrence that seems almost absurd in the light of the success of Stephen Frears' *The Queen* in 2006 (cf. Lawson).

Since the Theatres Act of 1968, the British stage has witnessed a number of increasingly violent and provocative plays. While the absence of pre-censorship and the (so far mostly) unsuccessful attempts at post-censorship through the courts seems to suggest that in a permissive society no taboos are left to be broken, the controversies sparked by the so-called In-Yer-Face Theater of the 1990s and beyond (cf. Sierz) paint a slightly different picture. Plays like Sarah Kanes' *Blasted* (1995) or Mark Ravenhill's *Shopping and Fucking* (1996) still manage to shock and demonstrate considerable transgressive potential. And in the light of inter-community tensions and racial strife, some commentators fear that despite the repeal of anti-blasphemy legislation in the United Kingdom, private prosecutions similar to *The Romans in Britain* case might meet with more success in the future—and lead to renewed self-censorship. The narrative of taboo, transgression, and censorship remains an ongoing one.

Notes

1. For an overview refer to Thomas, Conolly, Clare, Johnston, and de Jongh.
2. In practice, the right to forbid the production of an already licensed play was rarely exercised. Cf. Johnston 31; Shellard et al. 17.
3. Later that year an unaltered version was published by Grant Richards in the collection *Plays: Pleasant and Unpleasant*. Cf. Kelly 40f.

Works Cited

Ahrens, Rüdiger. "History and the Dramatic Context: John Osborne's Historical Plays." *Fu Jen Studies* 16 (1973): 49–75.

Beacham, Richard. "Brenton Invades Britain: *The Romans in Britain* Controversy." *Theater* 12.2 (1981): 24–37.

Bennett, Alan. "A Question of Attribution." *Plays Two: Kafka's Dick, The Insurance Man, The Old Country, An Englishman Abroad, A Question of Attribution*. London: Faber and Faber, 1998.

Bond, Edward. "Saved." 1966. *Plays: 1. Saved, Early Morning, The Pope's Wedding*. London: Methuen, 1983.

Brenton, Howard. "The Romans in Britain." 1980. *Plays: 2. The Romans in Britain, Thirteenth Night, The Genius, Bloody Poetry, Greenland*. London: Methuen, 1996.

Clare, Janet. *"Art Made Tongue-tied by Authority": Elizabethan and Jacobean Dramatic Censorship*. Manchester: Manchester UP, 1990.

Conolly, Leonard W. *The Censorship of British Drama 1737–1824*. San Marino, CA: Huntington Library, 1976.

De Jongh, Nicholas. *Politics, Prudery and Perversions: The Censoring of the English Stage 1901–1968*. London: Methuen, 2000.

Dukore, Bernard F. "A Patriot for Me. By John Osborne." *Theatre in Review* 22.1 (1970): 104–5.

Findlater, Richard. *Banned! A Review of Theatrical Censorship in Britain*. London: MacGibbon and Kee, 1967.

Foucault, Michel. *Discipline and Punish: The Birth of the Prison*. New York: Pantheon, 1977.

———. "Of Other Spaces." Trans. Jay Miskowiec. *Diacritics* 16.1 (1986): 22–27.

Innes, Christopher. *Modern British Drama: The Twentieth Century*. Cambridge: Cambridge UP, 2002.

Johnston, John. *The Lord Chamberlain's Blue Pencil*. London: Hodder and Stoughton, 1990.

Kane, Sarah. *Blasted*. London: Methuen, 2002.

Kennedy, David. "British Theatre, 1895–1946." Vol. 3 of *The Cambridge History of British Theatre*. Ed. Baz Kershaw. Cambridge: Cambridge UP, 2004. 3–33.

Kerensky, Oleg. *The New British Drama*. London: Hamish Hamilton, 1977.

Kershaw, Baz. "British Theatre, 1940–2002: An Introduction." Vol. 3 of *The Cambridge History of British Theatre*. Ed. Baz Kershaw. Cambridge: Cambridge UP, 2004. 291–325.

Kosok, Heinz. "Traditionen und Konventionen des 19. Jahrhunderts im englischen Drama und Theater des 20. Jahrhunderts." *Drama und Theater im England des 20. Jahrhunderts*. Ed. Heinz Kosok. Düsseldorf: August Bagel, 1980. 9–24.

Kruger, Loren. "'Our National House': The Ideology of the National Theatre of Great Britain." *Theatre Journal* 39.1 (1987): 35–50.

Lawson, Mark. "One Is Ready for One's Close-up." *The Guardian* September 8, 2006. February 17, 2009 <http://www.guardian.co.uk/film/2006/sep/08/3>.

Maack, Annegret. "Das Drama des kommerziellen Theaters: 1900–1940." *Drama und Theater im England des 20. Jahrhunderts*. Ed. Heinz Kosok. Düsseldorf: August Bagel, 1980. 25–40.

Marshik, Celia. *British Modernism and Censorship*. Cambridge: Cambridge UP, 2006.

Murray, Oswyn. "The Romans Back in Britain." *Times Online* February 22, 2006. February 17, 2009 <http://tls.timesonline.co.uk/article/0,,25352–2053163,00.html>.

Osborne, John. "A Patriot for Me." *Plays Three: Luther, A Patriot for Me, Inadmissible Evidence*. London: Faber and Faber, 1998.

Powell, Kerry. "New Women, New Plays, and Shaw in the 1890s." Vol. 3 of *The Cambridge History of British Theatre*. Ed. Baz Kershaw. Cambridge: Cambridge UP, 2004. 76–102.

Ravenhill, Mark. *Shopping and F***ing*. London: Methuen, 2005.

Sharine, Richard. *The Plays of Edward Bond*. London: Associated UP, 1976.

Shaw, George Bernard. "Mrs. Warren's Profession." Ed. Sandie Byrne. *George Bernard Shaw's Plays: Mrs. Warren's Profession, Pygmalion, Man and Superman, Major Barbara*. New York: Norton, 2002.

Shellard, Dominic, Steve Nicholson, and Miriam Handley. *The Lord Chamberlain Regrets: A History of British Theatre Censorship*. London: British Library, 2004.

Sherek, Henry. "Can the Modern Theatre Be Commercial?" *The Journal of the Royal Society for the Encouragement of Arts, Manufactures and Commerce* 111 (1963): 441–55.

Sierz, Alex. *In-Yer-Face Theatre: British Drama Today*. London: Faber and Faber, 2001.

Thomas, Donald. *A Long Time Burning: The History of Literary Censorship in England*. London: Routledge, 1969.

Trussler, Simon. *The Plays of John Osborne: An Assessment*. London: Gollancz, 1969.

Tynan, Kenneth. "The National Theatre." *The Journal of the Royal Society for the Encouragement of Arts, Manufactures and Commerce* 112 (1964): 687–702.

Wallis, Mick. "Social Commitment and Aesthetic Experiment, 1895–1946." Vol. 3 of *The Cambridge History of British Theatre*. Ed. Baz Kershaw. Cambridge: Cambridge UP, 2004. 167–91.

CHAPTER XIII

THE HOLOCAUST AND AESTHETIC TRANSGRESSION IN CONTEMPORARY BRITISH FICTION

Lars Heiler

The Holocaust marks *the* traumatic event in twentieth-century history because it has become the ultimate test case for the viability of Enlightenment values held up by Western societies since the eighteenth century.[1] As it represents the transgression of cultural taboos, that is, the infringement of basic human rights and values, the forms of commemorating the Holocaust as an exceptional scar on the 'skin of civilization' and as a "watershed event" (Bernard-Donals vii), are supposed to serve as a warning to subsequent generations. Consequently, the Holocaust memory culture has itself become a ritualized taboo area under protection of the law and public morality.

In Britain, there has been a growing awareness in recent years that the legacy of the Holocaust does not only include the Germans as perpetrators and the Jews as victims, but that it constitutes a pan-European—if not universal—obligation to combat the seeds of racism and prejudice. The inauguration of an annual Holocaust Memorial Day by the British government in 2001 testifies to this new dimension of envisaging the Holocaust.[2] Unfortunately, the mere fact that the government deemed it necessary to introduce such a day cannot be seen as an unambiguously positive signal. Rather, the rise of anti-democratic and anti-Semitic forces in Britain as well as in other Western democracies seems to require a new sense of alertness and historical consciousness in the face of ignorance and intolerance. Recent reports that school teachers in Britain often avoid controversial subjects such as the Holocaust in history lessons for fear of

244   *Lars Heiler*

provoking anti-Semitic reactions from Muslim pupils (cf. www.telegraph.co.uk) represent cases of passive Holocaust denial which may be considered even more alarming than the libelous and disparaging statements of active Holocaust deniers such as David Irving, if one takes into account the long-term effects of such downplaying strategies on the cultural memory.

Artistic—particularly filmic—representations of the Holocaust run the risk of turning the suffering of millions into a spectacle, of trivializing it, or of not managing to capture the whole scope of the atrocities committed. Generic questions such as rendering a Holocaust narrative in (tragi-)comic form can quickly turn into issues of decorum and moral decency.[3] On the other hand, the Holocaust has often been considered an event so unprecedented that it is impossible to approach it through conventional artistic forms; what is therefore needed is a turn to

> obliqueness in representation that approaches the abstraction of abstract painting without yet conceding its goals, to the uses of allegory and fable and surrealism, to the blurring of traditional genres not just for the sake of undoing them but in the interests of combining certain of their elements that otherwise had been held apart. (Lang 2000, 10)

This essay attempts to show how the re-writings of the Holocaust in three contemporary British novels work as aesthetic transgressions of an incomprehensible historical event. It analyses how the selected texts try to remember the Holocaust in individualized narratives which avoid epic proportions and claims to universality, and how they approach their subject matter through forms of re-writing objectified history and of distorting realistic narrative conventions. Also, it will deal with the impact these aesthetic transgressions have with regard to the ethical dimension inherent to the three narratives, following Berel Lang's observation that "writing which takes the Holocaust as its subject requires moral as well as aesthetic justification" (1988, 4). As the transgressive intensity of the three texts in question decreases in accordance with the publication dates, Ian McEwan's *Black Dogs* (1992), Martin Amis' *Time's Arrow* (1990), and D.M. Thomas' *The White Hotel* (1981) will be presented in chronologically reverse order.

In *Black Dogs*, Ian McEwan establishes two former Gestapo dogs as a recurring image for human evil, including the unspeakable

Holocaust and Aesthetic Transgression ❧ 245

horror of the Holocaust, which is not captured metonymically, as a realistic enumeration of murders and corpses, but metaphorically, through the dogs which haunt the imagination of the central characters. The novel does not follow a linear time scheme and is composed of four separate parts, shifting backward and forward in time: in part I, which is set in 1987, the homodiegetic narrator Jeremy introduces the life-long estrangement and ideological struggles between his parents-in-law, June and Bernard Tremaine, as a starting point for his desire to write a memoir of the terminally ill June. Part II sends Jeremy and Bernard to Berlin in order to witness the fall of the Berlin Wall in 1989. In Part III, Jeremy relates how he met his future wife Jenny on a trip to Poland in 1981 which culminates in a visit to Majdanek concentration camp, and Part IV contains Jeremy's memoir of June, in which her religious and spiritual devotion is explained as a direct result of the "mythological encounter" (Slay 142) with the black dogs on her honeymoon in France in 1946. What welds these four parts together is a gradually increasing awareness of the nature of evil and the mechanisms of violence, along with a symbolic expansion of the image of the black dogs.

Acts of violence figure prominently in the novel, from the abuse of Jeremy's niece Sally by her father to the atrocities committed in Majdanek, thereby covering private and public spheres indiscriminately. Following June's cue, Jeremy comes to see all these acts as the work of the black dogs, a "malign principle, a force in human affairs that periodically advances to dominate and destroy the lives of individuals or nations, then retreats to await the next occasion" (*BD* 19). That the dogs should occupy such a privileged space in June's imagination is explained through her violent encounter with them in the south of France, where she faces death at the hands of the two giant beasts but manages to fight them back, while the unsuspecting Bernard is busy hunting caterpillars. June's very private near-death experience gains a more far-reaching quality when she learns from the mayor of the nearby village that the dogs were brought to the area by the Gestapo during the war in order to intimidate the locals; that, in addition, they were trained to rape women and had done so on one occasion. Although the second part of this story is fiercely rejected by June's and Bernard's landlady, who claims it was invented by the local men to disparage the reputation of the woman in question, the mayor's account elevates June's encounter with the animals into a more general confrontation of good versus evil, beyond the confinement of private experience.

246 &es *Lars Heiler*

Yet it is June herself who reminds Jeremy that the dogs cannot be read in mere mythical or allegorical terms: "'No, you clot. Not symbolic!' I hear her correcting me. 'Literal, anecdotal, true. Don't you know, I was nearly killed!'" (*BD* 28) Despite June's insistence on the physical reality of the dogs they gain an undeniable symbolic quality through two complementary strategies: first, by placing the concept of the black dogs into a traditional metaphorical frame of reference with eminent precursors in English history, as Jeremy learns from Bernard:

> But you know, I was the one who told her about Churchill's black dog. You remember? The name he gave to the depressions he used to get from time to time. I think he pinched the expression from Samuel Johnson. So June's idea was that if one dog was a personal depression, two dogs were a kind of cultural depression, civilisation's worst moods. (*BD* 104)

Second, it is by challenging a symbolic reading of the dogs that June herself provides the necessary cues for their intertextual and mythological interpretation *ex negativo*:

> I'm not saying these animals were anything other than what they appeared to be. Despite what Bernard says, I don't actually believe they were Satan's familiars, Hell Hounds or omens from God, or whatever he tells people I believe....I haven't mythologised these animals. I've made use of them. They set me free. I discovered something. (*BD* 59)

The reason why McEwan's novel is so preoccupied with metaphorical interpretations of phenomena such as violence, evil, and the Holocaust becomes evident in the Majdanek episode when Jeremy and his future wife visit one of the death camps. Interestingly, this site of commemoration and remembrance fails to bring about the intended cathartic effect in Jeremy:

> The extravagant numerical scale, the easy-to-say numbers—tens and hundreds of thousands, millions—denied the imagination its proper sympathies, its rightful grasp of the suffering, and one was drawn insidiously to the persecutor's premise, that life was cheap, junk to be inspected in heaps. As we walked on, my emotions died. There was nothing we could do to help. There was no one to feed or free. We were strolling like tourists. (*BD* 110f.)

Holocaust and Aesthetic Transgression ❧ 247

Overwhelmed and numbed by the metonymic signs of mass extermination, which evokes Jeremy's "inverted admiration" (*BD* 111) for the perpetrators, but no adequate moral or political response[4], he begins to acquire a taste for metaphorical, mythopoeic, and non-realist forms of communication in his own writing, particularly in his oneiric rendition of June's encounter with the black dogs and in forms of emplotment which highlight the uncanny parallels between this event and other confrontations with violence in the novel. For example, when Bernard is attacked by young fascist thugs at the Berlin Wall in 1989, Jeremy points out that the young woman who saves his father-in-law bears a certain resemblance to the late June, who is almost transformed into a guardian angel in the course of the novel.

What kind of ethical perspective on the Holocaust results from the novel's transgression of realist conventions, its stylization of evil forces, its structural complexity, and Jeremy's role as an unreliable narrator who tries to grasp the sheer scale of twentieth-century European history, politics and the psychology of violence, and to harmonize them in a narrative which eludes a coherent sense of closure?[5] What are we supposed to make of the metaphorical equation of everyday violence in the private sphere with the mass extermination taking place in the Nazi death camps, which is established by the symbol of the black dogs? One could argue that this form of symbolization represents an illicit attempt to contextualize and normalize the Holocaust, which may still remain unique in its magnitude, but since it springs from the same source as all the other, more trivial violent acts in the novel, becomes explicable as a multiplication of individual regression toward savagery and is contained in one single mythical image. Irving Howe, in drawing on Adorno's early rejection of literary representations of the Holocaust, illustrates the reservations and fears connected with such a position: "that the representation of a horrible event, especially if in drawing upon literary skills it achieves a certain graphic power, could serve to domesticate it, rendering it familiar and in some sense even tolerable, and thereby shearing away part of the horror" (180). But Howe also points out the difficulties which any writer, but the novelist in particular, faces when dealing with the Holocaust as their subject:

> In approaching the Holocaust, the canniest writers keep a wary distance. They know or sense that their subject cannot be met full face. It must be taken on a tangent, with extreme wariness, through strategies of indirection and circuitous narratives that leave untouched the

central horror—that leave it untouched but always invoke or evoke it as hovering shadow. (194)

McEwan seems to be acutely aware of this problem. Although *Black Dogs* is "not strictly a Holocaust novel" (Sicher 192), the Holocaust as "universal reference point of human depravity" (*BD* 37) forms the novel's background, even if it lurks in the shadows for most of the time. Jeremy's Majdanek experience provides a self-reflective confirmation of Howe's dictum that a face-on confrontation with the gruesome details of mass extermination is not a strategy that the novelist should pursue. To introduce the black dogs as an unsettling image for the ever-lurking danger of the outbreak of violence seems to provide the 'hovering shadow' that Howe demands of a narrative which deals with the Holocaust in a serious and ethically responsible manner.

With *Time's Arrow*, Martin Amis has written a much more experimental and stylistically transgressive novel than *Black Dogs*. Its central conceit, time flowing backward, allows the dying protagonist Tod Friendly, a former doctor at Auschwitz, to undo the crimes he committed during the war. Since he had to adopt various aliases after the war, Friendly's name changes several times in the course of the novel's regressive temporal structure, till he assumes his original identity of Odilo Unverdorben, the Nazi war criminal. The novel is told from the perspective of the split-off or repressed conscience or soul of the protagonist, which accompanies him on his trip to his dark past, with only a vague idea of where the journey is going:

> He is travelling towards his secret. Parasite or passenger, I am travelling there with him. It will be bad. It will be bad, and not intelligible. But I will know one thing about it (and at least the certainty brings comfort): I *will* know *how* bad the secret is. I will know the nature of the offence. Already I know this. I know that it is to do with trash and shit, and that it is wrong in time. (*TA* 73)

The narrator follows Friendly / Unverdorben in his various guises from late-twentieth-century America to the postwar period, the Second World War, and back to his birth, when the novel's trajectory changes and time begins to flow forward again, repeating not only the protagonist's life, but also twentieth-century history all over again.

The idea of temporal reversal, which Amis borrowed from an episode in Kurt Vonnegut's *Slaughterhouse-Five*, produces grotesque situations when taken to logical extremes: dialogues rendered in direct

Holocaust and Aesthetic Transgression ❈❈❈ 249

speech are produced in reverse chronology, cars have five reverse and only one forward gear, and Tod Friendly's working routine as a medical doctor in postwar America consists in injuring healthy patients which are sent home after being mangled:

> You want to know what I do? All right. Some guy comes in with a bandage around his head. We don't mess about. We'll soon have that off. He's got a hole in his head. So what do we do. We stick a nail in it. Get the nail—a good rusty one—from the trash or whatever. And lead him out to the Waiting room where he's allowed to linger and holler for a while before we ferry him back to the night. (*TA* 85)

Apart from emanating a bizarre sense of humor, the hospital episodes construct a highly negative image of the medical profession which points to the atrocities committed by Josef Mengele and other Nazi doctors in the concentration camps, under the guise of 'scientific progress': the supposed healer becomes the harbinger of death, pain, and destruction.

In the Auschwitz chapters Amis takes this grotesque mode of narration even further: the narrator observes how Odilo Unverdorben undoes the crimes he originally perpetrated, how corpses are saved from the crematoria, placed in the gas chambers to be reanimated by SS soldiers and doctors—in a scandalous countermovement, the Holocaust is transfigured into one large process of healing and regeneration. Aesthetically, Amis achieves one feat which is usually considered impossible: to "present the unrepresentable" (Finney 105), the mass extermination of the Jews, in a palatable form; to stage the obscene, simply by reversing the process of mechanized genocide and endowing it with an inverted interpretation provided by the naïve narrator. This strategy is not to be misunderstood as a cheap and tasteless form of provocation: instead, it foregrounds "the dreadful enormity of the project" (Parry 258) in its relentless mechanical progression. What is more, it provides a scathing critique of the Nazi ideology whose basic premises are grotesquely recuperated, but ultimately subverted in the creation of the Jews by Odilo Unverdorben:

> Tod's secret indeed has to do with trash and shit, but the narrator's point of view gets time wrong to make Odilo's crimes look right, to render the violent creation of a people easier than its brutal decimation. At the expense of the intelligibility of everything else, the narratorial soul of Odilo has made sense of the Holocaust, reliteralizing Nazi eugenics as good birth, recasting genocide as genesis. (Menke 964)

A closer look at the transgressive stylistic strategies which Martin Amis employs in *Time's Arrow* shows that the author has violated almost all written or unwritten aesthetic rules that ought to be observed when writing about the Holocaust. First, the novel adopts the perspective of the perpetrator, never that of the victims; then, it does not respect the central taboo of not presenting the death in the gas chambers (cf. Howe), but does something even worse: crematoria and gas chambers produce life and create Jews instead of destroying them; and finally the novel's artificial design tends to create ironic distance, an intellectual response rather than "pity that is inspired by individual histories" (Parry 258; cf. Des Pres 218).

In the light of these transgressions, one may ask whether the thought experiment developed in *Time's Arrow* with its rejection of representational realism proves a successful strategy for the presentation of an adequate fictional response to the Nazi crimes, the immensity of the Holocaust and the suffering of the victims. Most critics readily acknowledge the novel's courage in taking enormous aesthetic as well as ethical risks (cf. Henke 87). Interestingly, they usually approve of its ethical seriousness and integrity, even if they doubt its literary and aesthetic merit: Natania Rosenfeld calls it a "pointedly failed experiment," but inevitably so: "[T]he mechanical character of Amis' grotesque effort to invert history only exposes the helplessness of a literary *tour de force* to convey the sense of mechanized genocide. *Time's Arrow* shatters the dream of a work of art that would be both mimetic and redemptive" (128). Daniel Oertel emphasizes the "incoherent narrative structure" at the heart of the novel, but sees this as "a suitable metaphor for the incoherence of history" (132). Although she observes that "Dead or alive, the Jews are always 'off-stage', missing from their own tragedy" (258), Ann Parry concedes that the novel is able to grasp the caesura which the Holocaust signifies in twentieth-century history and that it alerts its reader to the dangers of a potential repetition of history:

> *Time's Arrow* represents a caesura in which the Jews have been deconstructed and are still stranded outside European history.
> The final moments of the book stress the perpetuity of this condition and that of the West.... Time resumes its forward direction, the tragedy is about to unfold once more. The caesura as it is articulated in *Time's Arrow* is forever imminent and the trajectory of European history is the possibility of its recurrence. (258f.)

Holocaust and Aesthetic Transgression 251

Brian Finney takes this argument further by pointing out that the book's ending enables, or rather, urges the reader to perform "an endless oscillation between past and present, incorporating the past into our sense of modernity" (III). In other words, by making the reader a co-writer of the novel who has to reconstruct its plot, to complement the narrative with historical background information and to interpret the one-dimensional and often erroneous judgments of the narrator, *Time's Arrow* sharpens our sense of moral judgment and historical awareness. Simultaneously, the "wishful restoration" (Rosenfeld 124) of a crime that "leaves us intellectually disarmed" (Howe 175) is exposed as a fanciful daydream in the act of reading:

> Our own efforts to read the backward tale frontward perpetuate the trauma; hard as the narrator may try to un-do, our very reading re-does atrocity. We become implicated in the crimes of the twentieth century, re-twisting what wishful thinking would untwist; but we are also fortified against revisionism as we ourselves, through reading, enact the trajectory from the germ or dot of an idea through to the extermination of a people. (Rosenfeld 125)

Therefore, the aesthetic challenges presented by *Time's Arrow* do not obfuscate its ethical concerns or shatter the massive taboo constituted by the Holocaust. Rather, the multiple artistic liberties that Amis takes in this novel serve a number of implicit didactic purposes: while the surrealist 'constructive' dimension of *Time's Arrow* throws into relief the finality and destructiveness of the real Holocaust, our emotive response to the narrative prevents us from seeing this finality as a completed chapter in the book of European history. Instead, we are urged to practice active commemoration by trying to 'undo' the Holocaust—not in the past, but in the present and the future.

Without doubt, *The White Hotel* is one of the most controversial Holocaust novels in the English language. It mixes different narrative forms—erotic fantasy, psychoanalytical case study, historical novel and surreal dreams of paradise after the hell of the Holocaust—into a quasi-mythical narrative, thereby transgressing the boundaries of genre, of the classic realist mode, but equally breaking taboos about the merging of sex and violence in fiction. The six chapters (plus a prologue) center around the fate of Lisa Erdman, a young opera singer who, in the 1920s, is treated for hysteria by a fictional Sigmund Freud. In the first two chapters (a long poem named "*Don Giovanni*" and "The Gastein Journal"), Lisa unfolds her powerful

252　❦　*Lars Heiler*

erotic fantasies about staying in the eponymous white hotel with Freud's own son. At the outset, the hotel is redolent of paradisiacal bliss and prelapsarian harmony, a state which is, however, soon punctuated by a series of disasters—fires and landslides—that kill many of the guests and leave their relatives traumatized. This juxtaposition of Eros and Thanatos induces the fictional Freud to pursue his concept of the death instinct, a hypothesis which he is about to introduce in his essay *Beyond the Pleasure Principle*. Chapter Three, entitled "Frau Anna G." and written in the style of Freud's famous case studies, sees the founder of psychoanalysis grappling with the treatment of Lisa Erdman. Based on the erotic fantasies depicted in her poem and journal, he attempts to unearth Lisa's childhood traumata and read the physical pains in her breast and abdomen as symbolic representations of unconscious desires (cf. 91), but grows impatient with her because her therapy yields little progress. Chapter Four covers Lisa Erdman's middle years between 1929 and 1936, a period of relative happiness in which she marries the widowed Jewish-Russian baritone Victor Berenstein and becomes the step mother of his son Kolya—although she has always been filled with an inexplicable dread of ever having children. Chapter Five takes the reader to the Second World War and the massacre of Babi Yar, a ravine outside Kiev in the Ukraine where in 1941 more than 30,000 Jews were machine-gunned and buried by SS troops and Ukrainian police force in one day. Lisa Erdman, who could have saved herself because she has a Ukrainian passport and speaks German, dies in the massacre because she does not want to abandon Kolya. Lisa's horrifying last minutes, in which she has to jump into the ravine, is kicked in the breast and pelvis, and raped by a soldier with a bayonet, are rendered from the perspective of an authentic eye witness, Dina Pronicheva, one of the few survivors of Babi Yar. For a few pages, Thomas abandons the mode of fiction and inserts her testimony as presented in Anatoli Kuznetsov's documentary novel *Babi Yar* (1970). The title of Chapter Six, "The Camp," raises expectations (or fears) which are not fulfilled. Instead of a concentration camp, the novel seems to return to fantasy and to a seemingly paradisiacal place in which Lisa and other victims of the Holocaust find rest and comfort after their violent deaths.

As the example of Lisa's pains—which a patronizing Freud misreads as signs of hysteria and which turn out to be her diffuse forebodings of a gruesome death at Babi Yar—demonstrates, *The White Hotel* establishes a complex, self-referential echo structure, in which each

Holocaust and Aesthetic Transgression 253

chapter provides a new variation of the same theme. By the end, the reader is able to decode the allusions to the landslide at the white hotel as a prefiguration of the burial of tens of thousands of people in Kiev, Lisa's lifelong refusal to have children is explained by Kolya's death, and her erotic fantasies of being "split open" (*WH* 20) by her lover and "impaled" (*WH* 23) crystallize in the most shocking scene of the novel. Unsurprisingly, Thomas' stylistic variations and the obscenity of some scenes have evoked impassioned reactions by readers and critics alike. Rebecca Scherr has found fault with the connection of sexual fantasy and the Holocaust in the novel, which she judges as a "gross...misrepresent[ation of] historical facts, even the fact of the Holocaust itself, by transforming the memory of the Holocaust into a 'sexy memory'" (11). Zsuzsanna Ozsvath and Martha Satz deplore that the novel "seems to be an exploitation of the Holocaust rather than an explication" because, as they claim, it "subsumes the horrors of the Holocaust under psychological illness and thus reduces moral and metaphysical atrocity to comprehensible human size" (210). I would argue that the relationship between psychology and history in *The White Hotel* works the other way round: the novel shows that history cannot be subsumed under individual psychology, and that Lisa's 'symptoms' articulate not individual ontogenetic suffering, but seem to confirm C.G. Jung's notion of the 'collective unconscious' which is supposed to contain the sediments of phylogenetic human experience (in this case, even future experience).

Lars Ole Sauerberg has criticized the novel's final chapter for its return to non-realist discourse after the quasi-documentary report of the Babi Yar massacre: "To the traditionally minded reader..., the last section must seem embarrassingly out of tune.... Had Thomas chosen to finish the account after the blood bath of Babi Yar, he would at least have achieved a kind of tragic unity" (6). Sauerberg's general problem with *The White Hotel*—that the novel fails to convey an idea of the atrocities of the Holocaust through the means of aesthetic transgression (and mental escape)—finds an obvious target in the design of the last chapter: "[H]e cannot unite persuasively the individual's wish for an afterlife with the historical certainty of the absolute, irrevocable, and *in casu* monstrous reality of death" (9). The "traditionally minded reader" that Sauerberg invokes might find it difficult indeed to reconcile the two opposing elements, but maybe it is the very incompatibility of inescapable collective horror and private fantasy which provides a suitable reality-testing for our conscience: as in *Time's Arrow* we know that the Holocaust is final, but

254 ❧ *Lars Heiler*

our sense of morality craves for a Utopian redemption from the horrors of the past. A second argument in favor of the last chapter would
be to emphasize that 'The Camp' is a blighted paradise, reminiscent
of a postwar reception camp in which the scale of Jewish suffering
becomes glaringly obvious since the influx of refugees never stops.
The camp is not depicted as a home, but highlights the diasporic
homelessness which is central to Jewish experience. What is more,
the number of orphans in this camp/netherworld reminds us of the
mass extermination of children during the Holocaust. Conversely,
their parents in the real world are now childless, that is, deprived
of the offspring that is supposed to symbolize their future. In this
sense, Chapter Six does not exclusively indulge in the "sublimation
of poetic fictionalization" (Sauerberg 9), but partly reliteralizes the
cruel fate of the surviving Jews after the Holocaust.

Linda Hutcheon views the final section more favorably than
Sauerberg. In her analysis of the narrative strategies employed in this
chapter she concludes that it provides

> the perfect anti-closure closure. All the narrative ends are tied up:
> characters meet and sort out their difficulties.... Yet it is fundamen-
> tally inexplicable by normal narrative logic, and its time (after Lisa's
> death?) and place (Israel?) cannot be fixed with any certainty. What
> this ending does is foreground the arbitrariness of traditional novelis-
> tic closure, while nevertheless allowing, even demanding, it. (90)

In other words, the indeterminacy of the final chapter reinforces our
desire for traditional closure, but illustrates at the same time that
such closure would be an inappropriate narrative device in *The White
Hotel*. One could even argue that conventional closure would, paradoxically, become an act of aesthetic transgression that the novel
could not afford.

A number of critics have evaluated the interplay between realist and metaphorical discourses in the novel in terms similar to
Hutcheon's. Laura E. Tanner stresses the fact that the two modes of
representing violence in the novel highlight "the horrific gap" (144)
between private fantasy and collective slaughter:

> In contrast with the earlier aestheticized violence of the novel, the
> violence in the Babi Yar section is immediate and undeniable; the
> reader is offered no alternative sight at which to gaze and no medi-
> ating framework through which to assess the violent experience that
> the novel describes. (145)

Holocaust and Aesthetic Transgression ❧ 255

For Rowland Wymer, the conflict between historical and mythical material in the novel underscores the privileged position that the Holocaust occupies in European history, because it resists any attempt at integration into the novel's mythical structure:

> Although enclosed by redemptive myth and fully organized into the novel's poetic pattern of archetypal images, the Babi Yar chapter has a force of actuality which refuses recuperation. History and myth, like Freud and Jung, or death and life, end up in a relationship which is more of a dualism than an integration. The first term in each pairing simply will not be swallowed whole by the second. (67)

These remarks may provide another clue as to why the novel does not end with the Babi Yar massacre. The novel's futile attempt at containing this episode in its mythical structure can only be exposed as a failure when the non-realist frame that is broken by history is actually offered in the last chapter.

K.J. Phillips raises the question whether the "consoling order" (197) supplied by the novel's intricate structure and metaphorical screening establishes an aesthetic distance toward the Holocaust which would prevent the reader from grasping the full scope of the Babi Yar massacre. Like Tanner and Wymer, though, he is convinced that the quasi-documentary technique employed in Chapter Five undermines the complacency of even the most underidentifying aesthetic reader: "Thomas may divert us and please us with his layered pattern in which to wrap falling bodies. Yet he withdraws the veils from Babi Yar at the necessary moment, to present a violent historical fact starkly, not evaded..." (200).

The proliferation of literary texts which dare to touch upon the tabooed area of Holocaust representation can be accounted for as a reaction to the deeply felt gap between the unique experience that the Holocaust constitutes and the often stated unspeakability of this experience. That "such a paradox... need not necessarily be a dead end, [and that] it can also be an impetus for the creation of anamnestic structures which... make their own principal inadequacy the condition of a new form of historical and aesthetic memory" (Kunow 247), is illustrated by Thomas's disturbing fictional exploration. Like *Black Dogs* and *Time's Arrow*, *The White Hotel* upholds the significance of the Holocaust as the pivotal event in twentieth-century European history. This centrality is reflected in the desire of these novels to re-visit, re-enact, and re-write one of the darkest

256 ❦ *Lars Heiler*

chapters in the history of mankind in order to approach its enormity, to come to terms with its mysteries, and to commemorate the suffering of those who were killed and those who survived. That such an enterprise is always provisional, incomplete, and doomed to failure is inscribed in the aesthetic transgressions in which these novels engage: by resisting a seamless and linear narrative structure, by privileging non-realist, metaphorical modes of representation over realist ones, the texts concede their incapacity to contain their subject.

If "the Holocaust, at the edge of moral boundaries, is where discourse stops before the unspeakable, but where it also begins" (Kushner qtd. in Kunow 268), then fictional reconstructions such as those discussed in this essay, which break the frames and trespass the limits of traditional 'Holocaust decorum', can contribute to enabling the aesthetic anamnesis of the Holocaust and to countering the risks of Holocaust amnesia. The novels' propensity for many kinds of transgression—fragmentation, narratorial disjunction, genre-bending, obscenity, symbolism, surrealism, mythopoeia, et cetera—and their lack of traditional closure thus present the Holocaust not as an event that can be relegated to the past and contained in history books, but as constituting an unfinished moral obligation and an ongoing commitment for future generations.

Notes

1. Cf. Gauthier 103: "The Holocaust brought about a profound shift in Western civilization's sense of itself. It challenged the "identity" that Western civilization had constructed for itself over centuries, and in which it had so much invested. In the light of acts of atrocity carried out in the name of science, rationalism and order, we are obliged to rethink precisely what it means to be 'enlightened'."
2. For a detailed look at the objectives of Holocaust Memorial Day cf. http://www.hmd.org.uk.
3. Cf. Des Pres 218: "A set of fictions controls the field of Holocaust studies and requires of us a definite decorum, a sort of Holocaust etiquette that encourages some, rather than other, kinds of response. One of these fictions dictates that anything pertaining to the Holocaust must be serious, must be reverential in a manner that acknowledges the sacredness of its occasion."
4. Cf. Müller-Wood and Wood 49f.
5. For readings of the novel's disrupted structure and epistemological uncertainty cf. Delrez 17; Head 116; Malcolm 153; Morrison 267.

Works Cited

Amis, Martin. *Time's Arrow*. London: Vintage, 2003.

Bernard-Donals, Michael. *An Introduction to Holocaust Studies*. Upper Saddle River, NJ: Pearson Education, 2006.

The Daily Telegraph. "No Lessons on the Holocaust." April 19, 2008. February 17, 2009 <http://www.telegraph.co.uk/news/uknews/1547369/No-lessons-on-the-Holocaust html>.

Delrez, Marc. "Escape into Innocence: Ian McEwan and the Nightmare of History." *ARIEL* 26.2 (1995): 7–23.

Des Pres, Terrence. "Holocaust Laughter?" *Writing and the Holocaust*. Ed. Berel Lang. New York: Holmes and Meier, 1988. 217–33.

Finney, Brian. "Martin Amis's *Time's Arrow* and the Postmodern Sublime." *Martin Amis: Postmodernism and Beyond*. Ed. Gavin Keulks. Houndmills: Palgrave Macmillan, 2006. 101–16.

Gauthier, Tim S. *Narrative Desire and Historical Reparations. A.S. Byatt, Ian McEwan, Salman Rushdie*. New York: Routledge, 2006.

Head, Dominic. *Ian McEwan*. Manchester: Manchester UP, 2007.

Henke, Christoph. "Remembering Selves, Constructing Selves. Memory and Identity in Contemporary British Fiction." *Journal for the Study of British Cultures* 10.1 (2003): 77–100.

Holocaust Memorial Day Trust. March 18, 2009 <http://www.hmd.org.uk>.

Howe, Irving. "Writing and the Holocaust." *Writing and the Holocaust*. Ed. Berel Lang. New York: Holmes and Meier, 1988. 175–99.

Hutcheon, Linda. "Subject in/of/to History and His Story." *Diacritics* 16.1 (1986): 78–91.

Kunow, Rüdiger. "'Emotion Recollected in Tranquility'? Representing the Holocaust in Fiction." *Emotion in Postmodernism*. Eds. Gerhard Hoffmann and Alfred Hornung. Heidelberg: Winter, 1997. 247–69.

Kushner, Tony. *The Holocaust and the Liberated Imagination: A Social and Cultural History*. Oxford: Blackwell, 1994.

Lang, Berel. "Introduction." *Writing and the Holocaust*. Ed. Berel Lang. New York: Holmes and Meier, 1988. 1–15.

———. *Holocaust Representation. Art within the Limits of History and Ethics*. Baltimore: The Johns Hopkins UP, 2000.

Malcolm, David. *Understanding Ian McEwan*. Columbia: U of South Carolina P, 2002.

McEwan, Ian. *Black Dogs*. London: Picador, 1993.

Menke, Richard. "Narrative Reversals and the Thermodynamics of History in Martin Amis's *Time's Arrow*." *Modern Fiction Studies* 44.4 (1998): 959–80.

Morrison, Jago. "Narration and Unease in Ian McEwan's Later Fiction." *Critique* 42.3 (2001): 253–68.

Müller-Wood, Anja, and J. Carter Wood. "Bringing the Past to Heel: History, Identity and Violence in Ian McEwan's *Black Dogs*." *Literature & History* 16.2 (2007): 43–56.

Oertel, Daniel. "Effects of Garden-Pathing in Martin Amis's Novels *Time's Arrow* and *Night Train*." *Miscelánea: A Journal of English and American Studies* 22 (2001): 123–40.

Ozsvath, Zsuzsanna, and Martha Satz. "The Audacity of Expressing the Inexpressible: The Relation Between Moral and Aesthetic Considerations in Holocaust Literature." *Judaism: A Quarterly Journal of Jewish Life and Thought* 34.2 (1985): 197–210.

Parry, Ann. "The Caesura of the Holocaust in Martin Amis's *Time's Arrow* and Bernhard Schlink's *The Reader*." *Journal for European Studies* 29 (1999): 249–67.

Phillips, K.J. "The Phalaris Syndrome: Alain Robbe-Grillet vs. D.M. Thomas." *Women and Violence in Literature*. Ed. Katherine Anne Ackley. New York: Garland, 1990. 175–205.

Rosenfeld, Natania. "Turning Back: Retracing Twentieth-Century Trauma in Virginia Woolf, Martin Amis, and W.G. Sebald." *Partial Answers* 2.2 (2004): 109–37.

Sauerberg, Lars Ole. "When the Soul Takes Wing: D.M. Thomas' *The White Hotel*." *Critique* 31 (1989): 3–10.

Scherr, Rebecca. "The Uses of Memory and the Abuses of Fiction: Sexuality in Holocaust Fiction and Memoir." *Other Voices* 2.1 (2000): 1–13.

Sicher, Efraim. *The Holocaust Novel*. New York: Routledge, 2005.

Slay, Jack. *Ian McEwan*. New York: Twayne Publishers, 1996.

Tanner, Laura E. "Sweet Pain and Charred Bodies: Figuring Violence in *The White Hotel*." *Boundary 2*, 18.2 (1991): 130–49.

Thomas, D.M. *The White Hotel*. London: Phoenix, 1999.

Wymer, Rowland. "Freud, Jung and the 'Myth' of Psychoanalysis in *The White Hotel*." *Mosaic* 22.1 (1989): 55–69.

Editors and Contributors

STEFAN HORLACHER is Professor of English Literature and Chair of the English Department at Dresden University of Technology. He holds degrees from Mannheim University, University of Paris IV (Sorbonne), and was Visiting Scholar at Cornell University, at Kent State University, and at the English and Foreign Languages University, Hyderabad (India). He has published widely on English literature as well as on masculinity studies and gender studies, media studies, psychoanalysis, and theories of the comic. His latest monograph, *Conceptions of Masculinity in the Works of Thomas Hardy and D.H. Lawrence* (2006, in German), won the Postdoctoral Award of the German Association of Professors of English. His latest publication is *Gender and Laughter: Comic Affirmation and Subversion in Traditional and Modern Media* (co-editors: G. Pailer, A. Böhn, and U. Scheck, 2009).

STEFAN GLOMB is Senior Lecturer in English Literature at Mannheim University, where he also completed his M.A. and Ph.D. He has had scholarships form the German Academic Exchange Service (King's College, London) and from the State of Baden-Württemberg. His publications include *Memory and Identity in Contemporary British Drama* (1997, in German), *Beyond Extremes—The Representation of and Reflexion on Processes of Modernization in the Contemporary British Novel* (co-editor: Stefan Horlacher, 2004, in German), as well as a number of articles, mainly on contemporary British drama and fiction.

LARS HEILER is Senior Lecturer in English and American Literatures at the University of Kassel. He holds degrees in English, German, Spanish, and Media Studies from Mannheim University (Germany), where he also completed his Ph.D. He has had scholarships from the German Academic Exchange Service (University of Stirling) and from the State of Baden-Württemberg. He has published a book on *Regression and Cultural Critique in the Contemporary British Novel* (2004, in German) and several articles on twentieth century fiction.

260 ❧ *Editors and Contributors*

He is currently working on a book entitled *Literature and Therapy: Precarious Negotiations.*

* * *

UWE BÖKER is Professor Emeritus of English Literature at Dresden University of Technology. He held Visiting Professorships at the Universities of Regensburg, Tübingen, Siegen, Munich, Mainz, Freiburg, Passau, Göttingen, and at the University of Northern Iowa, Cedar Falls, before becoming Professor and Chair of the English Department at Dresden University from 1993 to 2006. His most recent publications are: *Processes of Institutionalisation: Case Studies in Law, Prison and Censorship* (2001), *Of Remembraunce the Keye: Medieval Literature and Its Impact through the Ages* (2004), and *John Gay's* The Beggar's Opera *1728–2004: Adaptations and Re-Writings* (2006).

STELLA BUTTER is Assistant Professor of English and Cultural Studies at Mannheim University. She formerly worked as Manager International Relations at the International Graduate Center for the Study of Culture at Gießen University, where she completed her doctorate on literature as a medium of cultural self-reflexivity. Her research interests include literature and philosophy, science and literature, the British novel (nineteenth–twenty-first century) and literary explorations of anonymity as a cultural phenomenon. Her most recent publication is *Literatur als Medium kultureller Selbstreflexion* (2007).

FOLKERT DEGENRING is Assistant Professor of English Literature at the University of Kassel. He took an interdisciplinary degree in English and Business Studies at the University of Mannheim and was a visiting student at the National University of Ireland, Galway. He has published a monograph entitled *Identität zwischen Dekonstruktion und (Re-)konstruktion im zeitgenössischen britischen Roman* (2008) and his current research project deals with the interaction of science and literature.

JOHN DRAKAKIS is Professor of English Studies at the University of Stirling, and the Director of the Scottish Institute of Northern Renaissance Studies (SINRS). He has published widely in Shakespeare Studies. He is the editor of *Alternative Shakespeares* in the New Accents Series, the Longman collection *Shakespearean Tragedy*, the Macmillan New Casebook on *Antony and Cleopatra*,

Editors and Contributors ❦ 261

and the Longman Critical Reader volume on *Tragedy* (with Naomi Conn Liebler). He is currently the general editor of the Routledge New Critical Idiom series, and he has just completed the manuscript of Shakespeare's *The Merchant of Venice* for the Arden 3 Shakespeare Series. He is the joint editor, with Dale Townshend, of a new collection, *Gothic Shakespeares* published in the Accents on Shakespeare series in December 2008, and has been appointed general editor for the *New Narrative and Dramatic Sources of Shakespeare* to be published by Routledge.

MATTHIAS EITELMANN is Research Assistant at Mannheim University. He graduated in English and German Studies and received his doctorate from Mannheim University for a thesis which explores in the context of medieval literature the concept of cultural memory as exemplified by the Old English heroic poem *Beowulf*. His research interests include literature and memory, language history and theoretical aspects of language change. His most recent publication is *Beowulfes Beorh—Das altenglische* Beowulf*-Epos als kultureller Gedächtnisspeicher* (2010).

JENS MARTIN GURR is Professor of British Literature and Culture at the University of Duisburg-Essen and Chair of the Department of Anglophone Studies. He studied English and German at the University of Mannheim, and received his doctorate from the University of Duisburg for his thesis *Tristram Shandy and the Dialectic of Enlightenment* (1999). His post-doctoral thesis *The Human Soul as Battleground: Variations on Dualism and the Self in English Literature* was published in 2003. He taught at the universities of Duisburg-Essen, Bamberg, and Waterloo (Canada). His research interests include all periods of British Literature, twentieth-century American literature, film and popular culture, as well as twentieth-century Anglophone novels, literary theory, and urban studies.

SARAH HEINZ is Professor of English and Cultural Studies at Mannheim University. She taught English, Cultural and Media Studies at Passau University after receiving her Ph.D. from Mannheim University for a study on postmodern identities in A.S. Byatt's novels. Her research interests include critical whiteness studies, postcolonial theory, identity theory, and contemporary Irish and British fiction and drama. Her most recent publications are *Unity in Difference: Metaphor, Romance and Identity in A.S. Byatt's Novels* (2007, in German) and *Thinking Globally* (co-editors: Silvia Marosi, Oliver Preukschat,

262 ❦ *Editors and Contributors*

Barbara Storz, Sascha Becker, Amadou Oury Ba, and Elke Reinhard, 2006, in German).

ANNA-MARGARETHA HORATSCHEK is Professor of English Literature and Chair of the English Department at the University of Kiel. She holds degrees from the University of California (Berkeley), Freiburg, and Mannheim and taught as an exchange professor in Washington, D.C. She has published widely on knowledge formation, epistemology, ethics, and mediality, for example, in her books *Erkenntnis und Realität. Sprachreflexion und Sprachexperiment in den Romanen von Richard Brautigan* (1989) and in *Alterität und Stereotyp. Die Funktion des Fremden in den "International Novels" von E. M. Forster und D. H. Lawrence* (1998). She is co-editor of *Literatur in Wissenschaft und Unterricht* and co-speaker of the interdisciplinary research group *Discursivising Knowledge in the Early Modern Period* at the University of Kiel.

CLIVE SCOTT is Professor Emeritus of European Literature at the University of East Anglia and a Fellow of the British Academy. His principal research interests lie in comparative poetics (*Channel Crossings: French and English Poetry in Dialogue 1550–2000*, 2002; R.H. Gapper Book Prize, 2004), literary translation (*Translating Baudelaire*, 2000; *Translating Rimbaud's "Illuminations,"* 2006) and photography's relationship with writing (*The Spoken Image: Photography and Language*, 1999; *Street Photography: From Atget to Cartier-Bresson*, 2007). He is at present engaged in the preparation of a book on the translation of Apollinaire's poetry and shorter pieces on the relationship between voice in modern poetry and directions in modern music.

Index

The index does not include 'taboo' and 'transgression' as separate entries. For specific transgressions and taboos, please consult the relevant entries in this index.

Authors of primary texts and theorists or authors of studies on taboo and transgression are included in the index. For a complete directory of all cited authors the reader is referred to the lists of works cited at the end of each chapter. Page references printed in bold type refer to whole chapters that offer a substantial discussion of the relevant entry.

abject, 10, 13, 16, 19, 119, 136, 143–44, 146, **193–208**
abortion, 29
Ackroyd, Peter, 37
Adams, James Eli, 32, 36
addiction, 63
adultery, 31, 35, 59, 154, 164, 167–71, 198
aesthetics, 4, 16–17, 120, 144, 224
Agamben, Giorgio, **75–97**
aggression, 124, 165; *see also* violence
alcohol, 31, 38, 40, 95
Allan, Keith, 160–61
Amis, Martin, 244, 248–51
anatomy, 170, 195; *see also* medicine
animality, see bestiality
anthropology, 4–6, 11
anxiety, 137, 139, 152
Ariès, Philippe, 137, 153
Aristotle, 55, 78–79
art, 14, 16, 18, 66, 68, 78, 145, 161, 198, 207, 211, 235, 238, 250
assassination, *see* murder
atrocity, 251, 253, 256
authorities, 7, 13–14, 18, 26, 31, 36, 49–53, 55, 76, 78, 80, 89, 95–96, 105, 107, 111, 154, 179, 190, 206, 227–29, 233–34, 238

Babcock, Barbara A., 212–13, 217, 221
Bakhtin, Mikhail M., 53, 68, 124, 148
ban, 5, 26, 79, 82, 99, 120; *see also* censorship
barbarity, 6, 142, 146, 247
Barker, Clive, 143
Barthes, Roland, 61, 177, 179, 186
Bataille, Georges, 16, 80, 84, 97, 120, 135–36
beauty, 122, 128, 131, 162, 164, 171–72
Benjamin, Walter, 78, 89
Bennett, Alan, 239
Bernard-Donals, Michael, 243
bestiality, 124, 130
Bettelheim, Bruno, 150
Betz, Werner, 18
bigamy, *see* polygamy
blasphemy, 24–27, 29–30, 40–41, 217, 224, 228, 236–37, 239
body, 6, 9–11, 19, 86, 94, 119, 139–40, 143–44, 146, **159–74**, 203–5, 216, 219; *see also* sexuality; gender
Bond, Edward, 3, 29, 235, 237–38

boundaries, 15, 31, 41, 55–56, 65, 68, 119, 161, 164, 166, 194, 211–12, 215, 219–20, 222–24, 256; *see also* liminality

Bradley, James E., 113

Brenton, Howard, 3, 36, 238

Bright, Timothy, 95

Bristol, Michael D., 28

Bristow, Edward J., 33

Bronfen, Elisabeth, 138, 142, 153

Brontë, Charlotte, 60

Browning, Robert, 159–60, 162–63, 166–68, 171

Bunyan, John, 17, 26, **99–114**

Burridge, Kate, 160–61

Butler, Judith, 193

Byron, George Gordon, Lord Byron, 24

cannibalism, 9, 39, 99

capitalism, 29, 55, 237

capital punishment, 37, 39; *see also* execution

carnival, 53, 148–49, 152, 154, 221

Carter, Angela, 137, 148–52

censorship, 17, 24, 26, 27–32, 35, **49–68**, 99–102, 108, 112–14, 119, 161, **226–40**; *see also* ban; Lord Chamberlain

Christianity, *see* religion

church, 23–24, 27, 30–31, 34, 41, 50, 106, 112, 153, 215, 237

Clare, Janet, 28, 52, 227, 240; *see also* religion

class, 26–27, 32–33, 38–39, 142, 162–63, 169, 212, 222, 228–30, 237

Coetzee, J(ohn) M(axwell), 49–50

Cohen, Ed, 33

Cohen, S., 27

colonialism, 11, 39, 221–22, 238

Conolly, Leonard W., 228, 240

Conrad, Joseph, 39, 50, 62, 64–65, 68

conservatism, 13, 159

constraint, 159, 161, 163, 166, 173; *see also* control

contagion, 6–7, 139

containment, 52, 54; *see also* control

control, 12–13, 24–27, 30, 34, 36–37, 94–95, 142, 163, 167, 170, 190, 227; *see also* law; repression; constraint; containment

conventions, 13, 15, 36, 50, 60–61, 121, 160, 169, 180, 204, 211, 218, 244, 247

Cook, James, 5

copulation, *see* sexuality

Crèvecœur, J. Hector St. John de, 187

crime, 23–26, 31, 33, 39, 79, 95, 137, 174, 205, 231–32, 238

crisis, 77, 159, 202

culture, 4–5, 13, 15, 18–19, 27, 119, 159–63, 186, 193, 196, 217, 222

death, 13, 23, 32, 36–39, 67, 85, **135–54**, 165–66, 198–99, 249–50, 252–53, 255

death penalty, *see* capital punishment

decay, 11, 14

decency, 59, 99, 244; *see also* propriety; decorum

decorum, 39, 62, 122, 244, 256; *see also* propriety; decency

defecation, *see* excretion

Defoe, Daniel, 37, 40, 58

De Jongh, Nicholas, 240

Deleuze, Gilles, 76

De Man, Paul, 68

Derrida, Jacques, 82

desire, *see* sexuality

destruction, 67–68, 147, 165–66, 168, 249

dirt, 8, 38, 112, 123–25, 221, 234

disease, 11, 33, 204–5, 253; *see also* health; medicine

displacement, 7, 146, 223

dissent, 65, **99–114**

Dollimore, Jonathan, 51–53, 68, 78

Douglas, Mary, 7–10, 119
drunkenness, *see* alcohol
Durkheim, Emile, 6, 7

Eco, Umberto, 223
Eggert, Hartmut, 5, 15–16, 120
Elias, Norbert, 118
Eliot, George (Mary Ann Evans),
    193–208
Eliot, T(homas) S(tearns), 184, 188, 190
Enlightenment, 13, 27, 55, 118, 126–31,
    142, 144, 216, 243
eroticism, *see* sexuality
ethics, 18, 90, 203, 224; *see also*
    morality
eugenics, 249
euphemism, 25–26, 37, 120, 215
evil, 6, 37, 87, 93, 102, 105, 109, 113,
    128, 206, 244–46
excess, 15, 83, 95–96, 107, 124, 139, 143,
    154, 164, 181
exclusion, 15–16, 77–78, 82, 85–86,
    88–89, 96, 161–63, 236
excretion, **117–31**, 211
execution, 38–39, 109; *see also* capital
    punishment
exhibitionism, *see* sexuality
experiment, 36, 58, 63, 100, 159, 161,
    183, 211, 229, 235–36, 248, 250

fear, 6, 10, 14, 18, 34, 81, 135, 137, 142,
    148, 152, 195, 197, 199
femininity, *see* gender
Fiedler, Leslie, 152
Fielding, Henry, 35, 37–38
filth, *see* dirt
Findlater, Richard, 231
Fluck, Winfried, 19
Foote, Stephanie, 34
foreigner, 6, 136, 221, 232
Foucault, Michel, 32, 119, 137, 140, 153,
    163, 174, 193, 230–31
Fox, William Johnson, 162
Frazer, Sir James, 6, 12

Freud, Sigmund, 4, 7, 10, 14, 18,
    135–36, 160, 173, 193–94, 201, 208,
    251–52, 255
Fryer, Peter, 159
Fuß, Peter, 151

Ganim, Russel J., 119
Gatrell, V(ic) A.C., 33, 39
gay, *see* homosexuality
Gay, John, **117–31**
Gell, Alfred, 3, 9
gender, 26, 40, 67, 139, 141, 149–51,
    154, 167–68, 170, 193, 198, 200,
    203, 215, 217–22
    femininity, 122, 150–51, 218
    masculinity, 67, 91, 150, 219
    misogyny, 121, 123
    patriarchy, 152–53, 179, 219
genocide, *see* murder
genre, 55–56, 148, 160, 251, 256
Goldsmith, Netta Murray, 33
Golec, Janusz, 15
gothic, 39, **135–54**
Graupmann, Jürgen, 18
Greenblatt, Stephen, 52, 159, 161
Griest, Guinevere L., 35
guilt, 65, 90–92, 168, 206

Habermas, Jürgen, 196, 208
Hardy, Thomas, 35
health, 40, 164, 170, 172; *see also*
    disease; medicine
hegemony, 25–27, 37–38, 152
Heinschink, Mozes F., 6
Henley, William Earnest, 164, 171–72,
    180, 182–83
Héritier, Françoise, 9, 19
Hoffmann, Arne, 18
Holden, Lynn, 18
Holocaust, 3, 66, **243–56**
homosexuality, 29, 33–34, 65, 68,
    139–40, 228, 236–37
    gay, 34, 36, 65–66, 148
    lesbian, 34, 164

266 ❧ *Index*

Hopkins, Gerald Manley, 180, 182
Hornby, Nick, 117
horror, 136–37, 143–44, 150, 194–95, 204, 245, 247–48, 253; *see also* terror
Houswitschka, Christoph, 39
Hutcheson, Francis, 127–30
Huxley, Aldous, 121
hypocrisy, 54, 57, 173

identity, 9, 13, 16, 40–42, 53, 57, 64, 82, 87, 139, 142, 148, 151, 180, 187, 193–94, 197–200, 202–4, 206, 237, 256; *see also* subjectivity
ideology, 28, 54, 80, 90, 92, 179, 229
illness, *see* disease
imperialism, *see* colonialism
impurity, 32, 119, 136
incest, *see* sexuality
indecency, 33, 238; *see also* obscenity
indictment, 24–25, 108, 112, 237
individuality, 31, 99, 109, 137, 153, 204, 237, 253
infanticide, *see* murder
innocence, 62, 109, 138, 220
insanity, *see* madness
institution, 12, 23–24, 35, 54, 83, 87, 93, 169, 239
interdiction, *see* prohibition
Iser, Wolfgang, 61, 68
Islam, *see* religion

Jenks, Chris, 15, 212
Jervis, John, 15
Johnston, John, 27, 230, 235, 237–38, 240
jouissance, 177, 186, 190
Joyce, James, 17, 36, **210–25**
Judaism, *see* religion

Kaltenbrunner, Gerd-Klaus, 3, 14, 18
Kristeva, Julia, 9–10, 16, 19, 119, **193–208**
Kushner, Tony, 256

law, 6, 15, 17, 24, 26, 32, 37–39, 55, **75–97**, 140, 147, 152, 160–61, 163, 166, 173, 181, 202–8, 215, 238
Lawrence, D(avid) H(erbert), 3, 154, 184, 186–88
Leach, Edmund, 7–9, 18
lesbian, *see* homosexuality
Lévi-Strauss, Claude, 18, 19
Lewes, George Henry, 59, 195
Lewis, Matthew, 136–47, 151
libel, 25, 29–30, 36, 56–57; *see also* slander
liminality, 77, 136, 153, 222; *see also* boundaries
Locke, John, 126, 129
Lord Chamberlain, 29, 228, 230–38; *see also* censorship
love, 34, 142, **159–74**, 207
Lowman, John, 27
lust, 63, 93, 168, 200; *see also* sexuality; eroticism

madness, 13, 89, 93, 121, 125, 135, 137, 166, 170
Mandeville, Bernard, 38, 130
Marcus, Steven, 163
marriage, 140, 154, 164, 169–70, 230; *see also* bigamy
Marsh, Joss, 24–25, 27
Marshik, Celia, 231
masculinity, *see* gender
masochism, *see* sexuality
masturbation, *see* sexuality
matricide, *see* murder
matrimony, *see* marriage
Matus, Jill, 19
Maurer, Oscar, 35
McDonald, James, 18
McEwan, Ian, 17, 50, 66–68, 244, 246, 248
McLynn, Frank, 38–39
Mead, George Herbert, 193
medicine, 33–34, 125, 137, 170, 249
Meigs, Anna, 9

Meredith, George, 164, 169–70
meter, **177–91**
Meyers, Jeffrey, 65
Milton, John, 17, 26, 30, **99–114**
misogyny, *see* gender
Mitscherlich, Alexander, 14
modernism, 16, 35, 61, 64, 195, 223–24
modernization, 3, 15, 32, 36, 40, 55,
　　137, 164, 169–71, 222–24, 251
Montague, Ashley, 29
morality, 7, 10, 23–24, 33, 36, 54,
　　59–60, 62–65, 92, 126–31, 142,
　　144, 147, 160, 163, 173, 194, 202–8,
　　224, 231–32, 243–44, 253–54, 256;
　　see also ethics
murder, 19, 39, 65, 194, 200–201, 208
　assassination, 92
　genocide, 249–50; *see also*
　　Holocaust
　infanticide, 26, 35, 39
　matricide, 138, 146
　parricide, 4, 39
　regicide, **75–97**, 100–101, 113
Murry, John Middleton, 121
myth, 51, 152, 208, 255

narcissism, 3, 65, 197, 203, 218
nationality, 40–41, 53, 167, 212, 237
nature, 5, 25, 83, 89, 91, 92–97, 106,
　　124, 126–30, 142, 144, 215
necrophilia, *see* sexuality
norms, 17–18, 26–27, 32–33, 38, 64, 76,
　　87, 159–60, 198, 229; *see also*
　　values
Norton, Rictor, 23, 31, 34
nudity, 228, 238

obscenity, 239, 256; *see also*
　　indecency
order, 12, 15, 28, 31, 38, 77–79, 85–88,
　　91–93, 95, 110, 119, 135, 159,
　　161–62, 197, 200, 203, 205–6, 212,
　　217–18, 220
Osborne, John, 29, 235–38

otherness, 15, 78, 93
Oxtoby, Willard Gurdon, 6

paganism, *see* religion
pain, 164–65, 170–72, 181, 249
parricide, *see* murder
passion, *see* sexuality
Patmore, Coventry, 164, 170–72, 182
patriarchy, *see* gender
Patterson, Annabel, 49
pedophilia, *see* sexuality
Perrin, Noel, 30, 35
Persels, Jeff, 119
perversion, 67, 94, 121, 135
phallus, 152, 216
pharmakon, 82; *see also* scapegoat
pleasure, 13, 15, 49, 63–64, 68, 135, 171,
　　177, 182, 186, 220, 252
poison, 82–83
political correctness, 3, 66
politics, 26, 85–86, 88, 94–96,
　　99–114, 162
Pollak, Ellen, 121, 140, 153
pollution, 8, 10–11, 19
polygamy, 26, 35
Pope, Alexander, **117–31**
pornography, 30
postmodernism, 3–4, 15, 223–24
Pound, Ezra, 184–86, 191
power, 16, 25, 32, 41, 49, 51, 53–54,
　　75–77, 79–85, 87–95, 112, 140,
　　224, 231
profane, 4, 13, 18, 29, 40, 86, 135,
　　171–72, 215, 217, 222; *see also*
　　sacred; religion
prohibition, 6–7, 12, 16, 18, 24, 85
promiscuity, 237
propriety, 25, 34, 59, 62, 64, 122, 127,
　　162–64, 169, 172, 174, 182, 211,
　　214–15, 233; *see also* decency;
　　decorum
prostitution, 29, 167–68, 218, 230–31
provocation, 67, 165, 168, 249
prudery, 159

268　　*Index*

psychoanalysis, 4–5, 11, 14, 252
psychology, 195, 253
punishment, 13, 15, 37
purity, 62, 119

race, 26, 40, 162, 212, 222
racism, 13, 243
Radcliffe, Ann, 136–38, 143–47,
　　151, 154
Radcliffe-Brown, Alfred, 7, 8
radicalism, 59, **99–114**
Radzinowicz, Leon, 38
Rafetseder, Hermann, 30
rape, 139, 146, 149–51
Ravenhill, Mark, 239
reason, 14, 93, 126, 129–31; *see also*
　　Enlightenment
rebellion, 53, 79–80, 85, 88, 94, 104–5;
　　see also revolution
reform, 24, 33, 159, 162, 239
regicide, *see* murder
regression, 67, 197, 202, 247
religion, 6, 10, 17–18, 26, 28, 55, 63, 138,
　　166, 201–3, 228
　　Christianity, 6, 10, 26, 110, 202
　　Islam, 40–41, 244
　　Judaism, 10, 206
　　paganism, 164
renunciation, 7, 18
repression, 7–8, 13, 26, 65, 90–91, 99,
　　136, 141, 163, 195–99, 204, 208
respectability, *see* propriety
revolution, 26, 85, 108, 162; *see also*
　　rebellion
ritual, 85–86, 182
Robinson, J., 28
Rolph, C.H., 30
Royle, Nicholas, 136
Rushdie, Salman, 3, 41–42

sacred, 4, 6–8, 12–13, 18, 135–36, 215,
　　217, 222; *see also* profane; religion
sacrifice, 86, 206–7
sacrilege, 19

Sade, Donatien Alphonse François,
　　Marquis de Sade, 147, 165
sadism, *see* sexuality
sadomasochism, *see* sexuality
Sammells, Neil, 49
sanction, 8, 49
Sartre, Jean Paul, 119
satire, 56, 58–59, 123
scapegoat, 13, 60; *see also* pharmakon
scatology, **117–31**
Schaffers, Uta, 195
Schmitt, Carl, 76, 79, 86
science, 33–34, 57, 126–27, 137, 203,
　　249, 256; *see also* medicine
Seale, Clive, 37
secret, 65
self, *see* identity
self-fashioning, *see* identity
sexism, *see* gender
sexuality, 23, 32–33, 36–37, 65, 119,
　　135–54, **159–74**, 193, 216, 218, 228
　　copulation, 36, 217
　　desire, 18, 79, 81–83, 85, 94–96,
　　　138–40, 164–69, 202, 204, 220
　　eroticism, 153, 162, 164–65, 251–53
　　exhibitionism, 217
　　incest, 4, 7, 18–19, 140, 146,
　　　149–52, 194
　　lust, 168, 200
　　masochism, 13, 68
　　masturbation, 32, 211, 220
　　necrophilia, 140–42, 164
　　passion, 171, 181
　　sadism, 13
　　sadomasochism, 67, 164
　　sodomy, 23–24, 31, 33–34
　　voyeurism, 63, 216–17, 220
Shaftesbury, Anthony Ashley
　　Cooper, 3rd Earl of Shaftesbury,
　　127–30
Shakespeare, William, 28, 39, 51–55,
　　75–97, 198–99, 208
Shaw, George Bernard, 29, 230–32, 237
Shellard, Dominic, 230–33, 235–38, 240

Shelley, Percy Bysshe, 24, 29
Sheridan, Richard Brinsley, 127
Showalter, Elaine, 35
silencing, 23–25, 32
simulacrum, 83, 93–94, 150
sin, 10, 23, 112, 202, 206
Sinfield, Alan, 27, 51, 53
slander, 56; *see also* libel
Smith, Sir Thomas, 75, 79
Smith, William Robertson, 6
sodomy, *see* sexuality
spirituality, 110, 124, 215
stability, *see* order
Stallybrass, Peter, 119, 124, 217
Stephens, John Russell, 27, 39
stereotypes, 139, 141, 148–50, 169,
    200, 215, 219–21
Sterne, Laurence, **117–31**
Stevenson, Robert Louis, 50, 62–64
Strachey, Lytton, 35, 173
subjectivity, 9–11, 18–19, 76, 84, 96,
    149, 164, 183, 193–94, 196–97,
    206, 220, 237; *see also* identity
sublime, 143–44
subversion, 15, 26, 50, 52, 54–55, 58, 63,
    93, **99–114**
Swift, Jonathan, 39, 50, 55–58, **117–31**
Swinburne, Algernon Charles,
    163–68, 171
symbol, 6, 9–11, 23, 65, 119–20, 141,
    206, 208, 217, 246–47, 252
symbolic order, 15, 19, 79–80, 194–96,
    204, 207; *see also* symbol
Symons, Arthur, 183, 191

Teichmann, Michael, 6
Tennyson, Alfred, Lord Tennyson,
    159–60, 162, 164, 167–70, 174
terror, 67, 135–36, 143–44, 148, 151,
    201; *see also* horror

terrorism, 19, 30, 38, 63
Testard, Alain, 9
Thackeray, William Makepeace, 35,
    50, 58–62
theatricality, 52–53, 61, 154
Thody, Philip, 4, 6, 14, 17–18
Thomas, D(onald) M(ichael), 244,
    252–53, 255
Thomas, Donald, 25, 30, 35, 240
Todorov, Tzvetan, 54–55, 159–61
totemism, 12, 194
transition, 51, 61, 159–60, 162, 173
trauma, 85, 251
Türcke, Christoph, 5

uncanny, **135–54**
unconscious, 7, 16, 18, 36, 90–91, 94,
    180, 194, 196, 204, 253

Valeri, Valerio, 6–11, 13, 19
values, 13, 17, 25–27, 32–33, 38, 63–64,
    66, 153, 186, 212, 217, 229–30, 243;
    see also norms
vice, 31, 59–60, 144, 213, 232, 238
violation, 18, 135, 139–40, 150, 212, 217
violence, 4, 67, 75, 78, 82–83, 85–87,
    89–90, 92, 94, 147, 150, 232, 245,
    247–49, 254; *see also* aggression
voyeurism, *see* sexuality

Wells, H(erbert) G(eorge), 34, 36
White, Allon, 119, 124, 217
whore, *see* prostitution
Wilde, Oscar, 25, 33, 50, 63–64, 174
witchcraft, 31, 90
Woolf, Virginia, 35
Wordsworth, William, 180–82
Wundt, Wilhelm, 4

Young, Iris Marion, 197